AF494916

10.7

The Wake Up Call

Global Jihad and the Rise of Antisemitism in a World Gone MAD

Israel Ellis

A WICKED SON BOOK
An Imprint of Post Hill Press
ISBN: 979-8-89565-130-8
ISBN (eBook): 979-8-89565-131-5

The Wake Up Call:
Global Jihad and the Rise of Antisemitism in a World Gone MAD
© 2024 by Israel Ellis
All Rights Reserved

Cover design by Pini Hamou
Editorial work by Mathew Channer, Dave Gordon and Limore Ellis
Author photo by Amos Ben Gershom, GPO

Post Hill Press
New York • Nashville
wickedsonbooks.com
posthillpress.com

Published in the United States of America

TABLE OF CONTENTS

AUTHOR'S NOTE

THE WAKE-UP CALL as I describe in this book, is the new reality of a world reshaped by the events of October 7. We are in a struggle that Holocaust survivor and psychiatrist Viktor Frankl, author of *Man's Search for Meaning*, characterized as the battle between the decent and the indecent. This about sums up the conflicts we must overcome to find a way through to the other side of the madness. Goodness, peace, reason, democracy, must prevail over evil.

At some point, I had to complete the final chapter and send the manuscript to the publisher. Some people mentioned in the present may now be in the past, and some predictions discussed in the book are now in the present. While much may change, the core message of this book remains.

One of those core messages is: We seem to be living in a world gone MAD. That is, the concept of mutually assured destruction loses its leverage over managing a situation where the lovers of life must confront the lovers of death. In such a world, finding a path towards a harmonious future is hardened and made complex, by lack of reason and indecency.

Since October 7, 2023, the surge in global antisemitism has been unparalleled in modern times, posing a threat not only to Jewish people, but to all. The "progressives," already seduced by radical woke ideologies, have infiltrated and hijacked the liberal banner. The radical left have dominated their presence at universities, in the media, within political discussion and corporate culture. Those who remain silent are abetting the problem, thereby emboldening the protests of masked hoodlums. I feel betrayed in the country of my birth, the place I call home.

Hatred is not unique to the Jewish people, but antisemitism has proven to be the proverbial canary in the coal mine. History shows that the downfall of civilization follows closely behind the persecution of Jews. No matter your background, beliefs, or religion, I implore you to heed the messages, before we are left saying, "We could have, should have, would have."

Iran continues to double down as the main sponsor for global terror, directly and through its proxies. I can still feel the vibrations in my chest as I waited in the stairwell of my Tel Aviv hotel, the double booms of the Iron Dome overhead countering the volley of Iranian missiles. This was a terrifying moment. These escalations are continuing with intensity, and if allowed to continue, could have devastating consequences for the entire region, and a most serious and deadly threat to global security. A sworn enemy of the United States, Israel and all free democratic countries, Iran is nearing nuclear capability. The head of Global Jihad seeks worldwide domination by any means necessary. The cost of life; be it Jewish, Muslim, Christian, or anyone for that matter, is acceptable to the Iranian regime, whose leadership has perversely interpreted the Qur'an, in the pursuit of Global Jihad. There are fewer and fewer options left on the table in our diplomatic bag of tricks, and I fear for what is coming.

I imagine the words of "Hear O' Israel" parting the lips of the targeted souls on October 7, as the fear of death loomed. It is a prayer that is both whispered and cried aloud. Mothers and fathers, sisters and brothers, grandparents, aunties, uncles, cousins and friends. Farmers, writers, doctors, lawyers, technicians, engineers, teachers, and therapists; everyday hardworking and kind people; perhaps the final words of the innocents who wanted only peace with their neighbors.

Lovers of life. Friends to strangers. Israel is a village, where its people raise each other from darkness to light, from sadness to laughter, from anger to love. "Shema Yisrael." Hear, O Israel.

This book is dedicated to every one of them; to every person in Israel who must live with the stress of their threatened security on a daily basis. To every person in the world who is witness to the betrayal. To every brave hero who stands for life and calls out the lies.

The Wake Up Call was written and edited between Israel and my home in Canada. There is a certain authenticity that comes from observing the facts on the ground, rather than from afar. Being in Israel for much of the drafting process, and returning there to complete the editing, audiobook, and cover design, allowed me to capture nuances that could have otherwise been missed. I'm deeply grateful to the many people I engaged with. Each received me warmly, and readily provided their insights so that I could write the story that forms much of the important messages this book will tell.

October 7 is a subject increasingly prejudiced and blacklisted by major media and many professional industries. In fact, a well-known publisher refused to publish this manuscript, and I quote here their exact words of rejection to me, "the information pool is polluted and that accounts of beheaded babies, serial rapes, and massacres on October 7 had been contradicted." This response was shocking to me, but in hindsight, not surprising. October 7 is backed up by eye witness accounts and indisputable evidence that support one of the most barbaric, brutal, and gruesome terrorist attacks of all time. It seems that both the mainstream media and our politicians are afraid to challenge the radicals propping up the terrorists, whilst hiding behind a movement that claims diversity, equity, and inclusivity—except, that is, for Jews.

I am grateful to Anthony Ziccardi of Wicked Son Press, who courageously took on this project, committing to sharing the truth. Special thanks to my editors—Mathew Channer, Dave Gordon, and Limore Ellis—for pushing me to clarify meaning and substantiate facts. To my children, Arielle, Eitan, Dov, and Dean, who broadened the book's appeal by offering generational perspectives. My gratitude extends to those who have reviewed my manuscript in advance and advised me on some key points. Above all, to Limore, my partner in life, whose support and critical insights helped shape this book. She has come to know every hostage taken by Hamas on October 7 by name.

One cannot and should not ignore the false narratives, often easier to overlook than to question. It takes courage to reject what we know is likely an untruth. In my book *Moving Through Walls*, I refer to the well known story of the emperor not wearing clothes. It is a simple parable where the most innocent in the crowd, a child, shouts out the obvious. We too must call out the hate around us, and not go along just to get along. Every person has a choice—to stand up for humanity, or remain silent. Find your strength, open your mind, and choose to be on the right side of history, even if it's not the popular position of the day.

In writing this book, I've strived for balance, supporting my views with facts and citing sources rigorously. This project became a personal mission: to convey a message that provides answers to the question of how, and what we do now. My hope is that the effort inspires others. Each one of us has the power to make a difference for the better.

ISRAEL J. ELLIS, NOVEMBER 7, 2024

"There may be times when we are powerless to prevent injustice,
but there must never be a time when we fail to protest."

–ELIE WIESEL (1928-2016), HOLOCAUST SURVIVOR,

AUTHOR, AND NOBEL PEACE PRIZE LAUREATE.

INTRODUCTION

WE HAVE A BUSINESS in Blue Mountains, Ontario, two hours north of Toronto. My wife and I are strolling the downtown area of nearby Collingwood under a fresh January sun. A middle aged, sharply dressed, attractive woman notices Limore's *Chai* and Star of David necklace. She leans toward my wife and whispers "Shalom." She pulls back and winks, as if we are part of some secret society. "Why so shy and quiet?" my wife asks the woman. "Well, you know," she says, "you can never be too careful." "Of what?" Limore asks. "We have to stick together," the woman says, and by way of explanation she tells us that she is an unaffiliated Jew living in Tiny, Ontario (it's actually a small town called that) and she has never felt both connected, and in fear, until now. This seemingly ordinary interaction made me pause for thought. Is this where we are? Jews needing to secretly identify themselves to other Jews in such a clandestine fashion? As we made our way home and caught our flight to Israel the next day, I thought about what happened on the streets of this small town in any city, North America. I could not quite put my finger on what I was feeling at the moment, until this book committed itself to me.

THE BOOK I NEVER WANTED TO HAVE TO WRITE.
In 1993, my final year of university, I took a course called the Arab-Israeli conflict. At the time, I truly believed The Beatles, that "all you need is love." I was all in when it came to peace and love, a student of socialist thought, resistant to the instrumental reasoning that came with an overindulgent society. We lived in an increasingly "me before we" world, but I truly believed that narrative could change. (I was young and naive, as one tends to be on the cusp of adulthood.) Such was my thinking when I proposed a year-end party at my humble post-war brick townhome on Bathurst Street, in Toronto, and invited the students from my class to attend. I baked a cake and decorated half with the Israeli flag and half with the Palestinian flag. I was determined to believe, and projected my own perspective, that we all wanted the same thing—to live a free life with the choice to practice our own religion and culture alongside each other. After all, this was Canada, a progressive, free land. That evening, I imagined I could feel this common bond of our togetherness as we danced the night away in my living room, moving our bodies uniquely, but to the same music. I think back now and wonder: was I dancing just with myself, to my own tunes, or were the others really dancing with me? The years have gone by, and I have become a realist. I have come to understand that any outcome depends on reasonable people, willing partners with openness, faith, a belief in the future,

and an opportunity to forgive. I wrote my first book about these ideas[1], and years later, a lifetime, I still believe in this truth, this realism: where there is a willingness, there is a way.

I wish that there would never have been a reason to write this book. That the terror of October 7 never happened. That the world did not go crazy and betray the truth. That 1,200 innocent people were not brutally murdered and that others were not mercilessly kidnapped; torn from their families and home, displayed in the streets of Gaza as a prize of Hamas, and used to torment and taunt Israel and the Israeli people. This book is the frustration, the anguish, the record of the bizarre dissonance of a world gone mad and the exposure of hate. I really wish I did not feel the need or have the reason to write this, because I am just a person amongst many, and this was a call I would have preferred to have taken a pass on if not for the responsibility to tell a story that needs to be told.

On January 18, 2024 I traveled to Israel with Limore, my wife. Our son, Eitan, an IDF reservist, was activated on the morning of October 7. When we got to Israel, I struggled with the need to do something, *anything* to help. I soon realized that more than anything, people wanted to talk. They needed to be heard. And so I listened.

The one word question on the tip of everyone's tongue is: *How.* How could such an attack take place? How could Israel's defenses have failed the people of the South?

The "*How*" of the October 7, 2023 Hamas terror attack on Israel's south is amongst the most pressing questions being asked in its aftermath. Over 1,200 people were brutally murdered in a single day and, according to the official IDF count, 251 people were taken hostage into Gaza. This book seeks to provide answers.

The Hamas attack on Israel did not happen in a vacuum. The antisemitism now rampant on the Western World's streets and campuses did not erupt overnight. This book is for those who want to

---

1   *Moving Through Walls*, MTW Press, 2022

understand how the violence and chaos of terrorism is spilling into the neighborhoods of North America and Europe, and may come to threaten the freedom and security of the free world. For those of you made to feel unsafe by the masked protestors chanting "death to the Jews" and brandishing placards of hate, this book is for you.

I have written this book to provide truth and counter the misinformation propagated by those hiding behind their flawed, arrogant, leftist ideology, one which does not include the Jew as an equal, or include Israel's right to defend itself. Perhaps in the face of truth we can openly discuss the impossible reality Israel is forced into. And finally, for the beautiful people of Israel and the Jews in the diaspora, my brothers and sisters; I want to provide context, strength, empathy, and tools, so that our pain does not become a lone person suffering in isolation. We are one *united* nation. *You* are not alone, and together *we* will *dance again*[2].

THE THREAT

I had never felt the threat of antisemitism so clearly than in the weeks and months that followed Ten-Seven. During a trip to Europe, we witnessed with alarm the level of anti-Israel protests flooding the streets and public squares, and then back home in Toronto saw these threatening protests on familiar streets. This is my home, I have lived here my entire life, and yet I am left feeling unsafe, unprotected, and unwelcome. It was even more troubling when visiting our daughter in New York, where we witnessed hundreds of pro-Palestinian protesters disrupting the flow of commuters at Grand Central Station with a sit-in during rush hour. At the time of the printing of this book, none of this has abated. In fact, anti-

---

2   Mia Schem, one of the eight hostages freed from Gaza after 54 days in captivity on November 30, 2023, penned the phrase "We will dance again" as a tattoo on her arm, commemorating her experiences and her optimism for the future.

Israel protests have devolved into Jew-hating mobs that have become commonplace. The public and media's appeasement, indifference, rationalization, and capitulation to the rampage of people who are spreading lies, hate, and the call for Israel's destruction feels more and more like 1939 post-Kristallnacht[3], Nazi Germany.

A telling moment occurred for me when I was halted by a police barricade at a highway entrance near my Toronto neighborhood in Jan. 2024. The officer told me to return home for my own safety. A group of masked protesters, waving anti-Israel signage, including the *"From the River to the Sea"* slogan[4], had commandeered the bridge to the 401 highway, a main transport artery to and from a Jewish neighborhood in the suburbs. The police response was to divert traffic away from the bridge. It was even more shocking when reports showed officers handing out cups of Tim Hortons coffee to the bemused protestors. (After all, it was chilly, and Jew-hate takes a great deal of energy.)

In subsequent weeks and months, the protests would grow across cities and university campuses in Canada, the United States, and Western Europe. The crowds grew bigger, chanting louder, with signage more provocative each week. I was surprised by the sheer numbers of our fellow citizens coming out to support hate.

---

3   "Kristallnacht," also known as the "Night of Broken Glass," refers to the pogrom against Jews carried out by the Nazi regime in Germany on November 9-10, 1938. During this event, Jewish homes, businesses, and synagogues were destroyed, and many Jews were arrested and sent to concentration camps. The name "Kristallnacht" comes from the shards of broken glass that littered the streets after the windows of Jewish-owned stores and buildings were smashed. It is considered a significant and tragic event in the history of the Holocaust, marking a major escalation in the Nazi persecution of Jews.

4   "From the river to the sea" is a slogan invented by the Palestinian Arabs advocating for the elimination of Israel. Though, if you asked most protesters, they would have little knowledge that it refers to the area from the Jordan River to the Mediterranean Sea, encompassing all of Israel, and the Palestinian territories. By calling for control of this entire region, the slogan suggests replacing Israel with a single Palestinian state. Given the history of conflict, this is seen as a threat to the existence of Israel and its Jewish population, implying genocide. Therefore, many perceive it as advocating for the destruction or eradication of Israel.

The call for the genocide of Jews was louder than any time I could remember in my lifetime. It was easy for every Jew to feel anxious about the situation, to feel unsafe; but then again, I guess that is the point of it all.

On December 17, 2023 pro-Palestinian supporters (at this point I might as well call them "Jew-haters") gathered in front of the Zara retail store at Toronto's downtown Eaton center, where a masked, hooded man approached police, who were securing the store's entrance. "I will take you six feet deep, man!" he shouted into an officer's bewildered face.[5] To my astonishment, the officers simply stood by, not responding to the blatant threat. The policing policy seems to be "the situation is volatile. Let's not aggravate *them* more than necessary." Meanwhile, the mayor of Toronto, Olivia Chow, literally cowered to the protests that disrupted her community skating party on January 7, 2024 at Toronto's City Hall. As protesters shouted epithets against Jews and Israel, all she had to say was that it was their democratic right to speak. Vile protests are going on, almost unabated, everywhere. The situation is out of control and bordering on the lawlessness of anarchy, and the only response to its increasingly violent messaging is apathy. Police and politicians, who should have been reining in the (sometimes unlawful) demonstrations, were either nowhere to be found, or acted as limp-wristed as possible. It therefore gave a permission slip to the haters to continue their behavior.

I experienced a gag reflex when I saw photos of Canadian foreign minister Melanie Joly joyfully holding hands with Palestinian Authority (PA) leader Mahmoud Abbas (March, 2024). With his other hand, Abbas cozily held the lower arm of the MP for my riding of York Centre, Ya'ara Saks, Minister of Mental Health, an

---

5   Caught on Camera: masked man threatens death, cops stand by as pro-Palestinians march in mall, YouTube, uploaded by Toronto Sun, December 18, 2023 https://www.youtube.com/watch?v=PmgtuZNPHnA

Israeli-born Canadian. There could not be a harsher insult to every Jew in Canada. It was like a knife turning in my heart. How can Canada, let alone any democratic country, provide a seat at the table with a known antisemite and Holocaust denier, who regularly and publicly calls for the destruction of Israel? At the printing of this book, he's in the nineteenth year of his four-year term. He has denied the atrocities of Oct. 7 and continues the "pay for slay" program—one where his government shells out huge sums of reward money to terrorists or their families for murdering innocent Israelis. Jews everywhere have every right to be angered by the perversion of morality as the world gives in to Hamas once again, allowing the cycle of terror to repeat.

THE MOTIVATION

I arrived in Israel on an overcast Thursday morning. Day 103 since the attack. After settling into our Bauhaus apartment, we ventured onto the Tayelet, Tel Aviv's famous beachside boardwalk. There is a wide selection of restaurants and cafes inviting you to sit on the beach for some of the best people watching anywhere. The Promenade, stretching over 3 miles along the coast line from the port of Old Yaffo to the northern port of Tel Aviv, is a 5-star walk. We passed open air gyms and volleyball courts backed by the blue-green tint of the Mediterranean Sea and the soft white sand. The sun emerged as we set off, its warmth adding to Tel Aviv's comforting embrace of love and acceptance. I observed the diversity of people, the life of Israel. For the first time in months, I could breathe.

As is always the case when we come to Israel, our social calendar was wonderfully filled with family and friends. As one would expect, all conversation centered on the events of October 7 and the developing aftermath. I met with a very close friend, an IDF General and a war hero many times over. He was onsite in Kibbutz Be'eri within an hour of the attack, organizing confused troops and containing the situation. For 18 hours he would fight wave after wave of terrorists, but not without the loss of many brave souls that were with him that day. I met with my friend Uri, a doctor, who invited me to join him on a tour near Gaza. I traced the steps of the terrorists from the Gaza border right up to the gates of Kibbutz Be'eri, where I saw the charred remains of homes, the banners and pictures for the hostages, and the green tent deciphering the ashes of human remains and running rigorous DNA testing to ensure proper burial of Israel's people and that no terrorist would be buried in a Jewish grave.

I met with Jacob[6], who despite his quiet demeanor, carries with him many things he knows but does not speak of. He has been very busy of late with his work in the Shin Bet, Israel's national security agency. We met for an off-record discussion, where he helped me understand where it all went wrong.

"Hamas has been telling us for years they are going to do this," he said. "They have been forthright with their intentions. The real question is: why did this take so long? Why did it not already happen?"

One night, two weeks into our trip, I woke abruptly, drenched in cold sweat. A regular anxious moment thinking of my son Eitan and all the other brave children of our village who are on active duty, including my sister's boy, Yonatan, and my youngest son's closest mate, Jake. It was precisely 4:18 am, I recall from tapping my phone on the night table. I quietly slipped out of the bedroom and sat with my computer at the dining table. Tears started to suddenly flow. I was crying for the loss in a village that is my home. In this moment of anxiety, in the private dark of the early morning twilight, I realized I wasn't just nervous about Israel, but there was a broader message for the world that needed to be heard.

I stared at my laptop, taking all these thoughts in, then tapped the keyboard, typing two words on the screen: *Shema Yisrael* (Hear

---

6   Name changed for anonymity.

O' Israel.) "Oh, Israel, are you listening?" I asked out loud. I then typed the letters H O W. I let these float on the screen, and then I typed W H Y.

How did this happen? Why do *they* hate us? What is it about the Jew that is so hateful? Is the world listening? Are we listening? What is the message? What is the lesson? What is going to happen now? My thoughts rambled as a thin orange glow started to peak over the uneven skyline of Tel Aviv, and the morning of the next day was born. At that moment, I typed vigorously with a hunger to get the words out of my head.

My flow of thought started with the power struggle between the East and West, following World War II. Moscow and Washington charged eagerly into a nuclear arms race that would lead to the 45-year era of The Cold War. I saw these powers racing to create alliances, staking claim to countries freshly independent from their former colonial masters. Egypt would be the first to receive its independence from Britain in 1922, followed by Syria, Jordan, and Lebanon between 1945-46, and Israel in 1948. I saw Russia and the United States dividing a world, waging war through their proxy nations, buying, demanding, and blackmailing for their loyalty. I saw Israel standing in many of those backroom deals, sometimes participating, at other times suffering the consequences of handshakes they had no part of.

I am going to say the quiet part out loud. I am not going to use the term Israel-Palestinian conflict, because Israel is not at war with Palestinians. I will not use the Israel-Arab conflict, because Israel is not at war with Arabs. I will, however, use the words "the Israel-Jihadist conflict," because this is precisely what Israel is at war with. And the real entity that Israel is at war with is Iran, who has become the de facto sponsor of Global Jihad in the most violent interpretation of its definition.

The liberals will claim that this war with Jihad is about land. But the real motivation here is the hatred of the infidel.

The spectrum of right and left ideologies became more pronounced in the wake of the Cold War between the Soviets and Americans. I am going to diverge here for an important historical context that sets the stage for one of this world's greatest betrayals of liberal values—the adoption of extreme leftist rhetoric. It was within these ideologies and sensitivities that the liberal cause was created in response to an attack on the civil liberties of Americans that dates back to the McCarthy *Reds Under the Beds* era[7] and the Korean and Vietnam war conscriptions[8]. The "stick it to the man" and "Peace & Love" movements of the Hippy generation grew into a popular front of center-left thinking. The liberal machine would eventually become the de facto conscience of America, taking on

---

7   The McCarthy era, marked by its Reds under the Beds fervor, casts a long, somber shadow over the annals of American history. In the 1950s, a palpable, pervasive fear gripped the nation—a fear that communists were lurking everywhere, from the government corridors in Washington to the smallest rural towns. Spearheaded by Senator Joseph McCarthy, this period was characterized by an intense suspicion and scrutiny that saw countless individuals accused of communist sympathies or activities, often with little to no substantiating evidence. Lives were upended as the accusations flew. Careers were destroyed, friendships severed, and trust within the community eroded. The air was thick with paranoia, the American ethos of liberty and justice strained as loyalty oaths and blacklists became the order of the day. People watched what they said and with whom they associated, lest they too fall victim to the witch hunt.

    The term "Reds under the Beds" vividly captures the almost irrational panic that someone, anyone, could be a communist agent—a fear that penetrated the very sanctity of American homes. It was a time of looking over shoulders, of whispered accusations and a society cleaved by invisible yet fiercely policed ideological boundaries. The McCarthy era remains a poignant reminder of the fragility of freedom and the devastating consequences when fear overrides reason and justice in the public consciousness.

8   Conscription during the Korean War (1950-1953) involved over 1.5 million Americans, broadly supported as a continuation of World War II efforts. The Vietnam War conscription (late 1950s-1975), particularly through the lottery draft system introduced in 1969, involved 2.2 million American men and saw the loss of approximately 58,000 military personnel. The war was centered around the containment of Communism. The draft was highly contentious, fueling widespread protests and revealing deep societal divides. It is widely agreed that America lost this war. It is likely that America has lost every war since when it comes to installing itself in international conflicts more about protecting its economic and political interests under the guise of promoting democracy.

responsibility for social equity and justice, which has since devolved into the now highly divisive DEI (Diversity, Equity, and Inclusion) movement that has produced cancel-culture phenomena.

It is this aggressive and hypocritical liberal dissonance that has strayed from its original ideology of inclusion of all peoples and their beliefs. They, the leftist influence of the now liberal movement, have chosen to adopt the Palestinian struggle, becoming their cause celebre.

"Those who stand for nothing will fall for anything" is a quote widely attributed to Alexander Hamilton, one of the Founding Fathers of the United States. The phrase conveys the idea that without firm beliefs or principles a person can easily be swayed or manipulated by various influences. The left has become a new religion, with a devout following, that appeals to those who will fervently grab onto its branches, in consequence to a free fall of a society that has grown to be without personal cause. It is an ardent faith that demands adherence and defies reason.

It is this infatuation that the liberals would form with the Palestinian cause that would ultimately create a monster that got out of its cage.

The disunity within Israel that predated the events of October 7 percolated into an embarrassing boil. That is to say, the judicial reforms debate and subsequent protests that attracted hundreds of thousands of Israelis. The diminished respect and love for and between each Jew has consequences. The Talmud relates a story of 24,000 students of the great Rabbi Akiva who perished because disrespect and jealousy ran rampant among them[9]. The destruction

---

9   Yevamot 62b

of the second Jewish temple[10] can be traced back to senseless hatred amongst the people. Our force field of protection is lost when we are divided as a people. The parting words of Moses to the Israelites about to enter the promised land was to remind them of the *Derech Eretz* (The Way of the Land): unity, respect, and human kindness, the founding Jewish principles for keeping us and our land safe.

I will discuss this in greater detail later in the book and offer my opinions for the solution of the Israeli system of politics that has failed to find a balance to represent all Israeli citizens by fair and just leadership. Meanwhile, the co-dependent relationship that Israel has with its Western backers has created a crisis in sovereignty, where Israel may lose its independent decision-making. One can go as far to claim that the country is constantly being blackmailed by the changing of the current and judged by public opinion as the political zeitgeist has Israel being played like a fiddle by powers outside of its borders. This political manipulation has Israel being strongly criticized at every juncture when defending its right to exist. I believe that this outside sphere of influence that has compromised Israel's defenses may have brought us to the steps of the massacre of October 7.

Hear O' Israel are the words we find ourselves mouthing when even God has forsaken us. We said these words as we shuffled into the gas chambers, and inside our safe rooms as terrorists banged on the door. It is time now, for we must listen to these words and help to heal a world that is divided. The reality and impossibility of the situation is upon us; we must counter the lies that are now so prevalent. If not for the love of the Jewish people and our fellow Jew, then for the love of humanity. We must maintain a strong force to defend the Jewish State, for Israel is the world's first line of defense against Jihadism. If Israel fails, we will all fall. There is a global Jihad coming; it will not take any prisoners, and does not have limits in

---

10   586 BCE and 70 CE respectively. More to come on this later.

its thirst to destroy and conquer. Mutually Assured Destruction[11] is not a theory we can rely on in our strategy to counter Jihad. We are a people of life and they, the Jihadists, are a people of death. We have a limited window to deal with the monster that is rampaging through our countries, cities, and streets.

That early morning, as I sat in front of my screen having this epiphany of purpose, I recognized that I can use my skill as a communicator to bring the past, the present, and the future into view, and I began to write. The aftermath of Ten-Seven is the wake up call at the crossroads of what we do next.

11 The theory of Mutual Assured Destruction (MAD) is a military strategy and national security policy in which a full-scale use of nuclear weapons by two or more opposing sides would cause the complete annihilation of both the attacker and the defender. Rooted in the concept of deterrence, MAD assumes that no rational actor would initiate a conflict that would lead to certain destruction for all parties involved. This theory played a central role during the Cold War, particularly between the United States and the Soviet Union, with each country maintaining a large enough arsenal of nuclear weapons to discourage the other side from launching a first strike. The underlying principle of MAD is that the threat of mutual destruction ensures that nuclear weapons serve as a deterrent to major conflicts, rather than as tools for war.

HOW?

HOW COULD TEN-SEVEN HAVE HAPPENED? The question is often asked with bewilderment, from those who expected more from the experienced forces of the IDF. This is the single most asked question I am hearing, both inside Israel and beyond its borders, by Jews and non-Jews alike. It is a perplexing and practical question, how a terrorist attack on this scale could happen in Israel, given the level of surveillance technology and security apparatus. I, too, have this burning question, and in my quest to find the answers I wrote this book.

October 7, 2023 will be known as the worst ever breakdown in Israel's military defense and one of the deadliest terrorist attacks in recent history. Such a cataclysmic and pivotal event could not, and certainly did not, happen spontaneously. Ten-Seven is not just the beginning of something, it is the earthquake that came only after a long series of warning tremors that began decades ago. The great failure is that we ignored the quivering beneath our feet. The terrorists who stormed across Israel's Gaza border are the army of Global Jihad. This book will examine seven key observations that I posit have led to the single worst terror attack in the State of Israel's 75-year history. These, I believe, best answer the question of *How:*

1. **The East-West battle for dominance:** The Russian and United States' race for hegemonic supremacy since the end of World War II has created alliances and ideologies that have divided the world into an ongoing East-West confrontation. It's all about the global sphere of influence. Russia, China and Iran are the new "axis of evil", and for Russia, these friends share the same goal as do the Jihadists: to bring down the West.

2. **Non-State terror proxies:** There is an international Party of Terror, and they are lining up on every side of Israel, screaming for the destruction of the Jewish State. They are funded, militarized, and armed with radicalized purposes. They are largely funded by the head of the snake, the Iranian regime. Until the leadership of Iran is disposed of, Israel and its Western counterparts will remain trapped in a constant game of terrorist whack-a-mole.

3. **Funding terrorism:** $2 billion in aid money pours annually into the Gaza Strip from the US, Qatar, and European countries,most of it diverted to sinister purposes. Hamas has used aid money to build over 300 miles of tunnels, for sophisticated munitions manufacturing, arms acquisitions, military training, and the lining of many personal pockets along the way.

4. **The Palestinian refugee crisis:** This "crisis" is a perpetuating myth by the United Nations and the United Nations Relief and Works Agency (UNRWA)[1]. Palestinian Arabs are the only group who can inherit refugee status four (and counting) generations after a war. They are the only group who has a "specialized" and dedicated organization (UNRWA) to oversee aid and staffing. The Palestinian cause is big business, and keeps Palestinians as pawns and victims. Leftist ideology loves a good victim, and especially loves it when the problem can be blamed on the Jews.

5. **The syllabus of hate:** Presidents, educators, professionals, unions, organizations; all are aiding or abetting anti-Israel and antisemitic sentiment. It has already long-infected our campuses and spilled into our streets. These keffiyeh-clad hoodlums hiding their faces is the Jihad that has already invaded.

6. **Israel's political system:** The electoral and political systems of Israel no longer serve the people effectively. The proportionate model of democracy yields the fringe and minority far too much power, leaving a vacuum in government checks and balances. Band-Aid policies from an outdated system can no longer hold together the heterogeneous needs of the modern State of Israel. The IDF and its security apparatus thereby suffers from poorly made decisions made at the top of the political chain.

---

[1] The United Nations Relief and Works Agency for Palestine Refugees (UNRWA) is a UN agency founded in 1949, tasked with aiding Palestinian refugees. It is a subject of controversy due to its plainly biased involvement in the Palestinian cause and its infiltration by Hamas.

7. **Jewish disunity:** The disunity and polarization in Israel prior to October 7 was modern time's highest of lows for the people of the book. The way of the land seemed to be lost. Jews divided make for weak and easy prey for our enemies.

This book will draw the connections that have been 75 years in the making. These pages are here to fill in the gaps and provide some reason, to consider what brought us to October 7 and the road map to address what is to come. This book is a statement of the Aftermath of Ten-Seven. This is the wake up call. I am hopeful the people of Israel and the world will listen, and act to protect themselves from Global Jihad.

I am writing this book because this is the time for action, and we cannot sit idly by. For me, it starts with trying to put into context the complexity of how October 7 happened.

During my time in Israel in the aftermath of Ten-Seven, I listened to the people of this land, who have endured yet another attack on their existence, *a barbaric pogrom that takes us back to medieval times.*[2]

Through this book I hope to speak with those disconnected from these events as a point of education. I want to speak to the people who have taken to the streets, protesting Israel with wrong information. I appeal to reasonableness. I want to warn the liberal lovers of social justice and inclusion that their principles are at stake and being misused by the haters of this world, who are very

---

2   I want to note here that describing a modern event as "a barbaric pogrom that takes us back to medieval times" evokes a powerful and stark image of regression into a brutal past. The term "pogrom" originally refers to violent riots aimed at the massacre or persecution of an ethnic or religious group, particularly Jews in Russia and Eastern Europe during the late 19th and early 20th centuries. Using this term in a contemporary context suggests a severe and ruthless act of violence, deeply infused with historical connotations of lawlessness, persecution, and communal violence. This statement draws a direct line between historical acts of savagery and contemporary violence. Despite advancements in civil rights and societal norms, this primitive hatred and cruelty, reminiscent of darker times in human history, still exists, especially when it comes to acts of terror, where there are no rules of war.

clever at creating false narratives, twisting truths, and fermenting a sentiment of lies.

This book is for Jews and supporters of Israel everywhere. I wish to give voice to these feelings of betrayal and seclusion. To articulate with objectivity a candid account of the reality and the consequences of global anti-Jewish sentiment, which is very real. It is easy to feel alone, and I hope this book will connect, comfort, and let you feel heard.

I am hoping that this book will dispel the myths, expose the lies, and honor the truth.

MY NAME IS ISRAEL

DO YOU HAVE A PROBLEM WITH THAT?

VERY SHORTLY AFTER THE OCTOBER 7 ATTACK, my wife and I
boarded a planned riverboat excursion down the Rhine with extreme
trepidation. The last thing that we wanted to do was take a vaca-
tion at this time. We spent most of our time huddled around our
phones as the stories started to unfold. It was a surreal time to be
in Europe at the start of the surge of protests, which erupted almost
immediately, as if planned well in advance.

Our plan was to come to Israel at the end of the cruise. Eitan,
our son, pleaded with us not to continue to Israel. He did not want
to worry about us while he was actively serving in the IDF, while

the country came under attack. It was a very difficult time; we were numb as the aftermath of Ten-Seven started to unfold. One afternoon I took a break from reality and joined a castle hiking tour through hilly terrain. We were in Germany at the time, the rolling green landscape before us rich in history.

I had a pleasant conversation with some people from Walnut Creek, California. Well-healed liberal lovers. All went well until…

"Hey, I'm Steve by the way, and this is my wife Linda."

I automatically extended my own hand. "Israel."

There it was; Steve blinked.

"That's my name," I smiled. "Israel, Israel Ellis."

You could have cut the silence with a knife.

"Where are you from?" He eventually asked.

"Canada," I say, and watch the relief in his expression, his hand moving forward once more for me to shake. We talked about family and kids. I got around to my second oldest.

"He lives in Israel?" Steve asked, his nose twitching.

"Yes," I responded, ignoring the oncoming distaste. "He works for a startup." Sensing the need to fill in the blanks, I continued. "He went (to Israel) when he was 17 to join the army. We call him a lone soldier. We are very proud of him."

With a flick of his wrist, Steve slid up the sleeve of his LuLu Dri-fit and made a show of checking his Breitling watch. He looked away from me with obvious loathing. "Hey man, sorry, we gotta cut." He ran off to his group, his contempt undeniable.

I have never thought twice about introducing myself by name. A hand is extended, I shake it. Not anymore. It is happening all too often that my introduction is met with pause, to the extent that I am anxiously unsure of what reaction I will receive. How bizarre that this is something I should experience as a third generation Canadian, some stranger hesitating at the announcement of my name.

I recently had to change my Uber profile to "Izzy." Every Uber I ordered while visiting London was canceled.

"I'm telling you, it's your profile," my wife said, a settled reality in her voice.

"No, it can't be!" I retorted with naive innocence.

"I'm telling you, honey. Change it, and you'll see."

I changed it. The next Uber picked us up. I sat quietly as we rode among busy traffic and red-double decker buses, deeply saddened by the reality of bias, dissonance, prejudice, hate, and ignorance.

These are not isolated events. They are happening every day, everywhere, to every Jew and Israeli. I met Ora during a waterfall hike on the Island of Koh Phangan. A young bright light, who projects simple innocence. We got to talking. She is from Israel, traveling for the first time, seeing the world through the eyes of someone new to everything outside of the village. She explained to me that she originally planned a walkabout that was interrupted by Covid, then again on October 7. "I completely lost my confidence to travel," she says. "It's my brother who gave me the courage. He came back from the East a changed boy. Suddenly he is into meditation and prayer. I was so impressed."

But Ora's innocence was broken early during her travels when she met a boy in a Berlin coffee shop.

"What language is that?" the boy asked, overhearing the end of a phone conversation with her mother.

"It's Hebrew," Ora answered.

"Hebrew?! Really? Cool," he exclaimed.

"I am from Israel," Ora offered, smiling, thinking privately, *maybe...*

But the boy shifted uncomfortably, adjusting the glasses that gave him the academic look she found so attractive. "Hey..uh... I gotta go..."

"Oh really, why is that?" Ora asked. She was surprised. She didn't understand just yet.

"You people are murderers," the boy said, getting up from his seat and unconsciously pushing the bridge of his glasses.

"Hey, hold on," Ora called. He half-turned, pausing just long enough to retort.

"Your country is murdering children, and are colonial occupiers."

Then he was gone, another ignoramus, waltzing to the fables of academia. But Ora cannot shake this conversation from her mind. "What does this boy know of my country?" she said to me. "Who is he to judge me? He has never even been to Israel."

Until now, I never thought twice about my safety in Toronto. I can only remember one antisemitic experience, when I was seven years old. I was wearing my *Kippa* (Jewish skullcap), and playing on the swings at a playground. A group of boys came up to me, swiped my beanie and called me a *kike*. I honestly never recalled this incident until I was sitting in my car at the intersection of my own neighborhood, being told by police to turn around and go home for my own safety.

The anti-Israel, pro-Palestinian gatherings of the ignorant and the haters unfold in my own community, on campuses across North America, and in city streets all over the world. The number of people gathering are in the hundreds—at times thousands. Their banners unfurl hateful messages that beautify the terror, perversely rationalizing the October 7 terrorist attack as an act of a *just* revolution. I take it personally, after all, people are calling for *my* murder. The disturbing reality, as I magnify the pictures I see on the news sites, is that many of these people do not seem remotely connected or indigenous to the cause. I see a throwback to the 1930's Nazi start, Germany's forever stain. I see the weakness of governments who are capitulating to and negotiating with Global Jihad. The Palestinian cause is simply a catalyst. They are being victimized and manipulated by the powers behind these protests, used to further an anti-Jewish sentiment, for without their story the narrative is lost and the higher purpose is in peril. What we are seeing today is the spontaneous combustion of embers that have been glowing in wait; it only took a little wind to fan the flames of senseless hatred.

The agenda of Global Jihad is not hidden. Global Jihad is a well-documented cornerstone of radical Islam. It is shouted from the pulpits and lecterns of Imams in mosques and by educators in classrooms. It does not make me a racist or Islamophobe to confront this. The world is at a crossroads, given its clearest opportunity yet to wake up and understand that this is not an exclusive threat to Israel. Ships of every flag are being attacked in the Red Sea. Europe is on a demographic crash course, and within 20 years its legislature will shift significantly. The United States is under constant risk of incursion from the inside. Canada is overrun by radicals who are just now starting to show themselves. There is a radicalization of youth and the disenfranchised that is normalized online and in some parochial institutions. This is unchecked because the West lacks the fortitude to define hateful rhetoric. It is this rhetoric that perpetuates hate and can lead to violence. We must act to stop this madness.

On September 4th, 2024, The Meta (Facebook) content court ruled that the slogan "from the river the sea" isn't hate speech. This is concerning on so many levels, firstly, that Meta is a for profit corporation that has now come off as its own legislative body to determine what is hateful language and what is not. From where I sit, should that not be within the jurisdiction of an elected government body? Secondly, it is commonly accepted that this term is highly derogatory in the sense that the establishment of a Palestinian state requires the complete annihilation of Israel and its people. This type of terminology only serves to perpetuate hate and create an unsafe place for Jewish people who must fear for their safety.

The normalization of anti-Israel sentiment (which is synony-mous with anti-Jewish sentiment) is being propagated on all fronts. For example, it is not okay for the largest union in Canada (CUPE) to let its executive members retweet hate. I first realized the extent of this when in my neighborhood a number of years ago I came across a CUPE rally in front of the B'Nai Brith building, and wondered to myself, "What does a union representing the interests of the Canadian working person have to do with what is going on in Israel?" and "Why are they defaming Israel and the Jewish people?" I would later come to the realization that this is the antisemitism my wife's grandfather, a Holocaust survivor, referred to. The haters coming out of the forest were always there laying in wait. Ten-Seven provided CUPE's anti-Israel sentiments even more pronounced opportunities to show their true colors.

THERE IS NO COMING INVASION. IT IS ALREADY HERE

Jihad has already been invited into our universities, professions, communities, and public institutions. October 7 was a wake up call. It is an example of the hunger for Global Jihad, and what can happen if it is allowed to be satiated. To think that these events are restricted to a narrow strip on the Mediterranean is a complete miscalculation of reality. The next statement by Global Jihad could be an attack on your city, your block, your street. There are no second chances here. No do overs. There is a confrontation of values and cultures that is heading for a collision course. The Western mindset is guided by reciprocal altruism and human rights. The Jihadist mindset is ruled by conquest and the elimination of the infidel. The two mindsets are incompatible.

Global Jihad is counting on the Western sensitivities to immobilize its response in the face of the civil liberties that the West stands for, which may have to be compromised in the face of the threat. In a world where freedom of speech, freedom of religion, and freedom of assembly are sacrosanct to Western society, there may be security and defensive measures that will curtail these rights. What do you do when the rights and freedoms given to society are abused by any one group? The radicals are having a big party, while laughing at our enablement of them.

THE WORLD ORDER

The challenge we face is existential to the extreme. The Western, or *free,* socio-political foundation is based on freedoms and rights, diversity and inclusion, and equality in justice. These are the ideological values within the social contract that people born into freedom are encouraged to expect. But how do you respond when you witness these values being used against us? When thousands of protestors take to the streets and the promotion of violence and messages of hate becomes the predominant use of the privilege of expression, we have a problem.

This is what the Jihadist is counting on. Therefore, the only way to fight back is to challenge these ideals that are so foundational to the West's moral code of conduct. Law enforcement must be given the tools to curtail the incitement and the law breaking. Yet right now, the political class has shown it does not have the will to fight, and that leaves our uniformed officers… handcuffed.

In special circumstances, it is necessary to find workarounds with freedoms and rights. This is what happened on Sept. 11, 2001 when nearly 3,000 innocent people were murdered by Jihadist hijackers. Politicians put in place safeguards in homeland defense, airports, and surveillance. Unfortunately, even profiling. While it's true that not all Muslims are jihadists, those who are jihadists identify as Muslim. But the idea of isolating Muslims contradicts the principle of judging people as individuals.

Republican President George W. Bush took to arms to bring justice to the Axis of Evil. During his two terms he made it the cornerstone of his foreign policy to bring in a zero tolerance to terrorism on the shores of America and anywhere. Then came the Democratic left-leaning President Barack Obama, who in his first 100 days bowed to the Saudi King Abdullah, and bent his knee to Iran. Obama believed he could sweet talk terror regimes, naively ignored the threats, and America was played like a fiddle.

We now must take measures to protect the values of free society.

But we must also avoid the type of McCarthyism paranoia seen in the 1950s. So what is the answer? Do we surrender to the left's peace-and-love convictions and take our ideals to the firing range? Or do we do the hard work now and announce the unpalatable reality that there is a Global Jihad taking place, where the first line of defense has already been breached, and we must act now to ensure that Ten-Seven, or 9-11, does not repeat itself.

The most important pathway forward is going to depend on leadership who will endorse the difficult work that needs to be done and find a way to defend, secure, and protect, without compromising the freedoms and liberties we hold so dearly as the soul of our morality. The United States is the lighthouse in an ocean of nation states who can set the tone needed to protect the Western way of life. The left-leaning administrations of the United States and Canada have opened the floodgates to the Jihadists, whose actions in the aftermath of October 7 speak for what is to come. The sheer numbers of protestors and squatters in the encampments across North America is alarming and should be recognized for what they are, the fissile material of the haters.

In 1990, I traveled to Berlin and camped on the Potsdamer Platz, where I celebrated the fall of the Berlin Wall with the newly-freed people of the East. We were holed up in what was once No Man's Land[1], where many people died trying to escape East German communist tyranny. I partied for five days with the likes of popular singers Sinead O'Connor, Roger Waters (another misguided brick

---

1 The No Man's Land between East and West Germany, particularly around the Berlin Wall, refers to the heavily fortified and desolate area that separated the two sides during the Cold War. Officially known as the "death strip," this zone was a restricted area between the inner wall (facing East Berlin) and the outer wall (facing West Berlin). It stretched along the length of the Berlin Wall and was designed to prevent people from escaping from East Germany to West Germany.

in the wall[2]), and half a million other citizens of the world. It was a defining moment for me. As a young idealist, I was energized by the belief that tyranny has its eventual downfall and the people will prevail. But what has happened since the end of the Cold War? The world has just got more complicated, scarier, and a bigger threat to humanity. The new world order of evil is made up of an even larger group of controlling totalitarian rule: Russia, North Korea, China, and Iran act against the interests of a coalition of Western free nations. The countries within the sphere of Africa are leaning toward the Eastern influence, and the South and Central Americas are more prone to the West. You could include pariah states such as Syria, potentially Lebanon, if you agree that Hezbollah is running the show. Yemen and the pan-African zealots are influenced by Iran. Turkey, though considered secular and a member of NATO, is a big question mark. The concentration of these powers, and the radicalization of so many peoples, is a very dangerous combination that in all likelihood may overwhelm the West. The irony of all of this is that we have created the beast that now hunts us. The West's consumption of oil has fuelled the riches of Pan-Arab countries beyond their wildest imaginations. Billions of dollars pour from the West into the Middle East, and some of those dollars, directly or indirectly, fund terror and the protests happening in our backyards. The gas I purchase for my car, the taxes I pay to a government sympathetic to UNRWA; all this money goes to people who want to murder me, my family, and other Jews. Don't make any mistake

---

2   Roger Waters, co-founder and former bassist and lyricist of the iconic rock band Pink Floyd, is often described in controversial terms like "a misguided brick in the wall" due to his outspoken political views and activism, especially regarding the Israel-Palestine conflict. This phrase cleverly plays on the title of Pink Floyd's famous song "Another Brick in the Wall," which criticizes rigid and oppressive schooling and societal norms. Waters is a vocal supporter of the Boycott, Divestment, and Sanctions (BDS) movement against Israel, which he argues is a protest against what he views as the oppressive policies of Israel toward Palestinians. His stance has led to significant criticism and accusations of antisemitism, which he has consistently denied. Waters contends that his criticisms are not of Jews or Judaism but specifically against the policies of the Israeli government.

about it, because there is no subtlety in the statements being made by the Jihadists, who at every opportunity can be heard calling for the annihilation of the Jewish people. Global Jihad is very much a direct threat on our lives, lifestyles, morals and values.

The complexity and challenges we face as a free world are enormous and deep. For free nations to place Israel under a microscope, constantly admonishing and frustrating its efforts to defend itself against the relentless attacks from enemies that surround it on all sides, is bizarre when you look at this picture from above. These rallying cries against Israel are a self-inflicted bullet to the head for the West, and yet the people waving their flags in city streets and on campuses cannot see it. But Jihadists are euphoric at the support. They have been planning the deaths of the infidel—including the useful idiots—for a very long time.

THE DISSONANCE

I STARTED TO WRITE THIS BOOK from our apartment overlooking Allenby Street, an avenue that has played a central role in the development of Tel Aviv culture, known for its vibrant mix of architecture, bustling markets, lively nightlife, and proximity to the Carmel Market and the beachfront. Taking up a short term residence in Israel was an on-the-ground opportunity to speak with Israelis and gain understanding and perspective of the aftermath of October 7. I realized very quickly that first and foremost the people needed to be heard. I did not realize how powerful it would be to simply listen to their voices and offer them empathy. Typical of Israeli society, everyone has a lot to say, and you cannot have 10 people in a room with fewer than 10 different opinions. From these conversations, on the streets, in restaurants and bars, with friends and family, and also random encounters, I have developed the story being told in these pages.

The whole world needs to listen. "Stop being used!" I want to shout. "Open your eyes!" This is so much bigger than just Israel and the terror groups in the Middle East. When Houthis attack ships and force them out of the Suez Canal and around Cape Horn, your cost of goods just went up by 30%. When menacing, masked protesters disrupt our city streets and threaten action, you should be worried. When the Parliament of Canada bends its knee to the Palestinian cause, a group of people completely opposed to our Canadian values and way of life, it should deeply scare you. I am sickened to see members of parliament sitting in *my* government buildings wearing the keffiyeh made famous by the godfather of terrorism, Yasser Arafat. This is not about the liberal values we have worked so hard to evolve, but a hateful agenda fuelled by the *woke* left targeting the Western way of life. It is anarchy. It is hate. And there will soon be violent clashes that will turn our cities into security zones.

The isolation and betrayal of the Jewish community by the governments who have allowed the demonization of Jewish people post October 7, and the normalization of rhetoric targeting Jewish people, are leaving Jewish citizenry with a very uncomfortable and unwelcome feeling. Every time Jews leave a country because they are persecuted, that country falls apart. It happened in Spain, Russia, Arab lands—and it could happen to the Americas. One only needs to track Jewish migration to see this pattern of downfall. I recently visited the once thriving city of Łódź, Poland, tracing the life of my wife's grandfather, Elias, a Holocaust survivor, a man amongst men. His family and everything he had known were torn from him without mercy. Yet Elias preferred to see the optimistic potential of all persons regardless of who they were or where they came from. He was a believer in humanity. This was his choice.

Łódź was a thriving metropolis home to 233,000 Jews, rich and diverse in culture. By the end of the war there were only 800 Jewish souls left in the ghetto and an estimated 10,000 survivors. Today's Łódź is a gray cloudy place. It reeks of the death it hosted more than 75 years ago.

The Spanish Inquisition saw the migration of almost its entire Jewish community, and with that the decline of Spain. If the Jews leave, with this departure will become North America's decline.

THE CONTRADICTIONS

From within Israel, and its liberal values, there is a contradiction that comes from the need for security and protection of freedoms. Israel is the only country in the region that holds regular elections, protects and encourages free speech, is host to vast numbers of ethnic people, and welcomes diversity and inclusion. There is no other country in the region that would allow a Pride parade, let alone the open display of affection between two people of the same sex. (In the Palestinian Authority and Hamas-controlled areas, this is a death wish.) Yet balancing national security concerns with individual rights and freedoms is a challenge in light of necessary checkpoints, security barriers, and counteroffensive urban military operations. These policing tactics are ultimately forced upon Israel by the constant threat of Palestinian terrorists.

Humanitarian and social justice policies cannot be at the exclusion of others. The movements who claim to be rallying for humanity and outwardly exclude Jews contradict their own morality. There are several examples of dissonance of the groups who say they stand for one thing, but not when it applies to Jews. Take the Boycott, Divestment, Sanctions (BDS) movement against Israel. While the movement claims to be advocating for the human rights of Palestinians and against what it describes as Israeli occupation, it clearly crosses the line into antisemitism. For instance, when BDS campaigns target Jewish individuals as in professors, or organizations like a retailer owned by a Jewish person regardless of their stance on Israel, or when they exclude Jewish groups from participating in broader human rights coalitions purely based on their Jewish identity, they can be seen as contradicting the movement's stated goal of promoting universal human rights. This selective exclusion undermines the moral foundation of the movement by engaging in the very kind of discrimination it purports to oppose. One prominent example was in May 2024 when a Jewish-owned restaurant in Montreal, Falafel Yoni, had its windows smashed.

Here is one that really makes me shake my head: Pride movements, where LGBTQ+ people advocate for inclusivity and equal rights, and yet certain communities exclude or marginalize Jewish participants or groups. During Pride events, there have been controversies when Jewish LGBTQ+ groups have been barred from marching with Jewish symbols, such as the Star of David, or from carrying flags that incorporate these symbols. This exclusion can be seen as contradictory to the Pride movement's core values of diversity, inclusivity, and equality for all. By excluding Jewish groups, these factions within the Pride movement undermine their own moral stance of advocating for the rights and acceptance of all marginalized communities. Fredericton, New Brunswick, in its July 2024 Pride, renamed its march in solidarity with Palestinians, included Palestinian flags, and returned funds from any corporate donations who are known to do business with Israel. Lt.-Gov. Brenda Murphy, the first openly gay lieutenant governor, sent a notice that she refused to march after organizers chose to share the parade with the pro-Palestinian cause. The parade did not happen, and was subsequently canceled by organizers citing "safety" concerns.

As long as there are calls for the destruction of Israel we will never have the dialogue that leads to peace. We simply cannot have discussions that do not recognize Israel's existence and its right to self defense. The same rights that apply to any other country must apply to Israel. No one is debating Ukraine's right to defend itself, nor was there an admonishment for the killing of several thousand poorly-armed and inexperienced Russian soldiers fed into the meat grinder on the front lines.

The liberal perception is in conflict with the Palestinian Authority[1], which fails to adhere to the liberal ideologies of democracy, freedoms, and equality. None of these values are respected by the PA. In fact, quite the opposite.

THE MANIPULATION OF THE QURAN

The contradictions between the core principles of Islam and the current conflict with Israel merits discussion. The foundational Islamic values of peace, justice, and the sanctity of human life are disconnected from the realities of the anti Jewish and wider inter-Arab conflict in the region. Islam teaches peace as a fundamental principle; the Quran emphasizes the importance of peace. Muhammad's recorded life includes instances of making peace agreements with his enemies. The reality today contradicts these principles, driving the important question of how Islamic leaders can reconcile their rhetoric of destruction and Jihad alongside the peace-orientated religious teachings of the Quran. The 'Jihad' concept in Islam originally referred to "striving in the way of God", and yet today has been widely adopted as a rhetoric of aggression. Even if you take the stand that "striving in the way of God" is interpreted as self defense, the Quran insists that any act of self-defense must be conducted within strict ethical guidelines that minimize harm to civilians and seeks peace as the ultimate goal. (I guess Hamas and the other proxies of terror overlooked this one.) The perversion of

---

1   The Palestinian Authority (PA) is a semi-autonomous governing body established in 1994 after the Oslo Accords, overseeing parts of the West Bank. It functions as a subsidiary of the Palestine Liberation Organization (PLO), which was previously considered a terrorist organization under Yassar Arafat due to its violent activities in the 1970s and 1980s but later shifted toward peace negotiations, especially after renouncing terrorism in 1988. Fatah, a dominant faction within the PLO, has played a leading role in the PA, advocating for Palestinian national interests.

Islam is how they rationalize their terror. In doing so, they insult both Islam itself and all Muslims.

COUSINS AND PEACE

One cannot understand the true nature of what is happening in the Middle East without first studying the history of the relationship between Muslims and Jews. There is consensus that Ishmael is the ancestor of Arabs, whose line descends to the founding prophet of Islam, and Isaac, the father of the Jews—both of whom were born from Abraham. We can therefore safely conclude that the offspring from these two men were cousins; and so we can also say with some degree of informed intelligence that the Muslim-Jewish relationship has been one of cousins learning to live together and settling differences. I have studied Islam and the relationship between Muslims and Jews rooted in a shared Abrahamic tradition, where Jews are acknowledged as "People of the Book." The Quran emphasizes peaceful coexistence and mutual respect, while historical conflicts are seen as isolated events rather than indicators of enduring enmity. As I have stated above, Islamic teachings in the Quran advocate for justice, kindness, and the protection of religious minorities, including Jews. The only reference that has come afoul of violence is within the Hadith description:

> "The last hour would not come unless the Muslims will fight against the Jews and the Muslims would kill them until the Jews would hide themselves behind a stone or a tree and a stone or a tree would say: 'Muslim, or the servant of Allah, there is a Jew behind me; come and kill him'; but the tree Gharqad would not say, 'for it is the tree of the Jews.'"[2]

---

2   Sahih Muslim, Book 41, Hadith 6985

The Hadith is the unwritten Quran, more like comments recorded offline (assumed from Muhammad), and this particular comment relates to an end of world prophecy that should be read within the larger framework of Islamic eschatological prophecies. Its interpretation, likely a metaphor, varies widely. It should not be used as a general statement about contemporary Muslim-Jewish relations, which are governed by broader Islamic principles of coexistence and respect. However, it is this passage that has become the thin thread of rationale used by radicalized Muslims. I use the word "thread" with purpose, because this almost invisible link to a written sanction for the murder of Jews continues to dangle there only because people will attach themselves to any argument, even the weakest, when it comes to hating on someone else. Any person who is knowledgeable and/or a true Muslim will know that using this justification in the current day is a blasphemous and unjustifiable departure from the Quran.

The Gharqad, known scientifically as *Lycium*, is a thorny shrub that grows in arid and semi-arid regions, particularly in the Middle East, and is commonly referred to as boxthorn or wolfberry. Symbolically, this tree refers to people or groups loyal to Jews. Perhaps in a modern sense this could indicate the support of the United States, however there are countries within the Pan-Arab world that have also transcended the lunacy of this conflict and now appreciate what a peaceful relationship with Israel can produce for the greater good of their people and the region.

Egypt was the first to sign a peace agreement with Israel in 1979, for which President Anwar Sadat paid with his life when he was assassinated during a military parade in 1981. Thankfully, the peace treaty remains in full effect nearly 45 years later. The Israel-Jordan Peace Treaty was signed in 1994, ending the state of war that had existed between the two countries since 1948. It has succeeded its original author, King Hussein of Jordan, and is respected by his heirs. The former king became very close with Israeli leaders, and this open line of communication continues today. The relationship between Israel and Turkey has been more complex, characterized by periods of both close cooperation and tension. Turkey was the first country to officially recognize Israel in 1949. In 1996, the two countries signed a military cooperation agreement, leading to a close strategic partnership. However the relationship has been taken on a roller coaster of wide criticism and overt hateful incitement by Turkey's President Erdogan. The messages coming out of Turkey are a diplomatic strain, often leading to political conflict between the two nations.

The 2020 Abraham accords[3] were a major milestone, and is perhaps the best news to come out of the region since peace with Egypt and Jordan. The Accords were negotiated based on mutual economic interests and shared security. Say what you will about the Trump presidency, he was able to accomplish more in the peace process than any other recent administrations. Today, this critical deal is on shaky ground; the terrorist actors have put Pan-Arab nations in a difficult bind. There is not one secular Arab country that can tolerate a terror organization, and yet they are put into a position of needing to publicly express sympathy for the Palestinian people. This sensitivity has a volatile effect on the peace process. It is a sensitivity that Iran, through their terror proxies, uses against Israel and her newly-formed alliances in the region. Prior to October 7, Israel was possibly just weeks from signing an historic peace agreement with Saudi Arabia. Had it taken place, for the first time in 75 years every secular Arab country would have normalized relationships with Israel. It would have been a real win for peace and regional

---

3   The Abraham Accords, signed in 2020, are a series of agreements normalizing diplomatic relations between Israel and several Arab countries. This marked a significant shift in Middle Eastern diplomacy. The primary agreements were between Israel and the United Arab Emirates (UAE) and Israel and Bahrain. Later, Sudan and Morocco also agreed to normalize relations with Israel. It is noteworthy that Saudi Arabia was rumored to soon be signing the pact, which was put on the back burner after October 7th.

stability. There is no surprise, then, at the timing of October 7, which is likely to have been prematurely launched by Hamas, having been secretly pushed forward by Iran to undermine the Israel-Saudi Arabia peace deal. They were successful: the peace deal is now on the back burner. This is an example of the contradiction in intention, and how the cause of the Palestinians is being kept alive by any means, manipulated by Iran for its own goals.

ARRIVAL

Landing in Israel was an emotional experience of relief and love. A feeling of escaping something unsettling behind us. There is no country like Israel. She is one of the smallest countries by area but one of the most vast in history and world impact. Israel is also one of the most vocal places in the world. I am often pleasantly overwhelmed when I must give in to the chaos of several conversations going on simultaneously, each competing at a higher pitch. I will sit back with a smile, enveloped in the warmth and energy of the people who make up my village, and send a silent prayer of thanks to God for the gratefulness I feel in that moment.

It is not just for the sake of Israel's unique and beautiful culture, history, and people, that I ask the world to open its eyes. If Israel fails, the world's first line of defense is gone. This is not about Israel. It is about the ultimate fight between Good and Evil. Our morals and convictions, and the freedoms and liberties fought so hard for. Do not make the mistake of looking at the events of October 7 in a vacuum. What happened on that terrible morning was not the beginning, and if we allow things to continue as they have been, it most certainly will not be the end.

TEN-SEVEN

WAKING TO TERROR

HER STORY: You are just waking to the first light of the sun peaking through your window around the sides of the laced curtain your *Savta* sewed for you, blowing in the hot wind. Your eyes remain closed for another minute, feeling the warmth of your little ones snuggled against your chest. You open your eyes and smile at the vision of your 3-year-old and 5-year-old holding hands, the glint of the sun catching their angelic curls. In just twenty minutes you will be hiding beneath your bed amongst stored linens with your babies pressed against you, terrified they may make a sound, as four men dressed in black sit on your bed and unpack a bag filled with grenades and guns, speaking in a foreign Arab dialect. They are pacing the room frantically. One of them, he can't be more than 19, repeats over and over, "Allahu Akbar." Finally, they move outside, but before they leave they set the house ablaze. You move out from underneath the bed cautiously. Your children, mercifully quiet, regard you with terrified, deep dark eyes—one of them will not speak a word for two months. You recall your husband's kiss as he stealthily exited the bedroom to give you that extra bit of sleep, and wonder if he will ever again be coming to your side. They will find him later in a field with an almost imperceptible pulse, six bullets between his torso and legs. You will only know he is barely alive and in a coma, fighting to come back to you, after you and your children are discovered by the young soldiers who find you in the concrete storage room underneath the house that you barely reached via a trap door. The pop-pop sound of the gunfire will remain forever in your head. You will just make it into the darkness of the storage area filled with stale airlessness, and before you pass out from the smoke of your burning home you look down at those two beautiful faces—still holding hands, barely breathing.

His story: You are driving home from visiting with your parents, having brought your dad your wife's famous bone broth soup. He's been struggling with the flu. He will be fine, but you wanted to do this act of love to let him know you guys care. The streets are starting to fill with morning traffic. It will not get busier than this; today is a national holiday so many will be at home focused on family and community. You are eager to get back to yourself. There will be a treasure hunt for the kids on the Kibbutz. They are just now old enough to start enjoying the festivities. As you drive, you imagine their faces squealing in delight. A loud bang you cannot quite decipher breaks your daydream, then another much closer. You see a car up ahead lift into the air, one of its occupants flying through a window, and you skid to a stop. Your brain cannot reconcile what you see coming toward you through the smoke, a white Toyota pickup truck with the dark silhouettes of people standing in the tray. You see a flashes of light coming from the back toward you. Without thinking you floor the accelerator and drive into the field beside the road. You can only think now of racing home to where you left your sleeping wife and kids not even 30 minutes ago. The car gets stuck in some mud, the wheels still spinning as you exit into the field, running toward more smoke and shouts ahead. You hear the truck gears grinding as it follows, too terrified to look over your shoulder. Then you feel the searing burn, and you look down and see the massive holes opened up in your torso. You fall to the ground. Your last thoughts, the sweet curls you would press your face into as you breathe in that baby smell. Weeks later, as you struggle to awake amidst the beeping monitors and the strangeness of tubes protruding from your body, your heart will start to race madly, confused and terrified. You see the beauty of your wife's tears as she presses a small child against you. But your first thoughts are of nothing as you struggle to make sense of the moment.

A mother's story: Your daughter Yael and her two brothers Yoram and Noah have gone to a music festival in the south to join thousands of other young people in a celebration of life to the tunes of their day. It is drawing near 6am, and Noah, the younger brother, is starting to finally feel his beat. The night was a cold, bad idea, he's thinking, and the shrooms took too long to kick in, but in that moment, as he is shuffling his feet and raising his hands to the techno beat, a sliver of sun rises over the mountain and suddenly warms him, filling him with a gratitude and a feeling of total bliss. Just then, the wail of sirens. Long range missiles fly overhead, and Noah's heart drops as he watches them soar toward his home. But he is not panicking, he has seen this before, and knows there are effective countermeasures to neutralize them. But now he hears the sound of nearby explosions, the distinct pop-pop of gunfire. They are under attack, and he is seeing prisms. He feels his brother and sister grab his arms, and the three of them run toward the north field where the car is parked.

You start to panic as the news comes in, and you desperately call your kids on Facetime, relieved when they answer. They're panting, and beyond them you can hear people screaming, explosions and gunfire. Your heart leaps into your throat when you hear angry Arabic shouts in the distance. The kids find the car and race out. They will make several U-turns, not knowing where to go, while beside them other cars are engulfed in flames. They see bodies thrown from cars, riddled with bullets. The twisted faces of young party goers, heads hanging, still in their seats with frozen eyes.

Yoram feels the piss in his shorts sticking the fabric to his skin. He sees someone standing next to a car, waving his arms in the way you do when you want someone to stop and help, and as they get closer, they see the bodies around him and notice his black fatigues, the headband with Arabic scrawlings in green they only see on news reports. "Yoram, move! Move! Move!" you hear your daughter frantically scream just before the screen and phone goes dead. Yoram fights the terror and trusts his gut, "Keep moving until I can't," he tells himself. He drives straight for the terrorist, forcing a game of chicken. By some miracle they are able to find a path, and in the rear view mirror there is a split-second almost comedic scene of the lone gunman scrambling up from a ditch, pointing his gun and screaming as he sprays bullets in every direction. The car is flying 150km/h down the bumpy road; they see the highway and keep going without looking back. Within one hour of making it home and ripping away from your embrace, your son has his army fatigues on and is out the door.

Months later, I will drive by this exact site where Yoram is frantically trying to find an exit around the chaos, terrified for his siblings and their lives, thinking of his mother having to bury all three of her children. For each of the burned and bullet-riddled cars I now see lined up, there is a story of failed survival. Of sudden shock, terror, and panic as the music, dance and joy shifted to an apocalypse of sudden destruction, masked terrorists charging, gre-nades flying, RPG fire, machine gun fire. Screams of *Allahu Akbar! Allahu Akbar!* It must have been terrifying in their last moments. It is eerie, as the morning fog lifts, for me to see the multitude of burned out cars lined up for a mass burial. There are people taking samples for DNA, others making records for insurance. In some cases, the blood and body fragments are so embedded in the charred remains of the vehicles that to comply with Jewish burial law the entire car must be buried.

I will meet Noah in a hospital at Tel Hashomer a few months later. In the second month of the war he will find himself laying on the sandy ground, watching his own blood pooling around him as he slowly loses consciousness. They were able to save his leg, but the wound left him with a deformity that will always remind him. He proudly shows the shrapnel surgically removed, which he keeps in a small container next to his bed, perhaps as a reminder of what one little piece of metal can do to deform and end lives.

At the same hospital, I also meet Rubin, a strapping 25-year old police officer. He and his wife were staying with his parents in nearby Ashkelon on the morning of October 7. When they woke that morning, looking forward to the family celebration of the Jewish holiday of *Simchat Torah*, Rubin's phone on his side table was abuzz. When he answered, it took him a moment to comprehend the other side of the conversation. His police unit was under attack in the south. He was dressed, in his car and racing toward the action in less than five minutes. His only weapon was his private pistol; he would be outfitted, he figured, once he got to the station in Sderot. What he did not know was that the building was already on fire.

15 minutes later, racing down the two lane highway on the outskirts of Sderot, Rubin notices a cloud of dust coming toward him; he quickly pulls to a stop when he sees the white pick-up truck. A hail of bullets erupts from the Kalashnikov-wielding men standing in the open back of the truck; their trademark green berets

displaying the emblem and insignia of the Izz ad-Din al-Qassam Brigades can be seen from a distance. They come to a stop and open fire at Rubin's stationary vehicle. Rubin is out of his car and firing his pistol as soon as they come into range. By the time his last bullet is in the chamber, three of the terrorists are neutralized. Rubin stumbles back into his car. He has been shot 8 times. He turns the car around and is chased for 5 kilometers. He will call his wife and tell her he loves her. Two more bullets slam into his back, one of them lodging within millimeters of his spine. The terrorists, possibly realizing they are too deep into enemy territory, stop the pursuit. Another 5 kilometers and Rubin is pulling into the city of Netivot. His car rolls to a stop, and two bystanders rush over to see what is going on. As he is pulled from the now blood soaked vehicle, he hands his rescuers his cell phone and asks them to call his dad.

"I am sorry for the grief *Abba*, I love you. Tell mom."

Amazingly, Rubin does not lose consciousness as he is rushed to the nearby Soroka hospital in Be'er Sheva. His life is saved, he is happy to be alive, and remains hopeful he will not lose his leg. The bullet lodged in his spine is still there.

I will visit many soldiers in the hospital that day whose lives have changed forever, a new generation of cripples and amputees. Like Noah and Rubin, all of them tell me that they are the lucky ones. Hopefully, in the aftermath, when they are left alone in the quiet of their own spaces, they will still feel the same.

THE ATTACK

As I climbed the water tower overlooking the fields of Be'eri and the surrounding area, I was taken with the landscape before me. Parklands where families would normally gather for picnics and celebrations. Lush greenery of rolling hills dotted with saltbush trees, an off-roaders dream with its winding paths of varying elevations. These manicured, crushed limestone roads were the terrorists' gateway on October 7.

"10 minutes to this point, 10 minutes to the Kibbutz," Uri wakes me from my thoughts. "Less at high speeds, maybe 15 minutes to abduct people from here to there," he gestures in either direction, then his pointed finger rests on Gaza.

The skyline of Gaza is thick with smoke, and the boom of explosions echoes from across the border, just 1 kilometer away, reminding me I am in a war zone. And yet, there is a weirdly idyllic air of calm and beauty. It is the time of the red flowers, and usually, Uri tells me, there would be hundreds of tourists here to celebrate their short-lived blooming; a time for outdoor parties and barbecues with family and friends. But today the valleys are quiet, eerie, as if to pay tribute to the horrors of October 7.

"The first thing they did was launch the suicide drones," Uri says, his voice trailing, his head shaking in disbelief. Uri has been inside for nearly 6 months. A departure from his regular life as an ER Doctor and entrepreneur, now he is the doctor supporting an entire IDF company, following his charges into some of Gaza's most dangerous areas as they root out Hamas terrorists.

At 6:30am on October 7, 2023 Hamas launched the first phase of their attack with sophisticated, modified suicide drones and military UAVs (unmanned aerial vehicles) equipped with explosives and precision guided missiles. The UAVs targeted and destroyed the Israeli camera and communications systems along the Gaza border and neutralized the automated border gun turrets. Within minutes the Israel-Gaza front line was down, the defense technology disabled. In an effort to overwhelm the Iron Dome[1] defense system, an estimated 2,000 short range rockets were fired into Israel. The next assault, a wave of explosive-laden bulldozers, slammed into

---

[1]   Israel's Iron Dome is a sophisticated air defense system that intercepts short-range rockets and artillery shells, protecting civilian areas from aerial threats. Israel has developed additional air defense systems to complement it. These include David's Sling, which targets medium-to-long-range missiles, and the Arrow system, designed to intercept long-range ballistic missiles. Together, these systems form a multi-layered defense shield.

the border fences, blasting open multiple entry points. The ground attack came next, and thousands of Hamas foot soldiers streamed into Israel.

The ground troops were heavily armed with machine guns, RPG rockets, grenades, and machetes; they began inflicting mass casualties as soon as they breached the border. That morning, the entire 25-mile Gaza border was guarded by only 600 Israeli soldiers and intelligence officers, along with the gun turrets that were now useless, a poor match for the 3,000-strong, well-trained Hamas army now flooding in through the breaches. They immediately overwhelmed the IDF soldiers left to defend the border, along with unsuspecting security personnel and police targets in the area. Once these critical targets were down, it became open season for the terrorists as they piled into border communities and attacked unarmed civilians, most of whom were still just waking to the day. They brutalized, raped and murdered hundreds of unsuspecting party-goers at the nearby Nova Music Festival. They did so with glee and the pleasure of sociopathic madness. The estimates of the number of militants, as verified by several news sources including *Times of Israel* and *Al Jazeera*, do not include the numbers of Gazan civilians—some of them youth—who ran into the settlements, setting buildings on fire and pillaging what they could before returning back into Gaza.

Among the earliest casualties was a mobile intelligence unit of female soldiers who were immediately overwhelmed when terrorists rushed their caravan, stationed just meters from the border fence. I met one of these girls on a visit to the hospital. Michal was a beautiful 22-year-old with a boyfriend and, one can imagine, a future before they shot her in the head. She somehow survived, at least bodily. I tried not to stare at the void where her left eye used to be, or the concave shape of her head where the bullet exploded. While I spoke quietly with her parents, she stared mutely into the distance.

Michal is just one of the many victims of the unprecedented brutal attack with one singular goal in mind; to inflict as much pain, suffering, and damage as possible whilst transmitting in real time onto social media. People shot dead in the street, families burnt alive in their homes, rape, live dismemberments. In the chaos, Israeli soldiers and civilians organized themselves on the fly, fighting the terror onslaught with whatever they had, completely outnumbered by their attackers. These heroes held the line and fought to their last bullet, courageous actions that certainly saved many lives that day. In some areas, the initial battles raged for up to 18 hours. The heroism of the various ad hoc units cannot be overstated: they held the terrorists at bay, preventing them from advancing further into Israel.

It took 3 days for the IDF to clear Hamas from Kibbutz Be'eri. The terrorists who entered were well trained, an elite force known as the *Nukhba* within the Izz ad-Din al-Qassam Brigades, Hamas's military wing. Too late, it became clear that their training and their weaponry was much better than the IDF had assumed. The militants had markers within their ranks, specially trained to identify and coordinate targets. They used thermal tracers alongside the PK machine gun (a hand held heavy machine gun). Once they had occupied the border villages, they established high-ground advantages inside buildings, from which they rained heavy fire on advancing IDF units, who were unprepared for this type of urban warfare on their own turf.

"Where were the elite counter-terrorist units?" I asked Jacob, my friend in the Shin Bet. Contrary to what some may believe, Israel does not have an endless supply of special forces. Of the special units available, most are typically trained to deal with small-scale situations, not a mass-invasion. In a small extension of Kibbutz Nahal Oz, by chance, there was a 10-person Sayeret Matkal special reconnaissance unit, trained in counter-terrorism, hostage rescue, and intelligence gathering, that happened to be staying overnight as they were passing through. They were a ready team, meaning that they were armed and outfitted for a mission. This unit immediately took a stand, and with everything they had, stood their ground and neutralized several hundred terrorists. They alone likely saved this Kibbutz from further harm, and undoubtedly saved many lives with their heroism.

The efforts of the IDF and regular civilians who took up arms in Be'eri, Nahal Oz, and other communities, many of whom gave their lives, almost certainly prevented chaos and murder on a far larger scale. The Hamas attack was coordinated and planned using detailed knowledge of the area and critical targets within it, and was completely unanticipated by the IDF. The invaders came packed with enough supplies to sustain a days-long campaign. Israeli intelligence has since learned that Hamas was not targeting these border communities as its end goal, these were simply necessary conquests to advance much further into Israel, which, had they been able to do so, would have had far more devastating results. It is these communities that stalled the terrorist advancement, and those who died there are hailed as heroes for halting Hamas's offensive.

Following the pushback of Hamas, the IDF confirmed that 251 Israeli hostages were kidnapped, including children as young as 10 months, an 83-year-old great grandmother, IDF soldiers, party goers from the Nova Festival, and some foreign nationals, all smuggled back into Gaza in broad daylight in the trunks of cars, the back of pick-up trucks, on golf carts, and some carried or led on foot. The images of these kidnappings were recorded live and are some of the most despicable and cowardly acts of Hamas. What has become obvious is that Hamas is leveraging this kidnapping to continue to taunt and cause pain to Israel.

Hostage Square is set up outside the Museum of Art in central Tel Aviv, where families and supporters of the hostages gather for rallies and to raise awareness for those still held captive, pushing the government to do everything within its power to bring them home. Israel is placed in an almost impossible position as it tries to negotiate for the lives of these people, who simply happened to be in the wrong place at the wrong time. For their loved ones, the agonizing wait they must endure is simply another terror tactic used against Israel by its enemies. The hostages who have been released thus far tell stories of rape and torture. Of being kept in underground tunnels and in cages. The situation is complicated and volatile, made even more complex because there is not one central command holding the hostages. They were leveraged within the strip as valuable currency and divided up amongst various locations. It is believed that Yahya Sinwar, the leader of Hamas within Gaza, who is widely recognized as the architect of Ten-Seven, surrounds himself with some of the remaining hostages in the tunnels of Rafah. The lives of the survivors, the families of the living and dead, and the entire population of Israel, will never be the same. The PTSD of October 7 will reverberate for years to come.

As I walked the periphery of Kibbutz Be'eri, among the burned shells of houses and bullet-marked walls, I paused to acknowledge those that lived here, and those lost. My heart was in my throat as I saw the large posters of still-imprisoned hostages affixed to the doorways of many homes. There seemed no logical reason why some homes were spared and others not. It may not have been completely random; many terrorists were found with detailed notes and maps, including names, of who lived where. On what had once been a playground, I saw a large tent, a makeshift forensics lab where human remains were being sifted through and rigorously identified so that Jewish remains could be given a proper burial, and to avoid the cruel irony of victims and terrorists being buried together.

A new low for Hamas and terror were the shocking videos that were live streamed onto social media, documenting their crimes as they rampaged through Israeli communities. The frightful glee in the eyes of the terrorists as they performed their worst is obvious in the footage. The terrorists seemed raving mad; it has come to light that they were fed the drug Captagon, an ADHD-prescribed narcotic that when taken in higher doses deadens the senses and emboldens the taker. The media frenzy of recording and streaming was the same power and control strategy as rape: to humiliate, terrorize, dehumanize, and instill fear in every person globally. In some sick way these participants sought their 15 minutes of fame through these recordings. These videos are the legacy of Hamas. Yet, In a twist of the bizarre, despite the overwhelming evidence of the crimes committed against humanity, the highest echelons of political, educational and professional institutions would soon begin to rationalize these events as a defensive measure of the oppressed, and some now even deny the extent of the massacre that took place.

Judith Butler, a prominent academic in gender studies at Berkeley and recognized feminist, described the atrocities committed by Hamas on October 7, 2023 as acts of "armed resistance" during a discussion on the French YouTube show *Paroles d'Honneur*. She seemingly does not speak of the murders and rapes, and effectively downplayed the severity of the violence and the suffering of the victims.

Actress Susan Sarandon has been criticized for her comments. In an al Jazeera interview she said that Israel did not belong to the Jewish people, that Gaza was a concentration camp, and that the war against Hamas was a "genocide." All of these are outright lies. She was subsequently dropped by her promotion agency.

As a Canadian, I am disgusted with the Trudeau government's reaction and ongoing apathy surrounding Ten-Seven and its betrayal to its Jewish citizens. Trudeau and his outspoken illiberal Liberals could not bring themselves to immediately denounce the terrorists of October 7, and only did so with public demand. When speaking about these events, he cannot help himself but to speak in the same breath of the victims of "Palestine."

It was equally disturbing when media outlets quickly implemented policies around how Hamas must be described, especially those involved in the October 7 attack. Catherine Tait, CEO of the CBC, unabashedly created a formal guideline that requires journalists to refer to Ten-Seven's perpetrators as "militants." This, despite the fact that Canada has officially denounced the Hamas organization as terrorists. The term *militants* normalizes Hamas as legitimate warriors with a purpose. Let's be very clear about something here. The animals who attacked Israel on October 7 were murderous terrorists who, by their actions, completely satisfy the definition of a terrorist by any interpretation. Such acts were carried out as a mission to inflict as much harm and destruction as possible against unarmed civilians. These terrorists valued their death more than we value our life.

THE SECURITY BREACH

In retrospect, there were several critical security errors in the lead up to Ten-Seven. Militarily, it was a situation where a number of poor decisions and oversights collided, leading to massive consequences. That morning, too few soldiers and intelligence officers were stationed in the area. Another crucial mistake was the preoccupation with Hamas's tunnel system and its lack of preparation for an air attack. The drone attack was swift, unprecedented, and effective, quickly disabling the gun turrets and cameras, obliterating the first line of defenses and exploiting the over-reliance on defense technologies.

The coordinated breach of multiple border points was underestimated. According to IDF intelligence, the risk assessment of a breach focused on three possible entry points; in every simulated scenario it was always the same three main points of entry. But October 7 reports indicate as many as 20 points of entry. Each of these breaches concentrated access to several small communities along the frontier. With the towers taken out and such a small contingent of troops stationed in defense, the ground attack was a monster that got loose from its cage.

It is now widely reported by *Times of Israel* and other verifiable news sources that higher up intelligence failed to listen to the warnings of a team of female intelligence officers. These warnings, which detailed unusual activities and potential threats from Hamas, including training simulations directly targeting Israeli defenses, were allegedly dismissed or not adequately escalated by higher command levels within the military. This has led to criticisms of systemic issues within the IDF, including claims of misogyny, where the input of female soldiers was not taken as seriously as it should have been.

Despite some of the most sophisticated surveillance technology available, Hamas was able to train and arm itself directly under Israel's nose. Some reports suggest that the planning of October 7 took as long as two years. I have been told by security and intelligence sources about specific reports that mention Hamas building exact replicas of Israeli military assets, such as Merkava tanks, for training purposes. If this is true, it points to a high level of tactical planning and preparation. The scale and sophistication of the attack suggest that this was not a hastily planned operation but a well-coordinated assault that would have required extensive logistical and strategic preparation. So how could all of this have been missed by one of the most advanced intelligence communities in the world? Perhaps therein lies the problem. There are six salient points that could be seen as the intelligence downfall, all of which fatefully seemed to have occurred with simultaneous timing:

1. **Technological dependance:** Israel put too much reliance on the front line—the border walls, technology, gun turrets, etc, without any strategic backup plan.

2. **Misinterpretation of intelligence:** Some reports suggest there was a belief among senior IDF and intelligence officials that Hamas had become more institutionalized and less likely to initiate a full-scale attack, affecting the interpretation of the intelligence received.

3. **Downplaying of warnings:** Female soldiers at observation posts had reported unusual activities and preparations by Hamas, such as the use of drones and simulations of attacks on Israeli

military replicas. However, their warnings were reportedly not taken seriously enough by higher command levels.

4. **Complacency:** There appears to have been a degree of complacency within the IDF's leadership regarding the threat from Gaza. This may have been influenced by a broader political and military narrative that Hamas was focused on governance rather than initiating conflict.

5. **Organizational challenges:** The IDF faced challenges in integrating and responding to various types of intelligence from different units and ranks within the organization. The complexity of military intelligence processes sometimes leads to critical information being lost or undervalued in the broader strategic assessments.

6. **Political and strategic misjudgments:** There were broad political and strategic misjudgments regarding the stability of the region and the intentions of Hamas, influenced by political decisions and assumptions at the highest levels of Israeli leadership.

PAINFUL SHORTSIGHTEDNESS

The redeployment of troops to the Jewish settlements of Judea and Samaria (West Bank) only days prior to October 7 had entire brigades exiting from the Gaza area. Specifically, two companies of commandos from the IDF's Commando Brigade, which had been stationed at the Gaza border, were redeployed to the West Bank just days before the attack. This redeployment was part of the broader military focus and activities in the area, and has raised questions about whether this movement made the Gaza border more vulnerable at a critical time.

Two lawmakers with limited military experience may have influenced these fateful decisions. The endorsement of these lawmakers to positions they have no business occupying is a direct result of Israel's out-of-touch political system. Israel's security may have been compromised by inexperienced right wing radicals who were empowered through political deals. Those who may have been better suited for these difficult and complex security related positions were passed over. Giving Itamar Ben-Gvir and Bezalel Smotrich[2] seats at the table is like giving the controls of an Airbus A380 to someone with a single prop license.

Beyond politics, intelligence failures, and troop deployment, perhaps the biggest shortcoming that led to Ten-Seven is that we cannot understand, or choose to ignore, that the terrorist's love for death is greater than our love for life. There were no miscommunications from the Hamas command center; the fighters they sent into Israel from Gaza were to be martyred—none of them were coming back. This is an area where the logic of honoring and valuing life in the West is completely out of touch with the reality of on-the-ground Gaza. How can we in the West understand how a person can be so poisoned, that they run willingly to their deaths? This is the core of a misconception that still derails the most advanced military organizations in the world today. Terrorists and poorly-trained militias surprise and frustrate because they leverage the conventional wisdom of warfare against their much larger and more sophisticated foes. It's not the hardware and technology that will defeat them; it is the change in convention. Israel is actually exceptionally experienced at dealing with urban and terror incursion, and the IDF is often called upon to advise allies. What Israel did not train for, however, was the sheer numbers of terrorists involved in the attack on October 7.

---

2   Ben-Gvir is the Minister of National Security and yet he has never spent a day in uniform. In a country with conscription and hundreds of experienced career military people, it is hard to imagine that Gvir was the best person for such an important position. Smotrich is the Minister of Finance and well known for his extreme right wing agendas. He has no background or experience in finance or economics.

"Our training was always about a handful of terrorists infiltrating a Kibbutz, not thousands of well trained troops," Jacob explais. "The first wave (of terrorists) were well trained militia, but then the citizen mass frenzy came to loot, pillage and burn. The randomness of the situation created a chaos that could not be defended conventionally."

While the initial onslaught may have been successful for Hamas, it is the people in Gaza who would pay the ultimate price.

MORE QUESTIONS THAN ANSWERS

HOW DID ONE of the world's most advanced armies fail to defend against the October 7 invasion? How was Hamas able to amass the military hardware and supplies needed for the thousands of terrorists that took part in the October 7 massacre? How did they coordinate and train for this massive effort without being noticed? What will happen to the Gaza strip and its population once this is all over? What to do about Iran? What will the political fallout be in Israel? How will Israel be able to provide safety and security to the nearly 200,000 people who have been displaced in its north and south? Who will govern Gaza post-war? Will the Abraham Accords fall apart? What will happen to the people displaced in Gaza? The questions are dizzying without end. The answers are elusive.

The world's reaction to Ten-Seven will be noted in history as a turning point that will ultimately unite world Jewry in a powerful single statement of survival, not seen since the aftermath of the Holocaust. The tinderbox of antisemitism around the world has ignited, underlining the importance the State of Israel plays in the survival of the Jewish people, and revealing underlying senseless hatred and woke leftist ideology.

The *illiberal* liberals have lost their way. Their dissonance is obvious, and yet the narrative keeps changing to cover up the antisemitic bias. It seems that when it comes to the Jews, the liberal policies of inclusion and social justice do not apply. I recently read a statement issued from the York University faculty group, as reported by *The National Post* on April 17, 2024, which recommends defining support of Israel as equivalent with racism:

> *"York University is becoming a landscape of surveillance, fear, intimidation and repression for anybody advocating Palestinian liberation. Faculty members should not be pressured to condemn Hamas. More students have expressed or reported feeling that the university has become an unsafe environment…"*

It's like they took the narrative and turned it upside down. Now the supporters of Palestine are the underdogs who feel "unsafe"? How can this be true, when it is the Jewish students at York University and campuses across North America who are under constant intimidation by masked protests, demanding the annihilation of the Jewish state? I beg for evidence of one instance where Jewish students have intimidated anyone. Despite the injustice and unfair intimidation taking place everywhere, Jews are still being targeted and cited as controlling media and finance, including the same organizations that regularly and outwardly denounce Israel. As old and tired as this is, it is dangerous rhetoric that normalizes antisemitism and justifies hate against Jews.

The "Protocols of the Elders of Zion" is a fabricated tale of Jewish influence and world domination, and has been used to scapegoat the Jewish people since the 1903 publication in Russia. Originally written as a hoax, it was outed as a complete lie in 1921 by *The Times* in Britain, and by *Frankfurter Zeitung* Newspaper in Germany in 1924. This story of Jewish conspiracies is blatantly false, antisemitic propaganda, and yet remains widely circulated and has been used as a justification of acts of violence against the Jewish people. The document has been published and circulated in numerous Arab countries, sometimes endorsed by governmental and educational bodies, contributing to its perceived legitimacy in some circles. The text has appeared in school curriculums, television programming, and other forms of media across the region. For example, it was notably adapted into a television series in Egypt in 2002. It is often cited by Hezbollah's leader Hassan Nasrallah, by Hamas, and by other radical Islamic influencers. It is yet another bizarre false reality that many insist is real. In medieval times, it was the lie that Christian children were being murdered by Jews to use their blood to make matzah for Passover. And however ridiculous this may sound, these accusations were used to legitimize pogroms and the murder of Jews. The perpetrators of these lies would go so far as to plant the corpses of dead children in Jewish ghettos to implicate the community in the deed. This type of rhetoric becomes truth in the minds of people even though it is false—it is literal brain washing. It is dangerous, and must be stopped if we are ever to have a chance at lasting peace.

Today, Israel's staunchest allies stumble once again into the insanity of terrorist deal-making. Israel's defense becomes unpalatable for the career politicians, whose constituencies are filled with those unsympathetic to Israel. US Senate majority leader, Chuck Schumer, demanded Israel hold elections, claiming that Netanyahu no longer represents the interest of the Israeli people. This sentiment was later endorsed by President Biden. Where does the United States get off on the blatant influence of Israel's domestic politics? If Israel has issues with its political process and leadership, it is more than capable of managing and correcting them without US interference. One could never imagine Israel demanding that any US president is unfit for power.

President Biden withheld arms promised to Israel because he disagreed with the IDF incursion into Rafah, a Gaza enclave. What was not generally discussed is that Rafah became the Hamas command center and there is high likelihood that the hostages are believed to be held in Rafah. Hamas has every opportunity to end this. Returning all the hostages to Israel would have put them in a strong position to negotiate some peaceful form of surrender that would have saved many people in Gaza. Why is the use of human shields and treating people forcibly kidnapped as negotiating chips on a poker table not a subject of wide concern by the public? Why is Hamas's main narrative not fully discussed and exposed? In authenticated audio transcripts during an attempt at a deal to free the hostages, Hamas's top commander, Yahya Sinwar, was recorded as having said that the casualties among Gaza's civilian population is an "acceptable sacrifice" and that "We have them (Israel) exactly where we want them."

Israel's first priority is to protect the rights, safety, and peace of its citizens. The options available may not be very palatable, but who is at fault here? The Jews who are rightfully defending themselves, or the Gazans who are supporting Hamas and circulating rhetoric to pervert yet another generation of haters? What good can any solution have without the enforcement of a lasting peaceful narrative for future generations?

The questions about Ten-Seven burning in the minds of the Israeli citizenry will likely lead to major changes in the country's political, military, and judicial structures. There will hopefully be accountability, and already there is a changing of the guard in the military as top officers are resigning, admitting that it will be difficult for them to live with a military disaster of this level on their watch. The question is if the political administration will take its share of the responsibility. Given the nature of politics, that is highly unlikely, but hopefully change will be demanded by the people. I imagine that much will be learned in the aftermath of the wake up call of October 7, and as a result we can only hope that the security measures are put in place that will decrease the possibility of October 7 ever happening again.

In the immediate aftermath of Ten-Seven, it was rumored that Gazan laborers spied on the residents of the border communities and passed intel to the Hamas terrorists. However, Israel intelligence now denies this as the likely or singular source of this information. The sophistication of the attack is evidence that Hamas studied the area for quite some time and had advanced knowledge of the security risks that could be exploited. This information was gathered in a number of ways including surveillance drones; perhaps satellite imagery may have been shared or hijacked. How Israel intelligence missed all of this is going to be a significant focus of the investigation. One thing we will certainly conclude is that Hamas was severely underestimated. That Ten-Seven did not happen without significant external support by outside sources, including training, hardware, and intelligence. The presumed highest level culprit would ostensibly be Iran, however, the more mature Hezbollah organization may have mentored Hamas through the planning and execution of Operation Al-Aqsa Flood[1]. Any permanent cessation of hostilities will be meaningless if Iran's supreme council is allowed to continue its unchallenged support for terrorism. This will not just

---

1   This refers to the name of the October 7 attack. "Operation Al-Aqsa Flood" derives from the Al-Aqsa Mosque, a highly significant site in Islam located in Jerusalem. The term "flood" in the operation's name symbolizes a massive, overwhelming force.

affect Israel. Global Jihad is Iran's ultimate go-to proxy, and this is coming for everyone. Iran's ambition is world domination by Islam. Good luck to the entitled kids protesting for the cause, turning the key that will free the monster that will gobble them up.

THE STOCKPILES OF MURDER

It is perplexing that Hamas was able to amass the munitions and hardware capable of executing the single largest terror attack in history: the drones, missiles, rocket launchers, RPGs, guns and bullets. Each terrorist carried bags of munitions, hardware and food, prepared for a drawn-out conflict. That's at least 5,000 carriers, each with their own stash of supplies, and plenty more left behind in Gaza to continue the bombardment of Israel. Nearly 800 projectiles were sent into Israel within the first 80 minutes of the attack. In just the first few hours of the war, sources report 3,000 missiles launched at Israel. Compare this to a total of 4,000 missiles launched against Israel during the entirety of the 2014 Gaza war.[2]

CEASEFIRE INSANITY

Despite the horrors that have become known about October 7, the international community's support for Israel was short-lived. International pressure for a ceasefire was near-immediate, with little mention of the need to dismantle the Hamas terror network. Canada's New Democratic Party (NDP) introduced a motion in the House of Commons to recognize the Palestinian state, a direct reward to Hamas for its seditious and horrific terror attack. The NDP, which is supposed to be the front line when it comes to diversity, equity, and inclusion; women's rights, the Me Too movement, Black Lives Matter, LGBTQ+, etc. now endorses, without

---

2   The 2014 Gaza War, known as Operation Protective Edge, involved seven weeks of fighting between Israel and Hamas. The conflict resulted in significant casualties and destruction in Gaza, driven by airstrikes and a ground operation by Israel in response to Hamas rocket fire.

restrictions, admonishment or comment, a Palestinian state that will not be held to the same principles of democracy for which Canada stands. A Palestinian state that will commit crimes against women, criminalize homosexuality with punishment of death, who will violate all of the things the NDP stands for. It actually already does. What this Palestinian state *will* do in tandem with the NDP is to advocate and maintain antisemitic rhetoric. As a former candidate (1993) for Member of Parliament under the NDP, I am today entirely disgusted by the two-faced agenda that will have the NDP bed the devil to oust the Jew.

UN resolution 2728 was presented on March 25, 2024, with 14 members voting *Yes* and Israel's staunchest ally, the United States, muting itself with an abstention. The resolution called for an immediate ceasefire for the month of Ramadan, without any conditions relating to the recognition of Israel's right to defend itself and the cessation of hostilities against Israel. Instead, it instructed the "unconditional flow" of aid into Gaza. The Biden administration did not veto this resolution and instead allowed it to pass. While this resolution is purely symbolic, the United Nations has proven itself biased against the survival of Israel, and is no friend to the Jews. By demanding unrestricted flow of goods into Gaza, without seeking to ensure that these shipments will not rearm or empower Hamas, the UN is putting a loaded gun against the temple of Israel. Of course, this is the way of things for the UN, which admonishes Israel each year more times than all the combined other nations in the world. North Korea, China and Iran all receive significantly less chastisement. Meanwhile, Myanmar's militia had already been guilty of murdering 50,000 innocent citizens since the 2021 coup, while destroying hundreds of villages and displacing 2.3 million people. Just two UN resolutions have been passed against this brutalization, and the world is silent. You don't see protests in the streets or encampments on campus. If it ain't Jews, it ain't news.

Israel is judged harshly for its response, but no other country would have done anything differently. Alas, this is Israel, this is the Jews, and such rules and considerations do not apply to its right to defend itself or its people's survival. As far back as Biblical times, the Jewish cause and its people ultimately seem expendable.

AN IMPOSSIBLE SITUATION

THE LOVERS OF LIFE VS THE LOVERS OF DEATH

OCTOBER 7 was a massive Kamikazi-style suicide mission with the single clear objective to cause as much murder and destruction to as many Jews as possible. The attack had nothing to do with serving the interests of Palestinian people. Were that the case, then tens of billions of dollars of aid would have gone toward infrastructure, not tunnels and weapons. And hundreds of thousands of Palestinians would not purposefully be placed in harm's way by Hamas in order to maximize civilian casualties.

The impossibility of the situation has created pragmatic military choices that go from worst to worse. To simplify the predicaments faced by the Jewish state, it comes down to this:

1. Israel values life. Hamas values death.

2. There is no clear delineation between military and innocent civilians in the Gaza strip. The population is radicalized under a theocratic, violent regime. The majority of people in Gaza demand and celebrate the total destruction of Israel.

3. Hamas uses civilians as human shields.

4. Hamas is a direct proxy of Iran.

5. Hamas violates every human rights abuse, and yet it is Israel that is pinned constantly under a microscope and charged with these violations.

6. Israel is in a state of constant self-defense. If the Jewish state does not dismantle the terror and defend itself, it will be destroyed and all of its citizens murdered.

7. Anything the Jewish State does is highly scrutinized and almost always in a negative light.

8. Hamas plays on the Western world's naivete, and does so to further their agenda.

9. Israel recognizes that bribing for peace and prosperity did not work. Western societies continue to make this underestimation. Arab countries knowingly and continually allow for the flow of goods that will arm Hamas.

10. Israel is highly dependent on the United States. The majority of decision making regarding military response or the aftermath of this war will be highly influenced by whether the US allows or disallows certain plans.

The most fundamental and critical difference between Israel and Hamas is this: the love of life versus the sensationalism of death. There is significant disparity in how Israeli children are educated and how Hamas children are indoctrinated, how young adults live and dream, how adults live in their prime, middle, then senior years. When considering what is a reasonable response to October 7, one must take into account the harsh reality of the two very different lenses on either side of the border. The hope of Israel and her citizens for a long lasting peace and prosperity, and the despair of Palestinians who champion a deathwish ideology and perpetual victim status with no hope and dreams motivating their young people to change and produce a better future for their lives. These are not opposites imposed; there is a way of life that Israelis and Palestinian choose for themselves. Yes, it is well-documented that choices are enabled by the situation. But the situation itself can, and must, change. With an investment in the future, different choices can be made. It is within the realms of possibility that future generations of Palestinians can also become sustainable lovers of life instead of demonizing Israel and the Jews and championing a culture of hate. A relationship built on love, understanding, and co-existence is the only peaceful opportunity to resolve the Arab-Israeli conflict. If we truly want to provide Palestinians with a future, we must counter fanaticism and radical ideology. If the progressives really want to help the situation in Israel, they must focus on the non-political outreach between Palestinian and Jewish youth to bridge the divide. Not to say that this is not already happening; in fact, with some tragic irony, it is those people in Kibbutz Be'eri, who were committed to the peace process and a better life for Palestinians. The appreciation shown to them by Gazans was to murder them in their beds. The coexistence of Jews and Arabs depends on the institutionalization of education in the Palestinian and Israeli curriculum from the youngest of age.

In Israel, the social contract is designed to serve the betterment and best interest of its people. In Hamas-controlled Gaza, there is no social contract as we know it. Only subservience and intimidation. Perhaps the residents of Gaza lack choice and agency, but this is not the fault of Israel. The Gazans have been afforded every opportunity to build the Strip into a highly productive quality of life. Yet they are force-fed radicalization and brutality by a ruling party. Gaza was granted a self-ruling independence, as near as possible to the two-state solution that the Oslo Accords strived for. It took one of Israel's most hardened generals, Ariel Sharon, to become Prime Minister and make the incredibly difficult and fateful decision to disengage from the Gaza Strip. Sharon sanctioned this move in 2005, amid great contention. It was the ultimate poker play, and the Palestinians failed to trump an open deck. Had they been a faithful actor to the peace process, they would have achieved statehood. Peace is now likely further away than ever before. Hamas has been given billions of dollars to do with as they please. Instead of building up a beachside with luxury hotels, state-of-the-art hospitals and schools, and creating efficient infrastructure, they opted to build tunnels for terror. The international community knew full well what the money being transferred to Hamas was being used for, and yet no one protested. The enablement continued. But Ten-Seven was a line crossed. No longer could Israel ignore the obvious. Hamas effectively signed their own death warrant.

IN GAZA, THERE ARE NO INNOCENT BYSTANDERS

The tunnels of terror were not built solely by Hamas military, nor were the events of October 7 a purely military operation. The terror tunnels were built by civilians, and the events of Ten-Seven were perpetrated, alongside Hamas fighters, by everyday citizens. One only needs to review the footage of Shani Louk, the German woman who was kidnapped by Hamas from the Nova Music Festival. Her body was paraded through the streets clad in only her underwear after she was brutally raped and murdered. It was every day Gaza citizens who saw this, and who celebrated with candies thrown in the air. As the young Israeli babies, children and women were corralled in the streets of Gaza, the crowds gathered to jeer and pelt them with stones. How terrifying it must have been for 12-year-old Erez Kalderon, who had just witnessed horrifying crimes against his neighbors and family, to be forced by his captives into Gaza and paraded for all to see. Several hostages remain in the most terrible of conditions, held by civilian captors in Gaza, literally held in cages and starved as the family eats in the next room. These are not militants; they are ordinary Gazan citizens. Ironically, tragically, many of the victims from October 7 were peace activists who supported the Palestinian cause.

Complicity in crimes against humanity, whether from bystanders or terrorists, is a clear violation of international law. Individuals cannot escape accountability by claiming they were merely accomplices or indirectly involved in such crimes.

Some notable legal precedents include the Nuremberg Trials, where many Nazis were prosecuted for their roles in the Holocaust and other war crimes, establishing the precedent that "following orders" is not a valid defense for such crimes. Similarly, the International Criminal Tribunal for Rwanda (ICTR) and the International Criminal Tribunal for the former Yugoslavia (ICTY) have held individuals accountable for their participation in genocide and crimes against humanity. Why should these precedents not be applied in Gaza? Why does the international community continue to strive to find ways to rationalize the Gazans' responsibility and demonize Israel for rightfully defending itself?

A poll conducted by the Palestinian Center for Policy and Survey Research (PCPSR)[1] confirmed that 72% of Palestinians supported the October 7 attack. The same poll highlighted that if

---

1   Agencies and TOI Staff, *Times of Israel*, December 13, 2023, https://www.timesofisrael.com/poll-shows-soaring-support-for-hamas-in-west-bank-as-90-say-abbas-should-resign/

a presidential race were held, Hamas leader Ismail Haniyeh would be a popular choice. Though, that choice is now off the table. The survey also revealed a stark increase in support for Hamas in both Judea and Samaria (West Bank) and Gaza. We now have a generation of young people in Gaza who have been fed a litany of lies; Hamas, having extorted their quality of life into one of hatred, teaching them it is better to die killing Israelis than to live and make a better life for themselves.

Prior to October 7, Israel issued 18,000 work permits to Gazans[2], giving them the opportunity to earn far more money in Israel than they could in Gaza. The economic impact of Gazans working in Israel is quite significant. Each day, prior to October 7, Gazans working in Israel contributed approximately $1 million to Gaza's economy. A Gazan worker in Israel earned about 400 shekels per day (roughly $110 USD), whereas in Gaza they might earn only 40 shekels ($10.50 USD) for the same job[3]. Israel unknowingly allowed entry to Gazans hell bent on killing Jews.

On October 7, the Gazan population lost these economic advantages, and all Arab workers, including 100,000 permitted workers from Judea and Samaria (West Bank), were no longer allowed to work within Israel. The impact for both Palestenians and Israelis is significant. As a result, 80,000 permits are being issued to foreign workers from India, Sri Lanka, China, Thailand, and Moldova to replace the reliance on Arab labor.

October 7 pushed Palestinians into further despair and hardship.

WHEN WILL THE WORLD WAKE UP?

While there are almost certainly many people in Gaza who would choose peace with Israel, the majority of public sentiment remains

---

2   Nifal Al-Mughrabi, *Reuters*, Nov. 3, 2023

3   Aaron Boxerman, *Times of Israel*, June 16, 2022,

anti-Jewish and pro-Hamas. Yet the United States, Canada and Western Europe seem unwilling or unable to understand this. When the Western powers demand a ceasefire, how exactly do they expect this to work when Hamas will use whatever reprieve it is given to rearm itself? Israel has been a willing partner many times and each time the situation ends the same way, with renewed hostilities.

Let's take a look at some of the more notable failed deals between Hamas and Israel:

1. The Oslo Accords (1993). This was perhaps the greatest opportunity for a lasting peace between Israel and the PLO, but the ideas and intent that brought them together quickly unraveled. Its failure strengthened Hamas, which was not a party to the agreement but opposed its terms.

2. Israel's unilateral withdrawal from Gaza in 2005 was not an agreement with Hamas but was expected to reduce tensions. Instead, it led to increased hostilities, with Hamas taking control of Gaza and escalating attacks against Israel.

3. 2008-2009 Gaza War (Operation Cast Lead). A ceasefire agreement ended the conflict temporarily, but it broke down within months. Hamas continued its violence against Israel.

4. 2012 Ceasefire Agreement (Operation Pillar of Defense). This agreement was brokered by Egypt and aimed at ending the eight-day conflict. However, the truce was short-lived; once again Hamas began launching missiles into Israel and sponsoring terror attacks.

5. 2014 Ceasefire Agreement (Operation Protective Edge). Another Egyptian-brokered ceasefire, another war Israel was forced into to dislodge Hamas. This deal sought to end the

50-day conflict. This was the most significant and fierce fighting that came at great cost to Israel. Israel only agreed to withdraw after intense international pressures and guarantees to maintain the peace. It did not take long before the Hamas hostilities began again.

6. 2021 Ceasefire Agreement (Operation Guardian of the Walls). After 11 days of an intense Israeli defense operation, Egypt again brokered yet another deal that convinced Israel to back off. Days later missiles are being launched at Israel from Gaza.

7. In 2021, Qatar provided the Qatari Aid Agreement, which allowed for Qatar to provide financial aid to Gaza for strictly humanitarian purposes. Despite assurances, these funds very likely ended up being diverted by Hamas for military purposes.

8. March 2022, another ceasefire deal was brokered in response to further escalations in violence. The deal lasted a couple of days before renewed rocket fire into Israel.

9. August 2022, another ceasefire brokered by Egypt to end the three-day conflict. This deal, like others before it, ended the same way, with rockets being fired from Gaza and into Israel.

10. Since October 7, 2023 there have been several attempts at ceasefire agreements. Some have shown brief promise with the release of hostages. But unfortunately as of the date of this writing, there has been no lasting peace agreement. The release of hostages and the demilitarization of Hamas must be the key points of any deal. Why would Hamas agree to something that ends its leverage and hold on Gaza?

The evidence is clear, and the insanity of doing these deals is expecting a different outcome each time. Hamas does not act in good faith. They are a terrorist organization, and Israel is literally dealing with the devil. There is no deal-making with Hamas, and it's time that the world stops providing them a seat at the table. Doing so legitimizes their cause of destruction and death.

What other response can Israel bring to the table other than the cost that comes with defending itself from people who all day long celebrate death and martyrdom, who vow death to the Jews, and who cannot be trusted to honor a ceasefire? When will the Western powers demand the unconditional retreat from hate and terror, denounce the call for the destruction of the Jews, and demand an unequivocal acceptance of the State of Israel?

There is a complex relationship between benefactor and patron. Israel has long since been pulled between the United States's twin motivations of recognizing Israel's right to defend itself and balancing its own international relationships. The US typically has a short-lived appetite for Israel's management of threats, instead of accepting long drawn out campaigns. Each of the last three major military operations into Gaza were cut short of achieving its goals because of a change of narrative and heart by the United States.[4] A

---

4   **Operation Pillar of Defense** (2012): This operation was conducted over eight days in November 2012 following an escalation in rocket attacks from Gaza into Israel. The operation primarily consisted of airstrikes aimed at eliminating Hamas' military leadership and reducing the group's rocket-launching capabilities. A ceasefire was eventually brokered under Egyptian mediation after intense international pressure to end the violence.

Operation Protective Edge (2014): This operation began in July 2014 and lasted for 50 days. It was initiated by Israel in response to increased rocket fire from Gaza into Israeli territory. The operation involved a combination of airstrikes, naval bombardment, and a ground invasion aimed at targeting Hamas' military infrastructure, including tunnel networks used to infiltrate Israel. The conflict resulted in significant casualties and destruction, particularly in Gaza, and drew international attention to the humanitarian situation.

Operation Guardian of the Walls (May 2021): This operation was launched in response to rockets fired by Hamas toward Jerusalem and other areas, which marked a significant escalation in the conflict. The operation involved airstrikes by the Israel Defense Forces (IDF) aimed at Hamas targets in Gaza, which were met with continuous rocket fire from Gaza into Israeli territory.

Operation Swords or Iron (October 2023) is the current ongoing and longest operation in Gaza in response to the attack of October 7th.

consistent and typical scenario is unconditional American support of Israel, until the damage reports start to come in and public opinion shifts. The narrative then quickly becomes highly conditional, and the rhetoric between the US and Israel is negatively heightened. One thing the bigger brother cannot stand is not being listened to. In a recent exchange, President Biden, plainly frustrated that he cannot reign Netanyahu in, privately called Netanyahu an "asshole" behind closed doors.[5] According to NBC News he has gone as far as claiming that the Prime Minister of Israel is a "bad fucking guy." Biden cannot write the checks for a conflict that he cannot dictate the terms to.

The end result of this power dynamic is always the same: Israel is forced by the United States to sit at the table with terrorists and negotiate bad faith deals. Each time allowing Hamas to rebuild itself at the cost of Israeli lives.

It is entirely thanks to international pressure that Hamas was able to gather the resources it needed to amass the army, tunnels, missiles, hardware, drones and munitions necessary to carry out October 7. The reality is that Israel capitulated. Israel allowed foreign powers to meddle in domestic politics and military policies, a compromise that is a factor in the murder of over 1,200 Israelis. The aftermath of this damage will take years to unfold. Blood is on the hands of anyone who turned a blind eye knowing full well what Hamas was doing. Europe, the US, Canada, Russia, and Pan Arab countries all have a hand in the rebuilding of Hamas; gaining license, opportunity, hardware, money and the resources to execute October 7—and beyond. What is Israel to do in the face of the impossible situation they are put into? Short term peace for prosperity policies that perpetuate the cycles of Hamas aggression? Destroy. Negotiate. Rebuild. Attack. Destroy… and repeat.

---

5   Lee, Carol E, et al, NBC News, February 12, 2024, https://www.nbcnews.com/news/investigations/biden-disparages-netanyahu-private-hasnt-changed-us-policy-israel-rcna138282

JUSTIFIABLE DEFENSE

Any sovereign nation is legitimately justified to defend itself against an attack on its people and land. Israel should be no different; the Jewish State has every right to defend itself against annihilation. Israel is a democratic country, with human rights and a justice system. It is irresponsible of the media and political leaders to jump to conclusions, without independent investigation and verification. It only results in the immediate criticizing and vilifying of Israel to defend itself, and plainly discriminatory. The dissonance and bias is obvious, and has been going on for so long that there is a normalization of Jew hatred and exception in the public judgment. The truth has faded into irrelevancy.

Israel was invaded. Terrorists entered civilian homes and brutally murdered women, children, and men. Israeli citizens were degraded by rape and barbaric mutilation. Random people were kidnapped from within Israel's borders, these souls were forcefully taken and many murdered and humiliated in the streets of Gaza. What would you do if you were the country of Israel?

A MORAL ARMY

Golda Meir, Israel's 4th Prime Minister (1969-1974) famously stated that she blamed the Arabs not for killing her sons, but for turning her sons into killers.

The act of killing another human being, for any reason, tarnishes the soul, and there is little moral comfort to the waging of war, even if necessary. The IDF goes over and above any expectation of moral standards in sometimes the most impossible of situations.

During the Syrian uprising that started in October 2011, as part of the wider wave of the Arab Spring[6], injured Syrians who

---

6   The Arab Spring of 2011 was a series of anti-government protests and uprisings across the Middle East and North Africa, sparked by demands for political freedom, economic reform, and an end to corruption. It led to significant political changes, including the overthrow of leaders in Tunisia, Egypt, Libya, and Yemen, significant reforms in Morocco and Jordan, and ongoing civil conflicts in Syria and Libya.

approached the Israeli border were taken to Israeli hospitals and given life saving operations and medicine. No money changed hands, and all of this was done under a veil of secrecy. Israel is always among the first to respond to global disasters. She does not differentiate, and has offered help to many of her enemies. Despite the blatant calls for Israel's destruction by Turkey's president Erdogen, Israel was one of the first countries to offer assistance to both Turkey and Syria following the devastating earthquakes in February 2023, where 54,000 people in Turkey perished. Israel sent search-and-rescue teams and humanitarian aid to Turkey. I will discuss *The Way of the Land*, the religious and cultural ideology that governs how Israel (and by extension the IDF) responds to calls for aid, extends peace, and helps its enemies, later in this book.

The Israel Defense Forces is the only military in the world that routinely provides warnings to civilians in areas affected by operations. This includes issuing evacuation orders using phone calls, text messages, and roof-knocking (a warning knock on the roof before a strike). These measures are intended to minimize civilian casualties during conflicts, particularly in dense urban environments like Gaza. There are very specific rules of engagement that IDF soldiers follow that involve warning shots and non-fatal deterrents in order to prevent and minimize non-military casualties. The IDF has a division known as the Military Advocate General's Corps (MAG Corps). This division was established prior to 1948 by the Haganah. The unit is responsible for investigating incidents of military engagement, ensuring that operations are conducted in accordance with both Israeli law and international law. The MAG Corps provides legal advice, handles investigations into misconduct, and prosecutes cases when necessary. It plays a critical role in maintaining legal and ethical standards within the IDF. There is zero tolerance for immoral conduct. Israel does everything to protect civilian life, even under the harshest of conditions.

It would have been much easier, and fewer Israeli soldiers would die, if Israel simply carpet-bombed Gaza. But that is not the standard or style of Israel. The concern for civilian casualties is a top priority. Hamas knows this, and uses Israel's high moral conduct against them at every possible opportunity. Israel's enemies are highly skilled at moving the public narrative against Israel and there is no price they will not pay to achieve this. The Hamas terrorist network has expanded over the last two decades to include women and children. Most Gazan citizens have been radicalized with one intent on their minds: to kill Jews anywhere.

OPERATION SWORDS OF IRON

Code named *Operation Swords of Iron*, Israel's response to October 7 is unprecedented in its very complicated ongoing war with Hamas. Gaza is quickly becoming a parking lot, likely uninhabitable for years to come. The IDF called up over 400,000 reservists in the wake of Ten-Seven, the fastest ever deployment of the IDF. They (the IDF) are forced to fight an urban battle, where they must adhere to the complex challenges of protecting the lives of Gazan civilians, rescue the hostages who are held within homes and civilian infrastructure, and flush out thousands of terrorists embedded within the population and inside the miles of tunnels they hide in.

Hamas will stall for time using the hostages, and I am certain that at the last minute they will try to save themselves with some deal-making that they will never conclude. Hamas will booby trap everything they can, there will be suicide bombers and gunmen laying in wait. As a parent, the idea of my kid facing this is terrifying. I have no doubt that the IDF will be successful in its mission, but at what cost? And will this really be the last we hear from Hamas? What happens after the destruction is another matter being heavily debated.

MAKING AN IMPOSSIBLE SITUATION BETTER

When the dust settles, Gaza must not return to a place of hate and deprivation of life. Israel and the world must acknowledge that the experiment of self-governance failed, and for the foreseeable future The Strip must remain under Israel's complete military administration. The price paid is too high, leaving no trust left to work with Gaza or the international community. There is, however, a real opportunity to rebuild Gaza for the better. This is a logical step-by-step approach:

1. **Demilitarization and security:** The number one priority for the future of Gaza is a completely demilitarized Gaza Strip. There can be no opportunity for any groups to rearm under the misguided banner of resistance.

2. **Interim political solution:** Israel will need to appoint a secular Gazan administration that will be strictly monitored and controlled by Israel, and will be a mix of Israel and Palestinian politicians who are committed to a peaceful co-existence, to oversee the next several years of rebuilding Gaza. Progress should be toward a sustainable system of government that can provide independence and also ensure the security of Israel.

3. **Human aid and rebuilding:** The two million citizens of Gaza will need to be immediately housed and have access to food, running clean water and medical supplies. All goods inbound will have to be closely monitored and audited for security. A rebuilding plan paid for by the international community will provide new infrastructure and housing, hotels, and public facilities including government buildings, hospitals and schools.

4. **Education:** Educational guidelines must include a positive perspective on Arab-Israel co-existence, including education about Jewish culture alongside positive Islamic teachings. The syllabus of hate must be removed from the educational system. Further education for Gazans should be readily available.

5. **Economic development and employment:** Fostering economic development to rebuild Gaza's economy could include facilitating trade, improving access to markets, and creating job opportunities for Gazans. This is crucial for long-term stability, and to reduce the allure of militant groups, which often recruit from economically disenfranchised populations.

6. **Social cohesion and community resilience:** Investing in community-building activities that promote social cohesion and inter-communal peace. Much healing will need to be done by both Israelis and Gazans, and there must be comprehensive psychological support for those affected by the conflict to heal social divisions and build a foundation for long-term peace.

Israel cannot afford to fail in the outcome, and to ensure success an invasive security apparatus will have to be implemented. Addressing these priorities requires a balanced approach that considers the immediate security needs while also laying the groundwork for long-term social, economic, and political stability in Gaza.

ANSWERS WE NEED TO LISTEN TO

AT THE BEGINNING OF THIS BOOK I posit seven observations to the question of "*how.*" How is it possible that the October 7 Hamas terror attack on Israel took place? In the coming pages, I will explore these observations and offer some understanding on how such a failure in Israeli security and intelligence could have happened. Ten-Seven did not occur in a vacuum. It was the eruption that was 75 years in the making. Hopefully, we pay close attention to these observations, because this attack is just the tip of the spear held by those who wish to dominate, destroy, and bend free people to the will of theocratic radical dictatorship.

September 11, 2001 was the coming out party, and October 7, 2023 was the breakdown of the first line of defense. I am writing this book as a wake up call well beyond the borders of Israel. The protestors and celebrants rallying in the wake of Ten-Seven have no idea what they are supporting.

Please do not jump to any conclusions due to my candor. If you are protesting a cause on Humanitarian grounds, then good for you, but make sure to do so including the many violations against humanity by all parties involved. As soon as there is hateful and genocidal rhetoric calling for the annihilation of Jews and the perverse glorification of October 7 as an act of defiance, all credibility with the humanity argument and cause is lost. One other note about me… do not assume that I am an Islamaphobe by any stretch of the imagination, that would be a gross misjudgement of my words. I am more concerned with the many people who are perverting Islam for their own means.

Regardless of orientation, pronoun, ideology, or political affiliation, Global Jihad is knocking on your door, and for those running to answer the call, beware of what you are about to let inside. There will be no compromise. You will not be spared. The Jihad will consume everyone in its path. It is occult in nature, and determined to subject the world to the will of tyrants. The world has been swept up in what will be known as the greatest dupe of all time. We stand at the nexus of evil against which goodness must prevail, or all will be lost to the onslaught of Global Jihad. Now, humanity is tasked with the monumental feat of stopping the momentum of terror. But first it must wake up.

THE EAST-WEST BATTLE
FOR GLOBAL DOMINANCE

THE EAST-WEST GLOBAL HEGEMONIC BATTLE for dominance and control began with the United States and Russia's challenge for world supremacy in the aftermath of World War II, a struggle that would change the global geopolitical landscape. The past 75 years has created alliances and established ideologies that have set the stage for the Global Jihad of today.

Both the East and West have created a monster that knows no master. This monster, Jihad, has no responsibility to humanity. Its reasoning is misunderstood because it is completely contrary to the instincts of survival that govern the MAD (mutually assured destruction) theory that has maintained the status quo of the superpowers. Jihadists are self-destructive parasites with the goal of succeeding at any cost.

THE IDEOLOGICAL DIVIDE

As the global dust cloud of World War II settled slowly over a shell-shocked and fractured world, two countries emerged from the haze that would become the new power brokers, and who would between them reshape geopolitics for decades to come. The United States of America, and the USSR (Union of Soviet Socialist Republics, or known in shorthand, as Russia).

Political theory emerged about aggression or capitulation via arms escalation, which would hopefully avert anyone pushing the button. In order to remain competitive within the theory of MAD, each side was required to continue to build its aggression capabilities and maintain the impression of being ready to launch its missiles at any time, or risk becoming outgunned, thereby ceding power to the other. The other main strategy of the Cold War was alignment. Both superpowers spread their sphere of influence, not through colonialism but through a quid-pro-quo: protection was available at the price of loyalty. This led to the formation of the NATO pack by the West, and the formal amalgamation of several countries under Moscow's banner ideologically bound by communism.

The discussion on the birth of modern liberalism and the Left-Right spectrum of political thought is foundational to understand the importance of how the ideological shift of the left veered so far from its origins. These origins, which include civil liberties, social justice, and equality, have now been turned upside down as liberalism comes to a place where it supports movements that are diametrically in opposition of its founding tenets. The following discussion is in an effort to provide some context on how this happened.

In the United States, communism, as a political and ideological force, sparked a homegrown paranoia and internal fear about the

Western ideals of freedom and liberty. By the early 1950s, Americans were brought to believe that communism was the enemy and this enemy was everywhere. Convinced that its freedom was at stake, America grew paranoid that Russian spies were lurking everywhere, and the concept of sleeper agents became very real. Your neighbor could be a Russian spy waiting to be suddenly activated. *Reds under the Beds* was the term coined for the paranoia that set in motion the McCarthyism period, named after Senator Joseph McCarthy, who led the anti-Communist movement in the US during the early 1950s. Were these suspicions simply unfounded paranoia? No, I don't think so. However when it comes to human emotions there will always be extremes. Russia was very quick to build a sophisticated spy network to maintain both its internal power and its external influence.

In the end, 1950s America would become what it accused its counterpart of, an internal spying agency hellbent on rooting out evil from within. Naturally, as American policy hardened against civil rights in its relentless pursuit of spies, real or imagined, public pushback increased. And so came the birth of the ideological war. The fronts were established between different types of thinking, and with that was born *the Right* and *the Left*. Red-blooded Americans and bleeding liberal diehards rallied on either side of the political-social divide. Over the years, each ideology would evolve beyond its origins of free world versus communism,beyond America, and expand into a broader global ideological spectrum: the protectionist, closed thinking of the right, and the open liberal ideals of the left. Each side evolved further away, fracturing into different sub-spectrums of governance, morality, religion, and free market economy. And with a widening spectrum grew extremism, where irrational behavior is driven by unreasonable thought. Ten-Seven, and the subsequent immediate rise of global antisemitism, was born through this ideological divide.

The liberal left, blinded by their own ambition, have now

licensed and in effect armed terrorists around the world, including Hamas. There is a fifth column congregating within the borders of Western countries; actually several columns. Sleeper cells are embedded with intense radicalization, because these columns have no mechanism to monitor or control the brainwashing of the disenfranchised on the campuses of our universities. Entire generations are forming their plans for activism based on manipulated narratives and false news that the Jihad is feeding the free press. Journalists and agencies eat up the news feeds without investigation, publishing and thereby giving legitimization to propaganda.

For example, when four of the hostages were rescued during a daring Israeli operation in Nuseirat refugee camp in central Gaza, the initial news that came out was that over 200 people were targeted and killed in an IDF operation. What was not mentioned was that this was a rescue operation in a residential neighborhood harboring hundreds of terrorists. Those killed were in battle with the IDF, not innocent bystanders as the first news reports would have you believe. The integrity of journalism has been sacrificed by a confirmation bias of the left liberals in favor of anti-Israel sentiment.

UNLIKELY BEDFELLOWS, DEADLY ALLIANCES

In the struggle for dominance between the East and West, alliances have been formed that ideologically can make little sense. For example, why is Putin playing in a sandbox with the Ayatollah? The simple answer is economics, and feeding each other's militarily industrial complexes. Both are needed to sustain their own agenda and power struggles. The result of these alliances is the de facto support of terrorism against Israel. The irony of this is that Russia has some dependency on Israel's survival. Russia has a considerable dependence on Israeli technology, particularly in the military and cybersecurity sectors. Additionally, Israel has not imposed sanctions on Russian oligarchs despite international pressure, particularly from the United States, to do so.

China, North Korea, Iran, and Russia: the axis of evil makes strange bedfellows. There is no honor amongst thieves, and certainly no honor amongst the nihilists, whose common ambition is to overtake the West. Eventually they will turn on each other—their loyalties are fickle—and will produce an endless volley of power struggles from within and in concert with each other. However for now, this alliance represents a clear and present danger to Israel and the rest of the world.

We know that Iran, China, and Russia have proxies at work, integrated within communities across the US and Canada. This may not come as a surprise for Europe, who some already say is a lost cause. Jacob, my Shin Bet friend, bluntly comments, "In twenty years the demographics of Europe will be its death. The clock cannot be turned back, there is little that can be done, it is too late." In some European neighborhoods, police will not interfere with Sharia law, the Islamic legal system. Unbeknownst to many Canadians and Americans, this uncomfortable reality is brewing within the concentration of Muslim neighborhoods.

I do not think the axis of evil membership is running co-ordinated agendas, but they do have a common purpose, and they are all immoral actors who seek world order. It is a well known fact that Iran and China have their own internal police mechanisms spying on their expats. Iran has carefully and patiently installed itself in the university campuses and has successfully manipulated public organizations such as CUPE (Canadian Union of Public Employees), either through idealist radicalization or with old-fashioned financial bribes.

China has been stealing technology from anyone and everyone. The downfall of one of our biggest tech darlings in Ottawa, Nortel, was the direct result of China stealing its proprietary information and creating products that they then sold back to Canada and the United States at lower costs than our own companies. What must be understood is that this is not about selling us back some hardware. This is about controlling communications infrastructure that is vital to our security, safety and protection. The very real fear is that China has created back doors into every piece of technology that we have purchased from them for military, medical, consumer, and telecommunications purposes. That means they can listen and influence outcomes on a domestic scale. At the time of the 5G network roll-out, the Chief Executive of Huawei was arrested, and we were faced with the reality that we knowingly allowed the Chinese to enter into the most sensitive areas of our security. We had rolled out the red carpet. Britain was the first to ban Huawei, the United States followed, and eventually Canada jumped on board.

In another brazen example of Chinese interference, Dr. Xiangguo Qiu and her husband, Dr. Keding Cheng, who were scientists at the National Microbiology Laboratory (NML) in Winnipeg, Canada, were fired in January 2021 following an investigation. They were secretly working in China, and were named on Chinese patents derived from sensitive work carried out at the Canadian biohazard laboratory. Canada has also been investigating the so-called China Police Stations[1] situated in Canada to spy on and intimidate Chinese Canadians.

I bring these instances up to highlight the ease with which foreign interference has installed itself in Canada, and how current Canadian policy seems unwilling or unable to prevent Jihadists, Chinese, and Iranian proxies on Canadian soil. The same intrusion has happened in the United States.

There is a real lack of understanding and education in both countries by immigration and customs officials to identify the import of radicals, there are little safeguards in place to identify and shut down online sources that radicalize, and there is almost no scrutiny of foreign funding of national institutions such as universi-

---

[1]   The China police stations operating in the US and Canada are often referred to as "overseas police service centers" or "Chinese overseas police stations." There are reports of threats using relatives and any means necessary to monitor, influence, and sometimes intimidate Chinese nationals living abroad.

ties and unions that rally on behalf of the Jihadist ideologies. These anti-Israel protests are blatant hate fests.

GLOBAL JIHAD VS COMMUNISM

The difference between the Jihadists and the communists is that communism was fought directly between two physical nations, Russia and America, which would eventually be defined through East and West alliances. You knew where the lines were drawn and you knew who your enemy was. The East-West conflict was a power struggle for a secular way of life, economic supremacy, and geographical control. The war was fought with an arms race, alliances, and ideological movements from within the enemy's borders that would serve to push opinion and sentiment. Ideology was more of a weapon the East could use against the West. Movements that threaten the East's hold on power are, even today, effectively illegal and severely repressed. Civil liberties are not on the menu in these countries. In contrast, American freedoms of speech and expression are leveraged by evil actors to spread their poisonous ideology as a weapon to undermine the West.

Jihad is very different, as there is no nation-to-nation war. Jihad is an unbordered, ideological movement based on the radical religious interpretation of world Islamic domination. Jihad is not bound by any conventions, it does not play by the rules of MAD as the Russians and Americans did, or by any modern rules of warfare. "By any means" justifies the end goal. This includes terrorism, the use of human shields, kidnapping, rape, and mutilation. There is no discrimination between young and old, male or female, or religious beliefs. In this way, there are no sides in Jihad, there are only the perpetrators and their innocent victims.

Radicalization is insidious; we often have no idea who has been radicalized until it's too late. But when those individuals stop acting as lone wolves and join the pack, coordinating their attacks, this is when we are at a total war from within. Not an easy war to win once it's already inside your borders and out of the box. I do not believe that victory can be achieved without impeding the civil liberties and freedoms we fought so hard for, back when liberalism was still true to itself, and before it had inadvertently become an enabler of Jihad.

NON-STATE TERROR PROXIES

AFTER THE HORRIFIC EVENTS OF 9/11, air travel security became the obsession of a shell-shocked and paranoid Western world. In today's world of terrorist plots, some foiled, many achieved, travel continues to become more restricted and stressful. The lines at airports have gotten out of control. Today, some flight check-in processes are longer than the flight itself. These days, anything under an 8-hour drive and I'm hopping in the car. What has not been dealt with enough is the root cause of our security concerns. The teaching of Jihad. Yes, eventually Osama Bin Laden was sent to his virgins, yet history will tell us that the world failed to see 9/11 for what it was: the appetizer for Global Jihad. The US figured if they took out Iraq's leader, Saddam Hussein, over some trumped-up charges of possessing weapons of mass destruction the problem would be solved. Don't get me wrong, Saddam Hussein was a very bad guy, but he was not the singular answer to stopping the disease of Jihad. Years later, the radical rhetoric continues to grow in brashness, the protests grow in disruption and intimidation, and the narrative seems to favor the victims of free speech when all they are spewing is hatred from the perch of their pulpits. As I watched the protests encamped on the lawns of university campuses, hearing that "negotiations" were taking place to get them to vacate, I got the awful feeling that the inmates were running the asylum.

This is not about a conflict over political or philosophical ideologies, this is a conflict about theological subjugation by any means necessary. The advantage of our Jihad adversaries is quite simple: we will never think like them. Afghanistan is a complete failure, spooled back into the dark ages, now back to being run by terrorists after the US abandoned the people of this country. Thousands of American, Canadian, and European coalition forces lost their lives in Afghanistan, and to what end? Nothing that was achieved stuck. What Hamas did on October 7 shows we are still living in a world out of control. What is going on in Yemen, compliments of the Houthis; how Hezbollah has taken Lebanon hostage; the red line that Syria's President Bashar al-Assad has crossed many times against his own people—all of this is further witness to the momentum of terror overtaking anything it touches. Closer to home, Canadian unions are outwardly in support of terrorist organizations like Hamas, manipulating people to go out and protest, based on misinformation about Israel and the rising of "Death to America" rhetoric. Islamophobia, a relatively small problem, is being discussed in the same breath as antisemitism, which has spiked hundreds of percentage points since October 7.

We are doing the jester's dance because the Jihad plays up the lover of death over the lover of life. How can we not lose? Until we start to think like a Jihdist and accept that MAD does not apply, we will not have the agency to do what must be done. Curb the education, disband the hate, charge the haters, stop the terror, take out Iran's radical theocracy.

IRAN

When I think of ancient Persia in the 5th Century BCE, I am transported to a golden era when Persia was the largest empire of the world under the stewardship of Xerxes I, known as King Aha-suerus (*Ach-ash-ver-osh*). I think about the story of *Purim* told in the chronicles of the *Book of Esther*. These events record the rise of Esther to queenhood, the plot by the evil Haman to destroy the Jews, and the eventual triumph of Esther and her Uncle Mordechai over Haman. It was a dark time for the Jews leading up to the miracle of their redemption. Haman was the hand of the king, and he convinced him that the Jews were a risk to his kingdom. His hatred likely stems from the loyalty the Jews showed to their God. He was jealous, and knew that they would never bend the knee to him. The king, being the king, was out of touch with what was happening in the streets, had no qualms in following Haman's suggestion to declare Jews enemies of the state, and signed their death warrant. And so it was declared with much fanfare and an edict issued to all 127 provinces that on the 13th day of the month of Adar (12th month of the Jewish lunar calendar), the purge (killing) of the Jews would be sanctioned by the highest court of the land. But before Haman's plan was enacted, in a divine turn of events, Vashti, the king's wife, fell out of his favor, and Haman suggested the king find a new queen. Eligible maidens were brought in from every corner of the kingdom for what would be the beauty pageant of all time. The winning contestant would become the new queen, and for one of the most powerful people on earth. When it was the maiden Esther's turn to appear before the king, he was enamored by her beauty and enchanted by her poise, brilliance, and character, and immediately declared her his queen. As directed by her Uncle Mordechai, Esther had hidden her Jewish roots, and did not reveal this to Ahasuerus until the last possible moment when she invited both king and his hand to a banquet she had prepared. At a pre-party at his home, Haman's friends and family noticed his melancholy.

"Why the long face?" asked his wife.

"None of this matters to me while that Jew Mordechai refuses to bend his knee and sits at the gates of the city in his sackcloth," Haman lamented.

His son jumped up and said, "Oh father, you are the most powerful person in the land aside from the King. Let's build a gallows today and we will hang that Jew when you are back from the party that the new queen has prepared."

Haman loved the idea, and his spirits soared. A gallows was erected in record time. But before the end of that day it was Haman swinging from the gallows prepared for Mordechai, and soon Mordechai, the new hand of the king, would be living in Haman's mansions. Clever Esther had already told Ahasuerus that someone wished to kill her and her family. Upon hearing this, Haman threw himself on her mercy. The king saw this as Haman trying to take Esther for himself, and that was the last time we heard from Haman.

The graves of Mordechai and Esther are maintained in Hamadan, Iran, considered a revered site for both the Jews and Muslims. The story of Purim is celebrated every year with a message for hope in the face of looming disaster. The concept of redemption is a big part of the Jewish culture. Miracles can and do happen.

The fall of Persia started with the conquest of Alexander the Great in 330 BCE and followed the Hellenistic period. The breakup of the once great empire saw periods of significant control over Persia by other empires, including the Parthian Empire (247 BCE-AD 224), and Sasanian Empire (AD 224-651), until the Islamic conquest in the 7th century AD. This marked the beginning of Islamic rule and the gradual conversion of the region to Islam, which significantly influenced the cultural and religious landscape. During the medieval Islamic period, the region became a center of Islamic culture and learning, contributing significantly to the Islamic Golden Age. Various dynasties such as the Abbasids, Safavids, and others ruled the area, each leaving a distinctive mark on its development. In the 20th century, Persia officially became Iran. The country underwent significant modernization under Reza Shah Pahlavi and his son, Mohammad Reza Shah Pahlavi. However, political unrest led to the Islamic Revolution in 1979, which established the Islamic Republic under Ayatollah Khomeini, who remained Iran's Supreme Leader until his death in 1989.

There are 995 miles between Iran and Israel. Iraq is located directly to the west of Iran, and is a buffer between Iran and Jordan, which is directly to the east of Israel and is a buffer between Iraq and Israel. Syria is north of Jordan and shares borders with Iraq. Syria is a close ally of Iran, and during the Syrian civil war, Syria was supported by both Iran and Russia. Iran is significantly larger than Israel, at 636,000 square miles compared to Israel's 8,000 square miles. Iran's population is 85 million people, more than 10 times Israel's population of 8 million. It is difficult to imagine what threat Iran feels from Israel, a tiny country nearly 1,000 miles away with less than 10% of Iran's population.

Iran has a long list of human rights abuses. The international community, including human rights organizations like Amnesty International and Human Rights Watch, have noted Iran's express disregard for civil rights and freedoms and its abuse of human rights. And yet, the United Nations saw it in their wisdom to appoint Iran to head a special symposium on Human Rights on November 2-3, 2023. Go figure. Here is a list of the ongoing abuses Iran is charged with:

1. **Political Repression:** The Iranian government has been accused of suppressing dissent through censorship, surveillance, arbitrary arrests, and detentions.

2. **Freedom of Speech and Press:** The Iranian government controls the media, blocking websites, restricting access to social media platforms, and regularly jailing journalists. There is heavy censorship of print, broadcast, and digital content.

3. **Treatment of Minorities:** Ethnic and religious minorities in Iran often face discrimination in various aspects of their lives, including employment, education, and freedom of worship.

4. **Women's Rights:** Women in Iran face systemic discrimination in law and practice. They are subject to strict dress codes and have few rights in marriage, divorce, child custody, and inheritance. Women activists campaigning for more rights often face severe penalties.

5. **Death Penalty and Judicial Process:** Iran has one of the highest rates of executions in the world. Charges that can carry the death penalty include murder, drug trafficking, espionage, and offenses related to sexual orientation and adultery. Juvenile offenders and political dissidents have also been executed.

6. **LGBTQ+ Rights:** Homosexuality is illegal in Iran, with severe punishments, including the death penalty, for consensual same-sex sexual acts. This community faces significant persecution, harassment, and discrimination.

7. **Use of Torture:** Reports of torture and other forms of ill-treatment in detention are widespread. These tactics are often used to extract confessions or as a means of punishment.

8. **Rights of Prisoners:** Conditions in many prisons are harsh and life-threatening. Overcrowding, limited access to health care, and abuse by guards are reported frequently.

Seyyed Ali Hosseini Khamenei is the current supreme theocratic leader of Iran, referred to as the Ayatollah. The President of Iran, Ebrahim Raisi was considered a possible successor to the Ayatollah, up until his recent untimely demise in a helicopter crash. The supreme council of Iran are puppets to the Ayatollah, and nothing happens without his blessings. He is, in a sense, to the Muslims what the Pope is to the Catholics, however he also has control of a significant army and military arsenal. He is a total zealot and the single most influential person dictating the vision of Global Jihad since his succession in 1989, the only succession for supreme leader thus far. The process for succession as well as the life of Khameini is a very private affair, but it is speculated that his son Mojtaba Khameini may eventually become his successor.

Where does the hate of Israel and the Jews come from? I have met a number of Iranian people over the years who appeared to harbor no antisemitic sentiment. I generally find Iranians to be very intelligent and warm people. I am really not sure where the disconnect is, and while my interactions have been with people outside of Iran, I cannot imagine people on the inside to be that much different. My suspicions are that the people of Iran may not share the same hatred of Jews their leadership does, nor, if asked, would they support the funding or terror and pressure to destroy Israel. This is yet another impossible situation Israel must resolve: how to deal with the threat of the Iranian regime without harming the supposedly innocent civilian population?

Member of the Ontario provincial parliament, Goldie Ghamari, is the first female Iranian-Canadian to hold office in Canada. She is a first generation Iranian, and is vocal about her opposition to Jihadism and the threat posed by the Islamic Republic. She noted, specifically for this book, the following:

"Since taking over Iran in 1979, the terrorist Islamic Regime has held the Iranian people hostage... Before the invention of the internet and social media, the Islamic Regime was able to successfully fool the rest of the world into thinking that the people of Iran supported the Ayatollahs and their Jihad against the West. However, nothing is farther from the truth. In fact, the empty polling stations and the historically low 10% voter turnout during the 2024 election in Iran is proof that the Iranian people completely reject the Islamic Regime. This widespread election boycott, which was acknowledged by the Islamic Regime, demonstrates the determination of the Iranian people to overthrow this illegitimate and anti-Iranian regime, and to take their country back from their terrorist Jihadi oppressors."

I believe there is a fantasy among Iran's leadership of rebuilding the former glory of the Persian empire. Historically, this is achieved through conquest. When the revolution of 1979 ousted the US-supported Shah, everything Western was decried as an enemy of Iran. Israel was a perfect target to vent this anger, and so an ideology was created to justify all of the resources necessary to distract the public from the domestic failings of the supreme leadership. It is a classic red herring. It therefore made sense for Iran to align itself with the Palestinian cause, even though they could care nothing about the plight of these people. When Iran launched 300 missiles, drones, and other air projectiles at Israel on April 13, 2024 there was no consideration for the Palestinians who would have been killed had the coalition of Israel and Western powers air defenses not managed to neutralize these projectiles with 99% accuracy. One of the inter-continental ballistic missiles was headed straight toward the Al Aqsa mosque in Jerusalem, and no one on the Palestinian side said a word about it.

Iran bankrolls Hamas, who have kept the Palestinian people living in Gaza in deprived living conditions and have served to perpetuate the Palestinian crisis. Without a crisis, Iran loses its anti-Jewish cause, and without a cause they have no footing to rationalize actions to undermine Western influences. At every turn of the peace effort, Iran is undermining and sabotaging the process. In terms of timing, Ten-Seven may have been launched prematurely to undermine and derail the imminent and historical peace treaty between Israel and Saudi Arabia, which would have further isolated the Islamic Republic. Middle East scholar, Mordechai Kedar, postulated as much in a *National Post* article of July 3, 2024, titled "Why Hamas went rogue on Oct. 7, and how the West could end the war."

Wherever there is terror, Iran has a fingerprint or two. The Iranian supreme leadership is responsible, in some form or another, for almost every terrorist attack on Israel and its citizens. Iran publically flaunts itself as sponsoring groups that are Jihadist and regularly threatens to take their "message" to America. It is likely that they are doing so already. Cancel the Iranian theocratic dictatorship and its terrorist entities, and the Jewish state of Israel will have a chance at peace. Iran's current security apparatus must be dismantled and its nuclear capabilities excluded from military enrichment. A tall order, but this is what must be done.

The battle against Global Jihad comes down to this: Iran is in the business of terrorism, and if we want peace and stability in the world, the Islamic Republic of Iran must be put out of business.

THE PARTY OF TERROR

Iran has been an excellent student of the Cold War era practice of forming alliances and spreading ideologies. They have perfected their own unique style of playing the game with the backing of multiple proxies, which I will aptly refer to as the *Party of Terror*. Proxies are necessary to Iran, allowing them to drive political and regional change across the world without inciting a military response against it. As long as Iran has proxies carrying out its dirty work, it avoids the optics of responsibility. So long as world leaders didn't really know the extent of the terror it sowed, Iran could be seen as a partner in negotiating the now flawed nuclear deal spearheaded by US President Barack Obama. Iran played the US and Europe like a fiddle. The diplomacy here seemed more about achieving short term gains at the expense of long-term consequences. No one wants this to turn into a never-ending conflict on their watch. But look at where we are now. The thinking must change soon, or we may find ourselves bending the knee in the direction of Persia.

The Party of Terror is not an exclusive list; there is a long list of fringe groups competing, always violently, for the favor of Iran's backing and the money of Qatar. Today, the main players are Hezbollah, Hamas, and the Houthis (the 3Hs), covering the north, central, and south of Israel respectively. When you add in Syria on the Golan side of the country, Israel is completely surrounded by some bad actors who hold rallies in the tens of thousands chanting death to Israel, death to America, death to anyone who stands in their way. The Party of Terror have built up extensive military capabilities and have no rules or boundaries when it comes to using terror and death to achieve their objectives.

Not to put too fine a point on it, but Iran creates these proxies to fight their dirty battles in order to distract the world from their plan to use Global Jihad to establish a new world order. Determined to become the main power-player in the Middle East, they seek to centralize their power via terror. The scary part of all this madness is that the liberal Western powers play right into their hands, as more of their proxies make their way around the world through "refugee" migration. Iran has eyes everywhere. By the time the free world comes to understand this, it may already be too late.

To achieve its goals, Iran creates situations that play on the moral conflict of the defenders of freedom. The situation in Gaza is precisely the right combination of impossibility and chaos needed to challenge Western morality, and we fall for it hard. For instance, most of those protesting against Israel or shouting pro-Palestinian rhetoric have no idea of the broader and bigger plan. Those who dare pull the mask off of the beast are quickly canceled and accused of Islamophobia. It is nothing short of brilliant marketing how Iran appeals to human rights sensitivities by making Gazans the victims. It's the perfect distraction, and the useful idiots play right into it without hesitation.

HAMAS

Harakat al-Muqawama al-Islamiya: generally known by the acronym Hamas. Translated, they brand themselves as the Islamic Resistance Movement. Hamas was founded in 1987 by three dodgy characters of the radicalized Muslim Brotherhood—not a favored Egyptian organization. Two of them, Sheikh Ahmed Yassin and Abdel Aziz al-Rantisi, have been sent off to meet their virgins. Mohammad Tahas is missing in action, location unknown. Hamas has a very straightforward mission: the destruction of Israel and the establishment of an Islamic state in what they deem to be "historic Palestine." Translated, Hamas wants to overthrow the legitimate Jewish state of Israel. This is not reclaiming an area. This is an overt and illegal military attack, and since Hamas has no legitimate state status, and targets civilians, this is also called terrorism. Despite what they may claim, the people who identify as Palestinian today were never indigenous to the area. (I will later show both ancient and modern evidence that the Jewish people are in fact indigenous to Israel.) Understanding Israel's history significantly and importantly shifts the context around Hamas's actions. They are not resisting; they are attacking.

The Hamas Charter is a clear giveaway: kill Jews, destroy Israel. In 2005, Israel fully disengaged from Gaza, leaving it to be run by the single party PA . Presently, the Life President is a "sweet" old man who also happens to be a dictator in his own right, a hater of Jews and a Holocaust denier. Mahmoud Abbas just wants to get his piece of the Greater Palestinian Area.

But his party, Fatah, lost in an electoral poker game with Hamas in 2006. Hamas violently overthrew Fatah in Gaza and staged elections. Hamas loved the Fatah model of running the place, but took things a step further by offering all citizens of Gaza a future in their genocidal mandate. Hamas is designated a terrorist organization by many countries, including the United States and Canada. It's telling how the authoritarian states of the world are the ones who do not consider Hamas a terror group.

HEZBOLLAH

1970s Lebanon was considered the Riviera of the Middle East. Beirut was the playground for the newly oil-rich Arabs. It was a significant trading port, and a unique vibe of freedom and wealth imbued the land up until the devastation of a civil war that lasted from 1975 to 1990, which led to a vacuum in leadership and an economy in tatters. The PLO (Palestinian Liberation Organization) and Syrian factions swooped in to use Lebanon as a base for its aggression against Israel. After the 1982 Lebanon war, launched preemptively by Israel in response to constant PLO incursions, Hezbollah eventually emerged as the main political and military presence. Under the leadership of Sayyed Hassan Nasrallah, Hezbollah is now firmly entrenched in Lebanon as a civil and military force, and is a recognized terrorist organization, one that vows Israel's total destruction.

Hezbollah was directly engaged again by Israel in the 2006 Lebanon War, also launched pre-emptively by Israel in response to a Hezbollah raid that resulted in the death of several IDF soldiers and the kidnapping of two others. The UN brokered a peace deal after 34 days of fierce fighting, which increased the buffer zone between Israel and Lebanon. Since then the clock has remained at 15 seconds to midnight, with several border skirmishes occuring, and the occasional volley of missiles launched into Israel.

Hezbollah has been very active in building its Iranian-trained army. In 2021, Nasrallah publicly claimed that the Hezbollah military force numbered 100,000 troops, making it the largest non-state army in the world. However, the true number is reported to be significantly less, perhaps fewer than 50,000 troops including elite, regular, and reservists. According to the Center for Strategic and International Studies in Washington, Hezbollah currently has 150,000 missiles pointed at Israel, but who knows? The real number could be much larger. Many of these missiles are long range and can reach almost anywhere inside of Israel. In addition to amassing arms and soldiers, it is believed that Hezbollah has also built an extensive network of tunnels that lead directly into Israel. On June 4, 2019, Israel sealed off the largest tunnel ever found as part of "Operation Northern Shield." The tunnel extended one mile and was 265 feet subterrain (approximately 22 stories underground). It was equipped with electricity and communication capabilities, and large enough that military vehicles could drive through it. It was designed for cross border incursions from Lebanon into Israel. Regardless of the government's assurances, it is possible that this is just the tip of the iceberg. The sophistication and extent of tunneling in Southern Lebanon may be a substantial threat to the Jewish state.

Given the post-October 7 security situation, the Israeli government has had no choice but to mandate the evacuation of 100,000 residents in the northern area.

"I cannot go back to my home," cries Leor, a resident of Kiryat Shmona, a city of 25,000 people within one mile of Lebanon's border. "There is zero seconds to safety when they launch a missile now."

She's not wrong. In January 2024, a mother and son were killed when a missile hit their northern home. They received no warning, and had no time to reach a bomb shelter. The average time an Israeli has to seek safety in a bomb shelter is 60 seconds. Every Israeli home, as per building codes, must have a *Mammad*, a safe room. Today, however, if you live next to Gaza, you have less than three seconds of warning to reach it. In the north, within 20km of the Lebanese border, you have 0 seconds to safety. When the levels fall under 30 seconds, residents have no choice but to evacuate for their own safety.

The situation with Hezbollah is quickly becoming entirely unsustainable for Israel. Constant security threats from a well-armed terrorist network that boasts an army larger than Lebanon's, and larger than many in the region, threaten Israel daily with total destruction. No one wants an escalation with Hezbollah, especially Israel. Regardless of the strength of the IDF, a war with Lebanon will incur a high cost in lives and regional consequences, but it is rapidly becoming the only option left on the table. I expect that the situation with Hezbollah will become a new front for Israel. It is not feasible to allow Hezbollah to displace the residents of the North, or amass more troops and weaponry. It is highly unlikely that Iran would give up its largest non-state terror actor in the region. Without Iran, Hezbollah would most certainly have a challenge to resupply and sustain any military offensive. As the range and sophistication of Hezbollah's missile capabilities grows, more Israelis are forced to evacuate from their homes. Hezbollah is winning its war without stepping a single foot inside of Israel.

Lebanon has concerns and they very well should. The Lebanese parliament is a pawn to both Hezbollah and Syrian influences. In 2005, Lebanese Prime Minister Rafic Hariri was assassinated in a dramatic attack when a bomb exploded in his motorcade in downtown Beirut, also killing 21 civilians. It is widely believed that Syria was responsible. I am honestly not sure what influence or independence Lebanese lawmakers today have outside of the Hezbollah army, but I can assure you that the people of Lebanon are not interested in seeing their country become a parking lot like Gaza. Surely, a military option is not something the Lebanese people want. The agency of the Lebanese people is reduced to being a victim of Hezbollah's aggressive stance toward Israel.

Interestingly, Hezbollah did not follow up and engage Israel on, or shortly after, October 7. It is unknown if this was a strategic calculation by Hezbollah, or if they simply were not included in the plans. "You did what?!" I imagine Sayyed Hassan Nasrallah screaming into his red phone. "And you did not invite me to the party?" Slam. Had they acted, Hezbollah would have seriously divided and limited Israel's response that day, but they would have also incurred the same wrath. War with Israel will result in a significant hardship to the Lebanese, and I cannot imagine that the people of Lebanon would be happy with this. So perhaps the question should be asked: to what extent can Lebanon control Hezbollah?

I do not see this situation ending well for Lebanon. The current situation is untenable, Lebanon's people should be freed from the tight grip of Hezbollah's power, and the people of Northern Israel must be able to return to their homes.

THE HOUTHI

The third major player in the party of terror is the Houthis, another non-state actor recently making a splash, using the Israel-Hamas conflict as a platform to gain more traction on the world stage with their "Death to Israel and America" narrative. The Houthis emerged in the late 1990s without any branding, a minority group from the religious Shia Muslim crowd located in the northern areas of Yemen, who were becoming increasingly agitated by what they perceived as the Yemeni government's too-close alignment with the West. Yemen's location by the Bab el-Mandeb Strait gives it significant geopolitical importance, overseeing one of the world's busiest maritime routes, crucial for international trade and oil shipments, making Yemen strategically important to Saudi Arabia and its consuming partners in the West, mainly the United States. It is this adverse influence of alliances that the emerging Houthi saw as another sell-off to Western interests, at the cost of their Islamic way of life.

Yemen has a rich history that dates back to ancient times. Somewhat ironically, in the 6th century CE after a very long period of Jewish influence, Yemen was ruled by a Jewish king. Dhu Nuwas, also known as Yusuf Asar, the last Himyarite king of Yemen, who converted to Judaism. His reign is generally placed around 517-525

CE. His reign did not last long, largely due to his dislike for the Christians. Had he better diplomatic skills, the Christians would have been kinder when they unseated him and his Jewish patronage. Yemen fell under the influence of the Ottomans until the 19th century, when the British established a protectorate in South Yemen, centered around the port of Aden due to its strategic location along the route to British India. This held up until the 1967 anti-colonial uprising, when South Yemen gained its independence, leading to the establishment of the People's Republic of Yemen, a Marxist state. In 1990, the North and South of Yemen unified to form the Republic of Yemen, but this lasted only a few years before the Houthi clan used its power base in the north to take over.

The Houthis are named after Hussein Badreddin al-Houghti, who led the group's first uprising in 2004. The Al-Houghti's strong extended family had numbers, local influence, and economic ties with other foreign powers in the region, who saw the rise of the Houthi clan as an opportunity to install their own influence. Who are we talking about here? It will not come as a big surprise that the Houthis biggest sponsor from day one has been Iran. Over the next 10 years the Houthis emerged as the horse to bet on when it came to overthrowing the Yemeni government, and with it their Western alliance. Salivating at the idea of controlling the strait leading to the Suez Canal, Iran naturally threw its full support behind the Houthi uprising. The payoff seemed likely when in 2014 the Houthi took control of Yemen's capital, Sana'a, and other parts of the country, forcing the government into exile. In March 2015, a coalition led by Saudi Arabia and backed mainly by the United States launched a military operation against the Houthis to restore the Yemini government, turning the Houthi insurgency into a major international conflict that resulted in widespread famine, displacement, and collateral damage, ultimately creating a humanitarian crisis. When the dust settled, Yemen was now controlled by two capitals. The legitimate ruling party led by President Mansour Hadi is now located in the south, governing from the city of Aden. He has the full military backing of Saudi Arabia and the support of the United States.

The Houthis, now firmly entrenched in Yemen's north, have created an administrative infrastructure complete with various ministries that govern the territories under their control. Their military influence is rapidly growing despite attempts to neutralize it. They potentially have an army between 25,000-45,000 troops, and I have read interviews with claims that since October 7 they have recruited 70,000 fighters to their cause. Human Rights Watch has brought forward 1,851 verified cases to the UN of child soldier recruitment by the Houthis, though these numbers are likely much higher. The Houthis have no moral issues with recruiting children as young as 10 years old; if you can carry a gun, you can join the Houthi. Yemen's desperate living conditions contribute to this crisis; with some parents giving up their children to the cause for a few dollars and bags of rice. According to a variety of sources and research available on the internet, they have short range, long range, and some guided missiles, drones, and attack boats. They have one F-5 jet fighter. Much of their armed display on social media tries and fails to give the impression of a formalized, professional military, though their inconsistent and varied uniforms, often including robes and jeans, do not reduce the deadliness of the Kalishkonovs they raise into the air. As I perused pictures of the Houthi war machine, I paused, drawn by the ceremonial daggers in the belts. They seemed out of place, like something from Arabian Nights, a throwback to when a good fight had to be up close and personal.

The Houthi have a promotional video on YouTube that is a real motivator to get involved. If it were a skit on Saturday Night Live it would be Borat funny, but the harsh reality is that these people are no joke. They have been armed by Iran with sophisticated weaponry and are holding one of the world's most important shipping routes hostage. A blockaded shipping route means rapid material consequences for consumer-driven economies. In response, the US and international forces launched "Operation Prosperity Guardian", a defensive coalition involving maritime forces. This has not stopped the Houthis from launching missiles, which are starting to be a cause of significant global concern to the supply chain. The Houthi are also firing guided missiles at Eilat, Israel's southern port. They announced that they are responding to Israel's fight with Hamas, and will not relent without a cessation of military aggression against Hamas. This is interesting, as they have nothing much in common with Hamas other than a shared interest in pursuing power through terrorism. However, the broader Sunni-Shia divide in the Muslim world, with Hamas being Sunni and the Houthis being Shia, complicates any potential for close collaboration.

The Houthis, like other regional players in the region, seem to be using the Palestinians to further their own cause. They couldn't care less about the life of a Palestinian, but it's good leverage to attract recruits and further their own mission of death to America.

The Houthis may be lesser-known on the world stage than Hamas or Hezbollah, but they should not be dismissed. Al Qaeda and Osama bin Laden were once underestimated too.

THE PARTY CRASHERS

There is no raver without the party crashers, and the vacuum of this Red Sea neighborhood has still more zealot radicals vying for their share of the pie. There is more than one biblical prophecy that divine intervention will play a role in the forces of destruction that will turn on each other. One notable example is in the Book of Ezekiel, specifically in the prophecy against Gog and Magog. In Ezekiel 38:21-22, it is written:

> "I will summon a sword against Gog on all my mountains, declares the Sovereign Lord. Every man's sword will be against his brother. I will execute judgment on him with plague and bloodshed; I will pour down torrents of rain, hailstones, and

burning sulfur on him and on his troops and on the many nations with him."

Another example is in the story of Gideon in the Book of Judges. In Judges 7:22, it describes how the Midianites turned on each other during Gideon's battle:

"When the three hundred trumpets sounded, the Lord caused the men throughout the camp to turn on each other with their swords. The army fled to Beth Shittah toward Zererah as far as the border of Abel Meholah near Tabbath."

These passages illustrate the theme of divine intervention causing confusion and infighting among the enemies of Israel.

Thankfully, these prophecies have played out throughout the modern history of the Middle East. Much of the death and destruction is actually caused through warring factions, not because of Israel or the West. Hamas brutally puts down any challenge to its power. Many Palestinians have been arbitrarily detained and murdered because they were thought to be working with Hamas's rival faction Fatah, or accused of collaboration (with Israel). This is just the tip of the iceberg. There are several branches of Islam that come off the division between Sunni and Shia sects, which both have their extreme factions that compete for who is the baddest Jihadist on the block.

Hezbollah and the Houthi are more of the extreme Shia sect, while Hamas adheres to the more extreme radical interpretations of Sunni, along with Al-Qaeda and the Islamic State (ISIS or ISIL). Religious divisions create strained bedfellows. The radical extremes of these groups share a common enemy in Israel and America; however, their own internal conflicts tend to (thankfully) undermine their potential to strike more effectively against the west. God help us should the day ever come when these factions find a way for lasting cooperation.

THE FUNDING OF TERRORISM

FOLLOW THE MONEY

I have talked about how Israel has been placed into compromised security positions by its allies for cessation of defense hostilities, and that not one of those ceasefire deals has stuck. Israel is forced into making deals with the devil, time and again allowing Hamas to rebuild itself.

Instead of building industry and sustainability, Hamas has used international aid to invest in terrorism. The real question is not how the Ten-Seven attack on Israel could have happened? Rather, how could it *not* have happened? I recall the live footage of money arriving from Qatar, multiple duffle bags of cash being offloaded for delivery into the Gaza strip. $30 million USD with the approval of Israel, the sponsorship of Qatar, and the blessings of Europe and the United States.

In May 2019 Qatar delivered $15 million in cash to Gaza. The money was transported in suitcases and handed over to Hamas officials under the supervision of Qatar's envoy to Gaza, Mohammed Al-Emadi. This event was widely covered by the media, with live footage showing the delivery. In November 2019 another installment of Qatari cash was shown on live TV. The same in September 2020, with the public announcement and transfer of $30 million in cash transferred into Hamas-controlled Gaza. In November 2021 another widely publicized event witnessed the transfer of cash and fuel into Gaza. The coordination with media and public display is no accident. These were PR planned events by Hamas and Qatar to showcase the absurdity of funding terror, with Israel essentially accepting the payment of peace policy and the blind eye of what the funds were really being used for.

All of this money was going through Hamas. While the stated intention was the relief of poverty, it was also widely publicized that these funds were to pay for Hamas public salaries. These are not the public servants we imagine when we think of the people that make our cities work. These public servants are deeply enmeshed in Hamas' terrorist agenda. There is no secret where this money was going or what it was building.

$360,000,000 annually over 10 years; $3.6 billion dollars has paid for miles of tunnels, weapons and equipment, with plenty left over for the top Hamas operatives to build their own nest eggs, many of whom preserved their newfound wealth in the real estate and equities of the countries they vow to destroy. Hamas did not just bite the hands that fed it, they consumed it with arrogance.

With its billions of dollars of aid money, Hamas built an estimated 1,300 tunnels, approximately 300 miles of underground systems. To put this into perspective, Toronto, one of Canada's largest cities, has only 44 miles of tunneled subway; Paris,141 miles. Given the relative size of Gaza, its tunnel system is one of the most extensive in the world. Hamas used these tunnels exclusively to support its terrorist operations, including the storage and manufacturing of weapons, food, water, generators, fuel, and other equipment. Undetected, Hamas leaders and fighters safely move throughout Gaza, smuggled in arms and goods (and everything else from porn to caviar), spring seemingly out of nowhere all across the area, and, most recently, used the tunnel systems to imprison and transport hostages out of sight and reach of would-be rescuers.

In certain places, Hamas's tunnels were large enough in some areas that Hamas leadership can drive cars from place to place and that high-end shopping takes place underground. There are many documented discoveries of these tunnels, their locations and uses. Many used for operations are strategically stationed under public institutions like hospitals and schools for human shielding.

How did Hamas pay for all this? Much of the money came from UNRWA's $1.6 billion, international payments, while Qatar and the blood money from Iran and its proxies made up a large part of funding for the terror enclave. Instead of these funds going to feed the population and build sustainability like they were supposed to, the money sent to Gaza was used by Hamas almost exclusively to further its mission of destroying Israel. Ironically, Israel is inadvertently one of their greatest supporters. Israel provides Gazans with 100% of the necessities of life: water, power, gas, internet, food aid. Gazans are entirely dependent on Israel for everything they need to live and fight another day. While Gaza is bombing Israel, Israel is forced to continuously power and sustain life in the strip. For years Israel has bent to international pressure, giving terrorists the resources to harm Israelis.

Hamas activity in the Gaza Strip has been the world's dirty secret for many years. Israel played the avoidance game as Hamas prepared for what was the worst single-day genocide of the Jewish people since the Holocaust. And all the while, Hamas leadership lined their pockets, jeering and sneering. Hamas' Former Chairman of its political bureau, Ismail Haniyeh, a billionaire, was considered one of the richest terrorists in the world. On the ground, carrying out the mandate of Hamas in Gaza, Yahya Sinwar, has become the top commander since his predecessor's demise in a daring administration of just retribution by Israel. Sinwar is another example of terror paying well, though I doubt he will have the opportunity to enjoy any retirement spending. In a perverse twist of irony, Israel provided the architect of October 7 with life-saving brain surgery when he was serving a life-sentence for terrorism. After 22 years of incarceration, Israel released Sinwar as part of the 2011 Gilad Shalit prisoner exchange.

THE SMUGGLING OPERATION

An advanced smuggling operation by road and sea under the guise of aid is how Hamas acquired goods under the noses of Israelis. Aid came into the strip via UNRWA foundations and, given UNRWA's status, these goods are rarely properly inspected. Parts for weapons and military equipment were smuggled into Gaza by being mixed in amongst other goods. Before Ten-Seven, approximately 600 trucks entered the Gaza enclave daily. Such an enormous volume of goods is almost impossible to effectively inspect, and anything endorsed by the UN would be seen as safe cargo and likely given only cursory inspection. Hidden among all this humanitarian relief, the equipment and weapons used to smash open Israel's border and wreak terror and death upon its people were smuggled into Gaza. Sources indicate that the operation was meticulously prepared and coordinated by Hamas's leadership. The *New York Times* and *Times of Israel* reported that the planning of the attack began at least two years in advance of October 7. In the months leading up to the attack, Hamas conducted drills and finalized logistics, which included stockpiling weapons, planning infiltration routes, and preparing to disable Israeli communications during the attack.

There is no way that all of the many organizations feeding and clothing the Gazan population were unaware that Hamas was smuggling in weapons and equipment. The international pressure to return to this model will effectively rearm and re-equip Hamas to continue its terrorist activities. As long as the world turns the other cheek to what is really happening, terrorism will continue.

The deception of humanitarian aid has been going on for some time. And regardless of Israel's intelligence and reporting on this to the world's intelligence communities and the United Nations, the response was mute. On May 31, 2010 the IDF intercepted boats in international waters ostensibly carrying humanitarian aid. The IDF had blockaded Gaza, necessary to prevent the smuggling of weapons and military materials that could be used by Hamas, and made it very clear that unauthorized transportation would not be tolerated. The Gaza Freedom Flotilla incident, as the event came to be named, happened in defiance of the Israeli government's ban. The lead boat, Mavi Marmara, flying a Greek flag and coming from Turkey, was boarded by an elite Israeli commando unit. During the operation, nine people were killed and several Israeli soldiers injured when the "peace" convoy opened fire on the IDF unit. Israel, who maintained that the incident was in self-defense, discovered a trove of weaponry. Following the raid on the Mavi Marmara, the UN Human Rights Council established an international fact-finding mission that concluded Israel's actions were in violation of international law, including international humanitarian and human rights law. The mission's report stated that Israel's enforcement of the blockade of Gaza was disproportionate. (Disproportionate?! Self-check for sanity in aisle 3 please!)

There have been several incidents where Israel has blocked aid ships or trucks and confiscated large amounts of weapons or technology for advanced weapon manufacturing hidden within them, and has immediately been internationally vilified for interfering with aid supplies. In some bizarre twist of the perverse, in the name of peace, Israel eventually forfeited the right to inspect goods, and up until Ten-Seven was allowing shipments across the border. It is preposterous that Israel was forced into these insane positions by the international community, when everyone knew precisely how Hamas was acquiring its weapons. Equally preposterous is that this expectation remains, even during negotiations for the return of hostages and an end to the war. The expectation by all actors involved is that Israel will once again allow goods to flow freely into Gaza. Hamas's cycle continues as it always has. Attack. Negotiate. Rearm. Repeat.

I received a desperate and frustrated WhatsApp message from my dear friend Rabbi Dovid Abrahamovitz. Dovid, who moved to Israel several years ago with his wife, Aliza, has become the go-to guy on the history of Jews of Eastern Europe, and leads many trips throughout the year to Poland retracing the horrors of the Holocaust.[1] So when Dovid and Aliza see truck loads of goods being delivered to Gaza in the wake of October 7, it understandably unnerved them.

"In the history of the world, was there ever a war where a country fed its enemies?" he writes to me. "Hamas is in need of food. They are negotiating for a ceasefire because they need to get food to their terrorists. When, God-willing, a miracle occurs, and all of the hostages are freed, how will we look them in the eye knowing we fueled their abusers? In 1943 when the Germans were depleted, should we have given out sandwiches and sent aid to help fuel their resistance?"

The pain in my friend's words is palpable. The son of their neighbor was just killed in action. To him and his family—to anyone who understands where the aid and money goes once it crosses the Gaza border—it is utterly ridiculous to sustain Gaza, knowing full well that Hamas would steal it to supply their fighters.

---

1   Abrahamowitz, Rabbi David. The World That Was European Tours Website. 2015. https://www.theworldthatwas.org/

WHERE TO LAY THE BLAME

The ability for Hamas to amass weaponry, troops, and equipment did not happen out of sight. It is perhaps possible that the powers of various security branches were caught off-guard, but it is impossible that all of this capability was not noticed or assessed as a significant threat. The munition manufacturing facilities were set up within the tunnel systems. Thousands of commercial drones were transformed into deadly suicide bombing squadrons. Much of the preparation for Ten-Seven occurred with Iranian assistance. There were Iranian specialists inside of Gaza, training, teaching, and supporting Hamas. How did these people get into the strip unnoticed? Tehran provided hundreds of specialists from the Quds Force of the Islamic Revolutionary Guard Corps (IRGC),[2] and support including financial backing, training, and weapons and military technology. According to the Foreign Policy Research Institute, Iran provided $70 million US dollars annually in direct military support to Hamas. The supreme leadership of Iran is directly responsible for the death and destruction on October 7. Just because it did not literally pull the trigger does not absolve it. This is not just a theory, it is legal precedent. Recently, in Michigan, James and Jennifer Crumbley, parents of school shooter Ethan, were charged with manslaughter in connection with their 15-year-old son's murdering spree in November 2021. Bottom line, if you provide the gun and the bullets, you will be charged with murder if someone uses these to kill. America applies this law to its own people, but not to Iran. Why should Iran be any different?

YOUR DOLLARS ARE AT WORK!

Anyone who has sent financial aid to Gaza, be it relief agencies, governments, companies, and individuals, can be credited with having helped prop up the deadly terrorist organization of Hamas.

---

2   The Quds Force is the extraterritorial military operative of Iran that conducts clandestine operations and provides support to non-state actors such as Hamas, Hezbollah, the Houthis, and other groups.

It is no secret, and yet many countries continued to funnel millions into the Strip. Not only did this enable Hamas, it gave them a voice and a seat at the table. It especially irks me that through my own tax dollars I too am complicit. In an article for the *New York Post*, Douglas Murray calls out how America was scammed into giving money to Hamas to build tunnels. He writes:

> "...our tax dollars helped build this system. It is American, European, and other taxpayer dollars that went into building this terrorist infrastructure…. billions of dollars have been given to them since that time. From a bewildering array of countries. All of whom seem to have thought that they were somehow helping the Palestinians in Gaza. Well, we weren't. All of this money was used by Hamas leaders to buy themselves luxury condos in Qatar and other foreign climes. Inside Gaza, almost none of this money went to help Palestinians in Gaza. Rather Hamas used the funds they didn't pilfer to build this underground terror network, which comes out in hospitals, mosques, and other places that the international community regards as sacred, but which Hamas does not."[3]

The funding of Hamas is death to the Jews by proxy. It is that simple. Every dollar finding its way into the pocket of Hamas is the ink signing the death warrant of Jews. The funding of UNRWA is aiding and abetting the murder of Jewish people. Hillel Neuer, of UN Watch, compiled dossiers that outline how UNRWA had direct ties to helping Hamas.

Here is a summary of the key points from these dossiers:

1. **Employment of Hamas Members:** The reports prove that many UNRWA employees are members of Hamas.

---

3   Murray, Douglas. "Hamas terror tunnels were built with your money". *New York Post*. December 21, 2023. https://nypost.com/2023/12/21/opinion/hamas-terror-tunnels-were-built-with-your-money/ .

2. **Use of UNRWA facilities by Hamas:** Several instances are cited where UNRWA facilities, such as schools, have been used to store weapons or as launch sites for rocket attacks against Israel.

3. **Educational material and incitement:** The dossiers show that the educational materials used in UNRWA schools promote antisemitism and incite violence. This includes textbooks and teaching practices that glorify martyrdom and Jihad against Israel.

4. **Social media Activity:** Evidence is provided of UNRWA employees posting content on social media that supports Hamas and praises terrorist attacks against Israelis. This includes sharing images and messages that glorify violence and hatred.

5. **Financial Irregularities:** Allegations are made about financial mismanagement within UNRWA, suggesting that funds intended for humanitarian purposes might be diverted to support Hamas activities.

6. **Calls for Accountability:** The reports conclude with calls for greater oversight and accountability of UNRWA operations. They suggest that donor countries should condition their funding on UNRWA's adherence to strict anti-terrorism measures and thorough vetting of staff.

UNRWA is one of the biggest elephants in the room when it comes to the direct support of terrorism, under the guise of alleviating the suffering of a people whose victimhood is perpetuated in one of the biggest scams of all time… the ongoing Palestinian refugee crisis.

THE "NON" REFUGEE CRISIS

IN 1949 the United Nations General Assembly created the United Nations Relief and Works Agency for Palestine Refugees (UNRWA) in response to what was considered a crisis of Palestinian refugees displaced during the 1948 Arab-Israeli conflict. The agency began operations on May 1, 1950, with a mandate to provide relief and support to the Palestinian refugees in Lebanon, Syria, Judea and Samaria (West Bank), and Gaza Strip. It is important to note here that as retribution for the establishment of the Jewish State of Israel, nearly one million Jews were forcefully expelled between 1948 and the 1970s from Arab countries, including Iraq, Egypt, Yemen, Syria, Lebanon,

Libya, Tunisia, Algeria, and Morocco, where they had resided for hundreds, and sometimes thousands, of years. They were stripped of their citizenship, robbed of their land and assets, sometimes tortured, and when fleeing allowed to bring with them only what they could carry. I do not recall any UN resolution or creation of a similar agency to handle the Jewish refugee crisis, yet the nearly one million expelled Jews is 50% more than the Palestinian refugees allegedly created in 1948. The actual number of Jews forcibly expelled from Arab countries is difficult to pinpoint, however various sources have pegged this number at between 850,000 and 1,000,000 people. I posit that the point is well made that one; there were many Jews who faced expulsion from their generational homes in Arab lands, and two; that this number far exceeds the claims of the so-called Palestinian refugees displaced by the legitimate defense of Israel in 1948.[1]

The seldom told story about the "Palestinian refugees" needs to be placed in the public's consciousness to deter the lies so often told about the conflict. In 1948, in preparation for an assault on the newly-formed country of Israel, the attacking Arab countries advised Arab residents to abandon their homes and leave the country to avoid danger (this is very different from being 'expelled', which is the current narrative of Palestine). Many of those who did took refuge in the Gaza Strip. Unfortunately for those who heeded this call, Israel won the war, and after the war those who had left their lands were denied entry to the Arab countries that had prompted their departure. They were now refugees, stuck in the Gaza Strip. Egypt took control of Gaza after the armistice agreements in 1949 and remained in control there for 19 years, during which it made no move to integrate or resettle the refugees.

The idea that Israel created the refugee camps of Gaza is false.

---

1   Mifano, Andrea. "The expulsion of Jews from Arab countries and Iran—the untold story". World Jewish Congress. February 2, 2021. https://www.worldjewishcongress.org/en/news/the-expulsion-of-jews-from-arab-countries-and-iran--an-untold-history

History has been corrupted to fit the narrative of the victim. A consistent trademark of the Palestinian cause is to solicit world sympathy. Despite the horrific barbarity of October 7, the Palestinians continue to win empathy from the world's liberal ideologists. The terror is even being rewarded as countries began to call for the recognition of a Palestinian state. On May 22, 2024 Norway, Ireland, and Spain announced their recognition of the State of Palestine. At the same time, I watched the NDP, a third tier minority partner, that enables the Liberal government of Canada with its votes pledge a vote to recognize a Palestinian state. All the while, some of the NDP's caucus added insult to injury, wearing the protest scarf (keffiyeh) in the House of Commons. This was for me one of the many reality moments of Canada's betrayal, I am no longer welcome in my home.

Originally intended to be a temporary measure to address the immediate humanitarian needs of the refugees created in 1948, UNRWA has evolved into a perpetual organization, deepening the victim status of the Palestinian cause. It has long been known that UNRWA, through its teaching of antisemitism in their Palestinian schools, has propagated the breeding of terrorists. UNRWA workers have worked hand in hand with Hamas. All the while claiming they have no idea about any of this. Israeli troops in Gaza City's Shejaiya neighborhood found a Hamas command center in an UNRWA school and health clinic, the IDF reported. Hamas turned these civilian sites into terrorist hubs. Troops from the Givati Brigade's Rotem Battalion discovered a weapons manufacturing plant and dozens of weapons, including mortars, machine guns, and grenades. The IDF also found Hamas intelligence documents hidden among UNRWA uniforms and equipment.

According to its website, the majority of the UNRWA's 30,000 employees are recorded as Palestinian "refugees." Since Ten-Seven, Israel has presented non-refutable evidence of at least 12 employees known to be directly involved with the killing spree of October 7, and over 1,200 employees suspected with good cause of working directly for Hamas, covering for Hamas, and participating in the military objectives of Hamas. In response, UNRWA committed to investigating allegations against its employees' involvement. Who are these guys kidding? For any other organization, this would be humiliating, and would be taken seriously. For UNRWA, it's a shrug.

The UNRWA budget in 2023 was $1.6 billion USD, according to its website, where they also offer a comprehensive 84-page document showing the funds the organization raises and disburses. However, unlike any other public institution of its kind, no auditor is signing off. There seems to be a complete lack of oversight and accountability. I was curious about UNRWA's executive salaries, and this was nowhere to be found. After doing some digging, I discovered that the average salary of an UNRWA executive is $236,000 USD. These 'executives' are residents of Gaza, earning on the upper scale of a North American professional salary, under the umbrella of Hamas. The CEO of UNRWA is Philippe Lazzarini, and his yearly payout is $700,000.[2] By comparison, the President of the United States earns an annual salary of $400,000. The Prime Minister of Canada, $379,000. The average CEO of some of the largest corporations in America earn between $630,000 and $1,074,000. UNRWA is big business for those that it feeds, and the inflated salaries of its top management alone constitutes a direct conflict of interest in maintaining, rather than reducing or even ending, the Palestinian refugee crisis.

THE PALESTINIAN REFUGEE DEFINED

In 2023 there were a reported 5.6 million Palestinian "refugees" being supported by UNRWA. It is a tenfold increase from the 500,000 registered in 1948. But at what point does someone *stop* being a refugee? The 1951 Refugee Convention relating to the status

---

2   Comparably.com.

of refugees, and subsequent 1967 protocol[3] by the United Nations High Commission, agrees that a refugee crisis has ended if at least one of the following five conditions are met:

1. When a refugee returns to their country of origin.

2. When a refugee permanently settles in their host country.

3. When a refugee settles in another country.

4. When the circumstances surrounding their refugee status cease to exist. In this situation, the individual rights are respected and they are not returned to situations where their life or freedoms would be threatened.

5. The revocation of a person's refugee status.

Let's take a look at where these 5.6 million Palestinian "refugees" reside.

In a 2021 survey conducted by the US, approximately 200,000 Palestinians had relocated to America. There are 3 million Palestinians in Jordan. There are 350,000 living in Kuwait. There's about 300,000 in Lebanon. About 500,000 in Syria. In Egypt, 100,000. 30,000 in Turkey. 400,000 in Saudi Arabia, and the same in Qatar. 100,000 in the Emirates. About 70,000 in Libya. About 40,000 in Yemen. They have all resettled in their host countries. There are a reported 2.3 million Palestinians living in Gaza, which was given

---

3   The 1951 Refugee Convention is officially known as the "Convention Relating to the Status of Refugees." The subsequent protocol that expanded the scope of the Convention is called the "1967 Protocol Relating to the Status of Refugees." The 1951 Convention initially limited its scope to protecting European refugees after World War II. However, the 1967 Protocol removed these geographical and temporal restrictions, making the provisions of the Convention applicable to refugees worldwide. These two documents are foundational to international refugee law, outlining the rights of displaced individuals and the legal obligations of states to protect them.

an independent mandate outside of any Israeli control as of 2005. Gaza, then, has become a permanent home, with infrastructure, community, and government. According to the standards set in 1967 by the UN, these people do not qualify as refugees. There are another 2 million Palestinians who live in the same land they came from, Israel, who are citizens of Israel, who receive the same benefits of citizenship, including the right to vote, as all Israelis. Combined, these populations account for approximately 4.6 million. The remaining difference is made up of "status unknown." If we accept that today's 5.6 million Palestinians are still refugees, then by the same logic the nearly 1 million Jews that were displaced in 1948 should also still be considered refugees, along with the millions of Jews displaced by the Holocaust. What about the millions of Indigenous people displaced by colonialism in various countries? If these populations are no longer considered refugees, then neither should those who identify as Palestinians. Result—I've just solved the 'refugee' crisis. Thank you UNRWA, your services are no longer needed, your cause is realized, and you may now dissolve. Unless, of course, you are part of another agenda. At best, UNRWA exists to continue to line its own pockets, like any big business. At worst, it helps Hamas to acquire the resources it needs to murder, rape, mutilate and terrorize Jews; not to mention their wider ambitions of Death to America and all infidels, who will be cleansed in the great Global Jihad. UNRWA is not part of the solution, they are a major contributor to the problem. This organization should be immediately defunded. The "crisis" of homeless or displaced Palestinians needs to be handled as a process with a plan to feed, clothe, house, educate, and chart a course toward sustainability. The term 'refugee' and the status of victim needs to be dropped from the narrative.

THE 'GROWING' PALESTINIAN REFUGEE CRISIS

Sisters Gigi and Bella Hadid are American models who became internationally renowned in the fashion industry. Their father,

Mohammad Hadid, was born in 1948 in Nazareth. The family fled to Syria as refugees. Though they are billionaires living a lavish life in Los Angeles; they are counted amongst the Palestinian refugee population. I bring this up because the one major mathematical flaw of the definition of the Palestinian refugee is subtraction.

The UNRWA claim of a growing refugee problem for the past 75 years is unlike any other refugee status of any other people. It is unique that a refugee crisis would continue to grow over a protracted period of time, and is highly problematic. In what can only be considered a blatant move to prolong the crisis, and secure its own survival, UNRWA has created a special definition for a Palestinian refugee. Unlike most other refugee populations, the Palestinian status is uniquely inherited. The UNRWA defines Palestinian refugees as:

> "Individuals whose normal place of residence was Palestine between June 1946 and May 1948, who lost their homes and means of livelihood as a result of the 1948 conflict, and their descendants, including legally adopted children."

This definition allows for the transmission of refugee status from parents to children, contributing to the growth of the population over generations. I have two issues with this. One, most people in 1948 abandoned their homes at the behest of the Pan-Arab forces that attacked Israel in 1948 en masse.[4] No one but themselves caused their displacement. Two, as we have already explored, UNRWA's unique

---

4   For further reading and a comprehensive view of the topic, I suggest you can consult these books and the following academic articles:

Morris, Benny. *The Birth of the Palestinian Refugee Problem Revisited.* Cambridge University Press, 2004.

Karsh, Efraim. *Palestine Betrayed.* Yale University Press, 2010.

Gelber, Yoav. *Palestine 1948: War, Escape and the Emergence of the Palestinian Refugee Problem.* Sussex Academic Press, 2006.

Sachar, Howard M. *A History of Israel: From the Rise of Zionism to Our Time.* Knopf, 1976.

classification of this inherited refugee status is a direct conflict of interest. It would not suit the interest of their business for the crisis not to grow. This is a blatant example of victimizing the Palestinian people for their benefit. UNRWA will do anything to keep their money rolling in, including supporting Hamas.

According to UNRWA, the natural increase in the population through births within the refugee community has significantly outpaced any decreases due to deaths, local integration, or resettlement in other countries. But at what point does a population's settlement confer settlement? If 75 years and three generations living in one place does not qualify for settlement, then by UNRWA's definition, everyone displaced from World War II and all their descendants would be considered refugees. My family was displaced from the town of Staszow, Poland, and from somewhere in Russia. My wife's family was displaced from Łódź after the Nazis killed almost everyone in their clan. I guess we, too, are refugees.

It is in the interest of UNRWA to prop up the numbers where they can to collect the money on headcount basis. These guys are like the biggest bookies of all time. UNRWA has set its own self-feeding policies, and somehow these have become hard truths about the Palestinians, truths that are now seized by a misguided liberal wave of social justice and used as fuel for the hatred of Jews.

Before the adoption of the 1967 UN Refugee mandates, a universal legal description for refugees was defined by the 1951 Refugee Convention. A refugee is a person who:

> *"Owing to a well-founded fear of being persecuted for reasons of race, religion, nationality, membership of a particular social group or political opinion, is outside the country of his nationality, and is unable to, or owing to such fear, is unwilling to avail himself of the protection of that country; or who, not having a nationality and being outside the country of his former habitual residence as a result of such events, is unable or, owing to such fear, is unwilling to return to it."*

Let's review. Palestinians in Gaza were governed by Hamas, who the population voted in. Palestinians in the West Bank are governed mainly by the PA. Israeli Arabs live with the full rights of Israeli citizenship. If there is any persecution going on, it is happening by their own people and is not a result of the 1948 conflict that the Arabs initiated against the newly-independent Jewish state of Israel.

Again, we see that the Palestinian refugee crisis is not a refugee crisis at all. It is big business, created for the purpose of perpetuating the conflict against Israel.

Ultimately, the sham of a refugee crisis covers the sick filicidal relationship the Palestinian people have with their sponsors, who will never allow for the goal that they preach. If they did actually achieve a two-state solution, it would end the big Palestinian business of UNRWA, which is chiefly concerned with feeding itself, including through funding terrorism. Sadly, the Palestinian people are the last to benefit from the billions of dollars UNRWA receives to rectify the crisis it has perpetuated.

UNRWA EXPOSED

The IDF recently exposed an UNRWA teacher, identified as Yusef Al-Hawajara, who was recorded boasting about his participation in the October 7 massacre, including his involvement in capturing female hostages. The audio clip has Al-Hawajara stating "We have female hostages. I captured one," and using expletives talking about female hostages. This evidence is a direct connection of UNRWA to Hamas amidst ongoing scrutiny over the agency's ties to the terrorist organization.[5] UNRWA suspended Al-Hawajara pending an investigation (there is no confirmation if this suspension is with or without pay). The statement by UNRWA is lip service, and there

---

5   Maggie Hroncich. "IDF Releases Audio Clips it says further connect UNRWA to October 7 Massacre". *The New York Sun*, March 4, 2024. https://www.nysun.com/article/idf-releases-audio-clips-it-says-further-connect-unrwa-to-october-7-massacre

are likely many other Yusef Al-Hawajaras being paid to be terrorists by UNRWA.

UNRWA has for a long time been known to support, or, at the very least, (and I say this with extreme charity) turn a blind eye to the Hamas terrorist network, including the Hamas command centers buried beneath their offices and hidden in their health and educational facilities. In 2010, the then-Conservative Canadian government under former Prime Minister Stephen Harper stopped all funding to UNRWA, citing concerns over corruption and terror sponsorship. A few months after being elected in 2015, Prime Minister Justin Trudeau restored funding to UNRWA despite the evidence of the previous government. In August 2018, the Trump administration cut US funding to UNRWA, describing its operations as "irredeemably flawed."[6] Within 90 days of taking office in 2021, President Biden resumed funding. The Liberals and Democrats prefer the path of least resistance, always attempting to dance at two weddings at the same time.

When the plain truth of the extent of UNRWA's staff involvement with the October 7 attack was exposed by Israel and others—including UN Watch—several countries immediately discontinued funding. Only after Austria, Estonia, Finland, Germany, Italy, Latvia, Lithuania, Netherlands, Romania, Sweden, Iceland, the UK, Japan, and Australia announced they were cutting funding did Canada jump on the bandwagon. It took no more than 30 days for Canada to resume funding, citing that "the investigations into these allegations are ongoing." Canada even had the audacity to fill in the back pay and complain that Israel was slow in assisting with the investigation and providing proof of corruption. Other countries to come back to the funding table are Sweden and the European

---

6   Wong, Edward. "Trump Administration's move to cut aid to Palestinian refugees denounced." *New York Times*, August 31, 2018. https://www.nytimes.com/2018/08/31/world/middleeast/trump-administration-aid-palestinian-refugees-.html

Union, while the UK and the US maintain that significant changes must take place at UNRWA for any funding to resume. Norway, naturally, has continued its funding, emphasizing what they believe to be UNRWA's critical role in humanitarian aid to the Palestinian people but saying nothing of their involvement with Hamas. I visited Oslo a few years back, a great clean city. Rich history for Jews. Everyone seems awfully nice. All was going well until I went to the government-run liquor store looking for a bottle of wine from Israel only to find out that they completely boycott Israeli wines as part of their role in BDS (boycott, development, and sanctions).

BDS is another smoke and mirrors acronym that provides cover for anti-Israel sentiment, which is in fact blatant antisemitism. It is another marketing tool dreamed up to sanction Israel for defending itself. Supporters cite BDS as a way of protesting Israel's "occupation" of Judea and Samaria (the West Bank) and its overall treatment of the Palestinian people. Perhaps Israel should treat the Palestinian people more like Hamas does. Would that appease the BDS movement?

Creative Community for Peace, a non-profit entertainment industry organization, notes online that the founder of the BDS movement, Omar Barghouti, wasn't shy about saying that the entire motivation behind this "movement" was to destroy Israel. It wasn't to negotiate a two-state settlement; rather, to encourage widespread economic harm to the Jewish state, to cause maximum damage.

Pouring salt on an open wound, I received this constituent's email in February, 2024 from my local member of parliament, Liberal Ya'ara Saks, who is also Jewish:

> *"With today's announcement, I've heard concern from constituents about funding for UNRWA. As Canadians, we are guided by our values and will make sure they (Hamas/Gazans) receive humanitarian support… We have a responsibility to ensure that Canadians have confidence in the organizations we provide funding to, which*

is why the government is supporting robust investigations into the serious allegations against UNRWA staff, and the implementation of improved oversight and accountability measures. The government has reviewed the interim report of the UN Office of Internal Oversight Services on this issue and looks forward to the final report. We expect UNRWA to meet its obligations and uphold the UN's value of neutrality."

Of course they will.

The guidance and values of Canadians she refers to, I suppose, apply to everyone but the Jewish people of this country. Saks goes on to parrot the government-issued statement that there are "ongoing investigations", and nothing has been concluded. Were there similar 'ongoing investigations when Trudeau knee-jerk accused Israel of bombing the Al Ahli Hospital in Gaza? Certainly not. The Gaza Ministry of Health (run by Hamas) reported over 500 casualties, and Al Jazeera backed it up. Trudeau described the strike as "absolutely unacceptable" and "illegal", squarely pinning the blame on the IDF Air Force.[7] Days later it was confirmed that the casualties were no more than 100, and, equally importantly, that the strike was an errant missile launched by Palestinian Islamic Jihad that landed in the *parking lot* next to the hospital. I do not recall Mr. Trudeau coming forward and being accountable for his words, which stoked even more incitement against the Jews. Not a word. It wasn't the first time, nor will it be the last.

It is upsetting to know taxes paid by Canadians are used by Hamas to fund their atrocities against Israelis to the tune of $30 million CAD per year. I got this number from the website of the CJPME (Canadians for Justice and Peace in the Middle East), an organization registered as a Canadian charity that hides behind

---

7   Reuters, Oct. 17 reuters.com/world/canadian-prime-minister-calls-israeli-strike-hospital-unacceptable-2023-10-17/

words like "Canada" and "justice"' while using the Palestinian cause for its own Israel and Jew-hating agenda. As I browsed the leadership section of their website, noting all the smiling faces and impressive resumes, I wondered where all the hatred and bias was coming from. I wanted to ask them, one at a time, how Israel had wronged them, or even someone close to them. Do they have any idea of the damage they are doing when they give resources and morale to terrorists? These people are just one example of Jihad invasion already here. There is nothing on their website that condemns Hamas or terrorism. There are many of these organizations in Canada, the United States, and Europe, who receive public funds that they later use to prop up the party of terror and the syllabus of hatred.

As a Jewish Canadian, a portion of the taxes I must pay is disbursed by a government who sends dollars to UNRWA, who protects and supports Hamas, who in turn wants to, and does, kill Jews. Hamas, who gets my dollars, wants to kill IDF soldiers, one of them being my son, who, as I am writing this, is part of an IDF ready team working in Gaza to protect a humanitarian corridor bringing food and critical supplies to Gazans. These supplies may end up feeding the Hamas terrorists whose only purpose is to launch attacks on IDF soldiers. So, in effect, I am paying money that is going to people who want to kill me, and my son is protecting the very supply chain of necessities that Hamas is using to try to kill him.

THE SYLLABUS OF HATE

RELIGION, RADICALIZATION, AND THE LEFT

MY WIFE AND I ARE GRATEFUL to live in a leafy suburban area of Toronto, built up in the 1950s and settled by a mix of mainly Italian and Jewish immigrants, hard working people looking for a peaceful place to establish community and raise families in a new country. When we moved in the early 2000s with our young family we could feel the legacy of those who built this neighborhood and the rising energy of the future generations of multi-ethnic people who make up Toronto. It is a place of peace, where people smile at each other in passing and stop to talk, earnestly inquiring about families and selves. It is easy to feel separated from what is going on outside these tree-lined streets and parkland paths; this is our place of refuge, where we can feel safe and appreciate simple things like breathing fresh air in the warmth of an early sun. So when I come across grafiti scribbled on safety barriers bordering our park, accusing Israel of genocide, I feel a personal violation. When I see masked people wrapped in the recognizable Kaffiyeh marching through my once idyllic neighborhood with megaphones, accusing my neighbors, in perfect anglo-English, of being baby killers, I am deeply disturbed. When I see police officers on bicycles gathering but doing nothing more than watching, ill-equipped to deal with the rallying voice of hateful intimidation calling for the destruction of my people, I am swept with anguish. My neighbors and I are left to feel intimidated, unsafe, and anxious, unprotected by police and government.

This scene is not limited to my Toronto streets, but is playing out throughout neighborhoods everywhere, with increased regularity, escalating quickly and alarmingly into outright calls for violence. Antisemitism, once hidden, is now officially normalized, a hair's breadth away from the actual violence that we know from experience will inevitably follow. I feel blindsided and betrayed by the anti-Jewish sentiment percolating with momentum in the place where I trusted to feel safe. This new reality for Jews everywhere outside of Israel is being freed by the syllabus of hate and allowed to spread unchecked.

MUSLIMS, CHRISTIANS AND JEWS

Islam was founded by its leader Muhammad (570 CE), often referred to as The Prophet, a title bestowed on him after his death (632 CE). He is the founder of Islam as the religion was to be called, its followers known as Muslims. Islam was established some 2,000 years after the giving of the Torah at Mount Sinai and some six centuries after the birth of Christianity. The chronology is important here because of claims made in the adaption of the Quran with regards to the prophets. Abraham is the father of both Ishmael and

Isaac, as stated in the Hebrew bible. God proclaims both to be the fathers of great nations to follow. It is believed that Ishmael's "great nation" referred to the future establishment of Islam. Though Ishmael was not a Muslim (as this predates), he is counted amongst the prophets, and the prophet Muhammad considers himself a direct descendant of Ishmael.

Both Islam and Judaism are monotheistic religions. Both religions share in the Abrahamic faith, sharing many historical and theological roots. There have been many periods in history where Muslims and Jews have lived in peace and unity, and these examples of peaceful coexistence reflect times of rich cultural, intellectual, and economic exchange. This includes the period of Medieval Spain from the 8th to 15th centuries, a 700-year period known as the Golden Age for Jews under Muslim rule. The atmosphere of religious tolerance allowed Jewish and Christian cultures to flourish alongside Islam. During the Ottoman Empire from the 15th to early 20th century, many Jews found refuge. The Sultan Bayezid II (1447-1512) was a protectorate of Jews, especially during the holy inquisition from 1492. There were various Ottoman sultans and some regional leaders that were kind or unkind to the Jews and Christians; however, it is well documented that Jews lived throughout the empire, contributed to economic activities and cultural identity, and enjoyed a degree of autonomy. Prior to the significant geopolitical changes of the 20th century, including the establishment of Israel and the subsequent Arab-Israeli conflicts, Jews lived in various parts of the Middle East and North Africa under Muslim rule. In countries like Morocco, Iraq, and Iran, Jewish communities often experienced periods of peaceful coexistence with their Muslim neighbors. Jewish communities also lived under Persian rule in what is now Iran during the Safavid (1501-1736) and Qajar (1789-1925) dynasties. While there were episodes of persecution, there were also extended periods of peace and productive interaction. This continued under the Reza Shah Pahlavi, though his alignment with Nazi Germany drew ire from the Jews and international community, eventually leading to his abdication in 1941, after which his son Mohammad Reza Shah Pahlavi ruled up until the revolution, when he escaped into exile in 1979. During this time the Jews lived a Golden Era in Iran.

Christianity is also a monotheistic religion, with the exception of the Trinity. Jesus is not considered a prophet but rather an extension (the son) of God. Viewing Jesus as a separate entity challenges the idea of monotheism. This is countered with the definition of the Trinity (the Father, the Son, the Holy Spirit) as the embodiment of one God. It was deemed an acceptable kind of monotheism for Muslims. Yet historically in Muslim lands, both Jews and Christians were considered *dhimmis*[1], essentially second-class citizens, tolerated because they were monotheists. Those with multiple gods were considered infidels and were not welcome to live amongst Muslims.

There were periods of Arab pogroms of Jews in Israel in the 19th and 20th century, though these tended to be about territorial struggles, not religious differences. It is only in these modern times that the rationale for Islamic aggression against the Jews leans on the narrative of a religious war, and this is not accepted by modern true believers who understand that there is no place for violence between the Muslims and the Jews. In fact, the term "Jihad" is the concept of the personal struggle with faith and observance. The struggle of fighting the evil inclination or achieving a higher spiritual goodness is Judaism's *"Yetzer Hara* and *Yetzer Hatov"*[2]. Christianity's

---

1 The term "dhimmi" originated in early Islamic rule during the 7th century, referring to non-Muslims under Muslim protection. It stems from Islamic jurisprudence, based on the Quran and Hadith, and denotes a protected status with specific conditions, notably paying the jizya tax in exchange for religious freedom and safety.

2 "Yetzer Hara" is the "evil inclination" in Jewish thought, representing self-serving urges, while "Yetzer Hatov" is the "good inclination," representing the desire to do good. These opposing inclinations highlight the moral struggle humans face.

concept of temptation[3] is similar in many ways to the Muslim's personal struggles. When you are a lover of life, it's natural to want to become the best of yourself in any religion. I believe that this is the true goal of religion; to learn from our ancestors and improve our relationship with God through evolving and healing yourself. The Jihadist perversely turns this idea into martyrdom[4]; the idea of sacrificing oneself, usually through violence. The cruelty and intent of radical Jihad is way outside the true teachings of Islam. The proclamations espoused by Nasrallah and Haniyeh, the terror leaders of Hezbollah and Hamas, by Khamanei, supreme leader of Iran, and by any cleric or radical Imam who uses their position to manipulate followers to do acts that completely defy the natural instinct for survival, is nothing more than the manipulation of human beings vying for power and enriching themselves personally.

The leaders of the Party of Terror twist Islamic teachings to line their personal pockets and turn young men into radicalized soldiers, murderers, and suicide bombers. These are the lovers of death, and we cannot view them in the same light we see ourselves. This is the reality that the world must recognize and counter with whatever means necessary, because like it or not, Global Jihad is coming for all of us. If we do not find the agency to impose a new order we will enter an era of destruction and death, driven by an endless supply of people willing to kill themselves for a cause they are misled to believe is true. This chain must be broken, and it is the responsibility of all nations to unify against terror and stop the rise of jihad.

---

3   In Christianity, temptation refers to the desire to sin or act against God's will. It is seen as a test of faith, with Satan often depicted as the tempter. Christians believe that resisting temptation strengthens their faith, and they seek God's help through prayer to overcome it, as exemplified in the Lord's Prayer: "Lead us not into temptation."

4   In radical Islamist ideology, martyrdom refers to dying in the name of Islam, often through violent jihad. It's seen as a path to paradise, glorifying those who sacrifice themselves for their faith, typically against perceived enemies of Islam. This belief is a distortion of mainstream Islamic teachings.

There are several Surahs in the Quran that outright comment on and instruct the followers of Islam to respect, engage in dialogue, and deal with people who are non-Muslims in non-violent ways.

Surah Al-Mumtahanah (60:8): "Allah does not forbid you from those who do not fight you because of religion and do not expel you from your homes—from being righteous toward them and acting justly toward them. Indeed, Allah loves those who act justly."

Surah Al-Baqarah (2:62): "Indeed, those who believed and those who were Jews or Christians or Sabeans—those [among them] who believed in Allah and the Last Day and did righteousness—will have their reward with their Lord, and no fear will there be concerning them, nor will they grieve."

Surah Al-Imran (3:84): "Say, 'We have believed in Allah and what has been revealed to us and what has been revealed to Abraham, Ishmael, Isaac, Jacob, and the Descendants, and what was given to Moses and Jesus and what was given to the prophets from their Lord. We make no distinction between any of them, and we are Muslims [in submission] to Him.'"

These texts imply fairness, respect, and common heritage. There is no justification for violence, and yet there are the false prophets of Islam who use the cover of the Quran as an excuse for their own murderous activities. These zealots of Islam are not the true believers they claim to be. The Party of Terror are the true infidels hiding under the cover of hate and personal gain through political power and conquest.

THE SYLLABUS OF HATE

The "Son of Hamas", Mosab Hassan Yousef, son of Sheikh Hassan Yousef, co-founder of Hamas, who fought as a Palestinian militant before coming over to Israel in 1997 as a spy for the Shin Bet, appeared on Dr. Phil Primetime on April 2, 2024 to debate with two student activists from the University of Michigan. Here is what he said during this conversation:

"It's very disappointing to see Americans supporting Hamas and thinking that Hamas is a cool thing... while those followers don't know that Hamas would torture them and massacre them with no mercy. They (Hamas) call them useful idiots. They don't know that Hamas is a dark black hole."

Despite Yousef's stark warnings, the hate-filled rallies and protests increase in ferocity. The rhetoric against Israel has been building, unchallenged by law, into a crescendo of hateful content and violent undertones. The aftermath of Ten-Seven bears witness to a wave of lawlessness. Police services appear defenseless against the growing crowds, which call for the destruction of Israel with perverse poetic chants and slogans on placards like "From The River to The Sea", "Long live Oct 7", and, "There is only one solution, intifada, revolution." All of these slogans have one meaning: the destruction of Israel, and/or violence against Jews.

Protester's faces are covered with keffiyehs, a symbol of the Palestinian "resistance" movement, which is now making its way as a statement of political support into the chambers of the Canadian and American legislatures. For example, Rashida Tlaib, the first Palestinian-American woman elected to US Congress, has worn a keffiyeh during official events and in support of Palestinian causes. In March, 2024 Tlaib and other members of Congress, known as The Squad, donned the keffiyeh in Senate chambers during Biden's State of Union address. In Canada, independent MPP Sarah Jama was asked to leave the Ontario Legislature for refusing to remove her keffiyeh. The Speaker of the Ontario Legislature banned the wearing of keffiyehs in April 2024, arguing that they were being worn to make a political statement. Several political figures and parties have called for the ban's reversal. Including, ironically, Premier Doug Ford (leader of the Progressive Conservatives), and leaders of other political parties. What is both ironic and moronic is that politicians don't really get it, but are constantly playing on both sides of the fence trying to make everyone happy and earn votes. My respect to the Speaker, Ted Arnott, for taking a position. There is no compromise for the Palestinian cause; it's everything or nothing.

The Toronto District School Board position, in 2024, on recognizing "anti-Palestinian racism" and "Nakba" are more examples of political infiltration influencing society. It's damn scary when I consider the weaponization of our young minds normalizing a call to support, empathize, and justify the call to Jihad. Children will now be learning about the glorification of martyrdom and violent resistance. Where do you think these "informed" kids will be 20 years from now when they are leading their communities, cities, provinces, and countries?

The above examples are emblematic of the lack of political will when it comes to hateful anti-Israel messaging and outright calls for violence against Jews. This only emboldens them further. Incidentally, all of those protesters that were dragged away and arrested after court orders deemed encampments illegal have since been fully exonerated and will suffer no penalties for the damage to property, the incitement of hate, and the trespassing on private and public properties.

The gatherings are becoming louder, the calls for violent uprising more aggressive. All of this normalizes prejudice and hate. It's no wonder Jewish schools and synagogues have been firebombed, vandalized, and shot at. Law enforcement slept while the haters kept putting more and more feet in the door.

At Columbia University, in Manhattan's Upper West Side, encamped protestors spent their hours chanting *"Fuck the Jews, Go back to Poland, We know where you live..."* and waving signs with slogans like *"Free Palestine"*, *"by any means"* and *"We love you Hamas."* Bizarrely, the president of Columbia University, Minouche Shafik, reporting to the House education and workforce committee of Columbia on April 17, 2024 stated an emphatic "No" when asked if the demonstrations were antisemitic.

Barely 80 years after the Holocaust, this is happening on American soil. It is shocking for any person to feel unsafe because of their religious beliefs, ethnicity, or orientation. It seems inevitable that these rallies will soon lead to direct violence; we saw the same signs in 1938 in Nazi Germany. The disturbing reality is that once the worst is over, whatever that becomes, these protesters will still be here. They are teachers, tradespeople, bus operators, Uber drivers, doctors, lawyers. They are the fabric of our society, and regardless of the land they live in, their education, and good fortune, like Haman in ancient Persia they are determined to see the Jew Mordechai swinging from the gallows.

In Canada's capital, thousands of people gathered outside the House of Commons in Ottawa, chanting slogans celebrating Hamas and the events of October 7. There are encampments at University of Toronto and McGill University in Montreal that are sealed off. Anyone entering must be aligned with their hateful beliefs. The protests and violence at the UCLA campus was covered by the Los Angeles Times, CNN, and NBC, who all reported Jews being openly attacked. This is the syllabus of hate and the lawlessness of anarchy.

THE USEFUL IDIOTS

On the morning of February 18, 2022, one thousand police officers from across Canada moved into position around the Canadian Parliament in Ottawa. Over the next few days, hundreds of Freedom Convoy protesters, campaigning against the Covid-19 laws that they considered an impingement on their freedoms, were arrested and dispersed. The protestors were labeled by Prime Minister Trudeau as far-right conspirators, and accused of harassing residents and disrupting local businesses. Trudeau shouted on X that these people were "thugs" and called the trucker protest "an insult to the truth." His promise to the Canadian public was to "do whatever is needed" to restore public order and protect Canadians. He held a press conference from his home, where he condemned the racism on display at the protests (I have not found any evidence of any racism). "Join your fellow Canadians," he said from his pulpit. "Be courageous and speak out. Do not stand for, or with, intolerance and hate." Then Trudeau goes all in and invokes the Canada Emergencies Act for the first time since its creation in 1988. The government froze $10 million raised for the Freedom Convoy and interfered with a GoFundME campaign, whose organizers were pressured into returning $24 million back to donors. I would imagine if the Truckers' target was the Jews, they would be invited to camp out. Of course, no "emergency" measures against antisemitism, no "emergency" measures against encampments, and no frozen bank accounts of protesters. The double standards of the Prime Minister of Canada are terribly disheartening.

Nor is mainstream media immune to this bias. With scores of examples of skewed reporting, lies, half-truths, manipulation and lazy fact-checking, where does one even start? As mentioned earlier, Catherine Tait, President of the Canadian Broadcasting Corporation (CBC), defended the newsroom's longstanding practice of not referring to attacks by Hamas as "terrorism" or "terrorists."

"The word is extremely politically charged, and if journalists use the word they enter into a debate that is not our business. Our business is to remain independent and fact-based," Tait said. This is despite the fact that Canada has designated Hamas as a terror group.

Terrorism is defined as the unlawful use of violence and intimidation, especially against civilians, in the pursuit of political aims. How else can you describe who Hamas is, and what Hamas has done?

CUPE (Canadian Union of Public Employees) has been a big supporter of the BDS campaign since 2006. The boycott, divestment and sanctions is a campaign against buying goods or services from Israel, which even extends to the hiring of Israeli academics. It is a blatant anti-Israel stance that singles out the Jewish State, while ignoring the world's worst perpetrators of human rights violations and a dozen other "brutal occupations" in the world. Ironically, it has done more harm to the Palestinians. The Israeli company SodaStream was faced with a boycott campaign against its products due to its main manufacturing plant being in the city of Ma'ale Adumim, located in Judea and Samaria (West Bank.) The company felt pressure to move its facilities to Lehavim (Southern Israel). This move resulted in the loss of over 500 Palestinian jobs—workers who had been employed at the facility for years. Cost to Palestinians equals a negative economic impact of over $100 million; cost to the BDS movement mandated by people outside of Israel equals zero. Another example of worsening the lives of the Palestinian people in the name of antisemitism.

The LCBO (Liquor Control Board of Ontario) banned wines from Judea and Samaria of Israel after being lobbied by CUPE. Where are the sanctions of Chinese goods for the persecution of the 1 million Uyghurs, who are rounded up and placed in detention camps? What about the sanctioning of the several other hot-list countries who are in violation of human rights? Why is Israel, the sole democratic entity in the Middle East, the only country that receives this unwelcome attention?

I wonder if Mark Hancock (National CUPE president) or Fred Hahn (VP Ontario CUPE), ardent supporters of BDS, would refuse PillCam, a capsule used for endoscopic imaging of the digestive tract, or Doxil for cancer therapy. Have they never used a USB drive or data storage device? These all come from Israel.

I want to scream every time I look at the York University diplomas hanging in my home office. CUPE has instructed teacher assistants what they must teach, regardless of the department or subject matter they are involved with. The union is offering legal and support services should any academics experience backlash. I quote from the instructions sent by CUPE:

> *"Israel's unrestrained confidence to carry out genocidal violence has only been made possible through the discursive legitimation and material support of Western imperialist nations, such as the Canadian settler state, and their institutions, including York University itself."*

The CUPE 3903 toolkit pamphlet goes on to instruct teachers to "denounce Israel at every available opportunity, even when it has no apparent relevance to the subject being studied."[5] It continues that all classes should be diverted to condemnation of the "Zionist Israeli state." The toolkit is filled with claims denouncing Israel as a genocidal "colonial project" and states that "The mere presence of Jewish groups on campus is evidence of York University's complicity in genocide." In other words, Jewish students and their clubs should leave, otherwise the university supports genocide. CUPE further claims that York University is an accessory to genocide because of its research links with the Hebrew University of Jerusalem.

York University's muted response to the growing attitude of antisemitism in the wake of Ten-Seven speaks volumes. Like York, most other North American university campuses, including the most elite institutions, have remained silent while their Jewish students are intimidated and accosted.

In stark contradiction to this ambivalence to and denial of antisemitism, the death of George Floyd during a police scuffle in May 2020 prompted a significant and widespread reaction from universities around the world, characterized by an overwhelming condemnation of police brutality and a renewed focus on the issues

---

5   Callan, Issac. "York University seeks meeting with union over 'toolkit on teaching Palestine". *Global News* January 30, 2024; https://globalnews.ca/news/10260045/york-university-union-palestinian-teach-in/

of racial justice and inequality. Many educational institutions issued statements expressing solidarity with the Black Lives Matter movement and committed to enhancing diversity and inclusivity within their communities. Some of these universities—Harvard, MIT, and Penn—were among those who remained silent in the wake of Hamas's attack on October 7, and whose presidents bristled when asked about the intimidation of Jewish students on campus.

In December 2023 the presidents of three American elite universities, Harvard, University of Pennsylvania, and Massachusetts Institute of Technology, were ordered to answer before the US House Committee on Education and the Workforce Congressional Committee. Despite the chastisement by committee chair Virginia Foxx, these leaders, who influence the stage for the ethical and moral compass of our young people and the future of America, refused to be accountable for the hate-fuelled antisemitic protests and intimidation of Jewish students happening on their campuses. Harvard President Claudine Gay, the first African American female president of Harvard, who until her plagiarism accusation was considered a respected lawyer, could not determine the actual and true legal status of the Palestinian refugee. "No," they assured us, they (antisemitic chants) do not cross the line of hate or discrimination or create an unsafe place for Jewish students. What followed was an ambiguous qualifier explaining to a Senate hearing that the call to violence is "dependent on context."

The barbarity and dehumanization of over 1,200 murdered Jews on October 7 is being rationalized across North America in rhetoric and protests, all of which are a prompt to violence. What comes next? A pogrom in a north Toronto Jewish neighborhood? If the current situation is allowed to continue, if the rhetoric of hate is not stopped at the source, violence is likely to follow. History has shown this countless times. Homicidal maniacs will wake up one morning and say to themselves "Someone has got to do something. Fuck it! I'll get it done myself." The more the hatred is stoked, the more people are apt to act on it. This is as true in Gaza as it is in Iran; as true in Paris as it is Pittsburgh. Parisienne Jews have been murdered for being Jewish, and a Pittsburgh synagogue, Tree of Life, was attacked, where 11 Jews were murdered by a gun-toting terrorist. There have been more than 45,000 Jihadist terror attacks around the world since 9/11, according to The Religion of Peace website. The meter on their site is a dark measurement of terror and destruction.

The rhetoric is raising the bar, prompting people to act out in reaction to what they perceive as a legitimate threat. On July 21, 2024 Zachareah Adam Quraishi, a Canadian citizen from the province of Alberta, arrived in Israel from a flight originating in Canada. Within 24 hours of his arrival he headed to the settlement of Netiv Haasara, located just 400 meters from the Gaza border, where 20 of its residents were brutally murdered by Hamas on October 7. He approached a checkpoint, where, despite warnings from soldiers guarding the community, he jumped from his car and charged at them wielding a kitchen knife and shouting "Free Palestine" and "you're murdering people in Gaza." He was immediately neutralized by the border guards.

As reported in the National Post, Canadian-born Knesset[6] member Sharren Haskel said the news that a Canadian citizen carried out a terror attack in Israel shouldn't be surprising. "The spread of radical Islam and extremist ideologies in Canada has created major cultural challenges for the country, including a plague of antisemitism that has spread, making it unsafe for Jews and Canadians to live their day-to-day lives without the fear of being attacked verbally and physically," she said. "With the lack of law enforcement and a turning a blind eye to the rise of hatred and violence by radical Muslims, Canada has become a hotbed for terrorists who are operating within and outside of Canada."

---

6   The Knesset is Israel's 120-member unicameral legislature, responsible for making laws, overseeing the government, and representing the public through proportional elections.

RADICALIZATION AND THE GLOBAL JIHAD

Radicalization tends to begin with the weaponization and manipulation of minds by cult-type fundamentalists. They'll institutionalize their ideas, which typically appeal to vulnerable people who may be going through a personal crisis, feel marginalized or discriminated against. From cult leaders to revolutionaries, the radicalizer generally has an agenda that is driven by some form of religious fanaticism. Radicalization most often adopts extreme political, social, or religious beliefs to justify their aims. As a result, the recruit is encouraged to engage in actions that involve some form of violence in an attempt to achieve the goals of these beliefs. The victim now feels a sense of belonging within the radicalized group.

Those who radicalize are often predatory, gifted at speaking, charming, and adept at reducing complex socio-political narratives to simplistic black-and-white explanations of good and evil. The victim then feels like their life's problems have someone or something to blame. The radicalizer plays on their victim's sense of injustice, encouraging them to feel abused and taken advantage of by the chosen enemy, be it a government, a nation, a religion, or a race.

According to a 2015 report from the National Bureau of Economic Research, around 30,000 fighters from at least 85 countries had joined ISIS at the time of the report's release. A large number of recruits came not only from the Middle East and the Arab world, but also from within the European Union, the United States, Canada, Australia, and New Zealand. Disenfranchised people will typically make first contact online, social media having become a mainstay of radical recruitment since its widespread adoption. The internet is a prominent tool for the radicalizer, as search engines provide immediate access to information, and targeted ads may appear to unsuspecting targets, drawing them in by appealing to their individual disenfranchisement and social rejection.

Shamima Begum is a British woman who gained international notoriety when she left the UK in 2015 at the age of 15 to join the Islamic State (ISIS) in Syria. Begum and two other schoolgirls from Bethnal Green, London, traveled to Syria via Turkey, where they crossed into ISIS-controlled territory. Their departure sparked widespread media coverage and brought attention to the issue of radicalization among young people in Europe.

Jake Bilardi, an Australian teenager, became known for his tragic journey from a seemingly ordinary life in Melbourne, Australia, to becoming a ISIS suicide bomber in Iraq in 2015. His story is often cited as an extreme example of online radicalization. Jake was described as a bright but lonely teenager, who struggled with social isolation after his mother's death. He turned to the internet to find a sense of belonging and purpose. Bilardi was drawn into extremist ideologies through online forums and propaganda, which glorified jihad and offered him a community and a cause to fight for.

John Georgelas, also known as Yahya Abu Hassan or Yahya al-Bahrumi, was an American who became a notable member of ISIS. Born in 1983 to a Greek-American family in Plano, Texas, Georgelas converted to Islam in 2001 during his studies at Blinn College in Texas. Georgelas met his future wife, Tania, on a Muslim matrimonial site. She was from a Bengali-British background and shared his radical views. They married in 2003 and lived in the US for a time before moving to the Middle East. In 2013, Georgelas took his family to Syria under the guise of a holiday, revealing their destination only upon approaching the Syrian border. Georgelas quickly rose through the ranks of ISIS, gaining notoriety for his involvement in their English-language propaganda efforts and his advocacy for the establishment of a caliphate. He reportedly died in October 2017.

While these people traveled abroad into the lion's den, Global Jihad is a globalized internal campaign that depends on the radicalization of people, communities, and entire populations, who stay in their native lands awaiting orders to carry out missions. Problematically, incidents of violence from radicalized individuals are often cited as "lone wolf" attacks, implying that the person acted alone and without formal affiliation. However, taken in a broader context, when we look at individual events, these lone wolf attacks are part of a larger, globalized campaign that plays itself out in a variety of ways. While not every attack may be specifically directed, they act together in the general idea of singular martyrdom.

___

September 11, 2001 was the worst ever terrorist attack on US soil. 19 Jihadi Saudi terrorists hijacked planes, which they rammed into the New York City Twin Towers, the Pentagon, and a field in Somerset County, Pennsylvania. The entire attack murdered 2,977 people in a single day, including 343 firefighters. Many more are believed to have suffered shortened lives as a result of inhaling the plumes of poisonous fumes.

The Bali Bombings occurred in 2002 and 2005. The first and most devastating has been linked to the Jemaah Islamiyah terrorist network, who carried out suicide bombings in the busy tourist district of Kuta. The attack killed 202 people, including many foreign tourists, and injured hundreds more. The second bombing in 2005 targeted restaurants in Bali, resulting in 20 deaths and numerous injuries.

The Madrid Train Bombings occurred on March 11, 2004 when coordinated bombings targeted commuter trains. The attack caused 193 deaths and around 2,000 injuries. The bombs were placed in backpacks and detonated by mobile phones, targeting morning commuters.

The London Tube Bombings, known as the 7/7 bombings, occurred on July 7, 2005. Four suicide bombers attacked central London's public transport system during the morning rush hour. Three bombs exploded on underground trains and the fourth on a double-decker bus, resulting in 52 deaths and over 700 injuries. This was the deadliest terrorist incident in the United Kingdom since the 1988 Lockerbie bombing, and the first Islamist suicide attack in the country.

The 2013 Boston Marathon was interrupted by a bombing attack carried out by Tamerlan and Dzhokhar Tsarnaev, two brothers of Chechen descent who were living in the United States. The bombings killed three people and injured several hundred others, including 17 who lost limbs. The Tsarnaev brothers were motivated by radical Islamist beliefs and the global jihadist movement. They constructed pressure-cooker bombs, which they detonated near the finish line of the marathon. The attack was part of what the brothers perceived as their fight against the US, which they believed was at war with Islam.

The Toronto 18 refers to a group of 14 adults and four youths, primarily from the Greater Toronto area, who were arrested in 2006, suspected of planning terrorist attacks in Southern Ontario, Canada. They were accused of plotting to bomb several high-profile targets, including the Toronto Stock Exchange, CSIS offices, and a military base near Toronto. The arrests were made possible by extensive surveillance and infiltration by the Canadian Security Intelligence Service (CSIS) and the Royal Canadian Mounted Police (RCMP). The investigation revealed that the group had conducted training camps and was attempting to procure materials to make explosives. The case drew significant attention due to its scale and the severity of the planned attacks. It raised concerns about domestic radicalization and the effectiveness of Canada's counter-terrorism measures. The members of the group were tried and convicted on various terrorism-related charges, leading to significant prison sentences for several of them. The Toronto 18 case remains one of the most notable terrorism cases in Canadian history.

On November 13, 2015 I attended a conference in Paris, France. I had just finished the Shabbat dinner with a small group of people. We were casually strolling through the Parvis de Notre Dame square in front of the Cathedral when several black vans screeched to a halt and black-clad military guys piled into the streets around us. For a moment my heart stuck in my throat. We checked our phones and realized we were standing in the middle of what would become the most devastating terrorist attack in Paris history. Nine terrorists executed a multitude of attacks across various locations. These attacks resulted in the deaths of 130 people and left over 400 injured.

The terrorists worked in three coordinated teams to carry out the atrocities at the Stade de France. Three suicide bombers detonated their explosive vests, killing themselves and one bystander. At the Bataclan Theater in the 11th arrondissement, a historic performance venue situated in a vibrant area known for its nightlife, bars, and restaurants, three gunmen armed with rifles and wearing explosive vests stormed a concert by The Eagles of Death Metal. They killed 90 attendees and took many others hostage. The siege ended when police stormed the theater, killing the attackers. The remaining attackers, armed with automatic weapons, entered several restaurants and cafés, including Le Carillon and Le Petit Cambodge, situated close to each other in the 10th arrondissement, resulting in 13 deaths at Le Carillon and 18 at Le Petit Cambodge. At another cafe, La Belle Équipe, 19 people were killed. At Café Bonne Bière and La Casa Nostra, located near each other in the 11th arrondissement, random gunfire resulted in the deaths of several people.

All nine terrorists were dead by the end of it all. Several other individuals were indicted for the planning and logistical support of the attacks, with further investigations leading to arrests and prosecutions of accomplices across Europe. The wider network included individuals who provided weapons, logistical support, and coordination, highlighting the complexity and breadth of the planning behind the attacks. ISIS later claimed responsibility for the attack.

I stood quietly outside the Café Bonne Biere in the 11th district of Paris the next morning. The flowers and candles were just starting to collect. I remember feeling numb, and a sense of disbelief. I was overcome by the senseless injustice and cowardice of the terrorist attack. My faith was shaken in humanity. I cried for those who will never again be able to cry for themselves.

On June 25, 2022 in Oslo, Zaniar Matapour opened fire on people at locations associated with the Oslo LGBTQ+ Pride event, killing two people and injuring 21 others. The attack, which took place at a popular gay bar and other nearby spots, was motivated by anti-LGBTQ+ sentiment and Islamic extremism.

The Crocus City Hall Attack in Moscow, Russia, on March 22, 2024 resulted in 145 deaths and over 550 injuries. Terrorists carried out a mass shooting and detonated explosions during a concert. Putin immediately tried to blame the attacks on Ukraine, however, responsibility for the attack was claimed by the Islamic State as part of its broader Jihadist agenda, which includes establishing and expanding its caliphate, retaliating against countries it perceives as enemies of Islam, and creating an atmosphere of terror and destabilization.

Iran, the franchisor of terror, is apparently not itself immune. Twin suicide bombings in Kerman, Iran, on January 3, 2024 were carried out by ISIL during a ceremony marking the death of Iranian General Qassem Soleimani, which claimed the lives of nearly 100 people. Iran publically tried to blame Israel and the United States for the attack. The US, however, had earlier warned Iran that the attack was a likely event.

Terror is not exclusive to the Islamic extremists, but in recent decades, they have been the main perpetrators by a landslide. There are other examples where the radicalization of individuals has led them down this grisly path. The attack on the Tree of Life Synagogue in Pittsburgh, Pennsylvania, occurred on October 27, 2018. It is considered one of the deadliest attacks against the Jewish community in the history of the United States. The assailant, Robert Bowers, stormed into the synagogue during Shabbat morning services and began shooting, killing 11 people and injuring several others, including four police officers who responded to the gunfire. Ironically, his motivations were his belief that Jewish people were helping immigrant invaders who were harming the United States.

In London, Canada, on June 6, 2021, Nathaniel Veltman drove his truck into a Muslim Pakistani-Canadian family during their evening walk, killing four members and seriously injuring a 9-year-old boy. Veltman openly admitted his hatred and paranoid delusions over the fear of Muslim immigration brought on by extreme Islamophobia.

Prejudice against Muslims is likely founded in the delusional paranoia that the Global Jihad cause is supported by the general Islamic population. This is not the case. The radical Jihadists are a problem for everyone. Terrorism does not discriminate against those who get caught in the crossfire. Muslims and non-Muslims have been murdered by the Jihadists.

To dismantle Jihad we must dismantle all forms of radicalization. It is within the power of governments to do this, but they must act. To do so, we must first understand what draws people into radical behaviors, and be actively concerned with their sources of information and those who publish and promote them.

ILLIBERAL LIBERALISM

WHERE WE WENT WRONG:
FROM MODERN LIBERALISM TO 'WOKEISM'

1950s AND '60s AMERICA was a period of unprecedented growth and economic prosperity for the country. After a quarter century of economic hardship in the wake of The Great Depression, the aftermath of World War II set the stage for America to pave the way into the future. It was a true *Make America Great* era. As mentioned earlier, it was also a time of social and political paranoia, ultimately spawning what became a polarization of the US political landscape and, socially, a significant generational gap. The Cold War era saw a clash of ideologies in American society. On one side, conservatives reacted with extreme vigilance against potential Russian espionage.

On the other hand, the post-war generation fiercely resisted this approach, viewing themselves as champions of civil liberties. This conflict gave rise to the liberal movement in the United States.

The 1960s counterculture was all about sticking it to the man. The Baby Boomer generation championed peace, liberalization of sex, popularization of drugs, and the introduction of musical genres that defined their cultural significance in history. Bob Dylan's *The Times They Are A-Changin'* is an anthem of the era, calling for social and political change. It reflects the upheavals of the time, urging people to embrace progress, highlighting generational divides and promoting activism against injustice, encapsulating the spirit of the Civil Rights Movement and anti-war protests. Those kids of the 60s would themselves become parents of the next generation, who would see further political and social shifts that defined the liberal left, the center, and the right. In the course of just two more generations, the ideological center eroded and the right and left divide deepened, paving the way for the post-2000 generation to become staunch allies of a liberal ideology that has become, at best, a parody of itself, evermore critical and less accommodating to those who did not jump on board. Hence, the birth of *Wokeism*.

The last quarter-century has likely seen the greatest ever social shift in acceptance and accommodation for the liberation of stereotypes, normatives, and acceptable social interactions. All of which is very positive, until you become that person who *forces* others to see your way. This is the great, modern hypocrisy of liberalism, the rapidly quickening slide from reason into fundamentalism and subjugation of the non-believers. The liberal ideology of "live and let live" is dead.

WHERE GOOD LIBERAL VALUES GO TO DIE

It sounds cliche: the liberal ideological movement has moved so far to the left, I have to look to the right to see them coming. The truth is that the modern liberal movement has been hijacked by leftist radicalists who wrongly refer to their beliefs as liberal ideology. The problem with this is that the actual liberals fail to see this, and can't seem to get off the bus that they unwittingly boarded.

American Author and radio host Dennis Prager argues that leftism and liberalism are fundamentally different. Here are the key points he makes to differentiate the two:

1. **Race:** Prager asserts that traditional liberalism believed race was insignificant, advocating for racial integration and equality. In contrast, he claims leftism considers race highly significant, sometimes viewing colorblindness as a form of racism.

2. **Capitalism:** Liberals have traditionally supported capitalism as a means to lift people out of poverty, though they favor a larger role for government in addressing social issues. Prager argues that leftists oppose capitalism and support socialism.

3. **Nationalism:** Prager highlights that liberals historically believed in the importance of the nation-state and protecting national sovereignty. Conversely, leftists often oppose nationalism, seeing it as a path to fascism and preferring international solidarity.

4. **View of America:** He notes that liberals have historically venerated America, recognizing its imperfections but valuing its foundational principles. Leftists, on the other hand, are seen as viewing America as fundamentally flawed and oppressive.

5. **Free Speech:** Prager claims that liberals strongly support free speech, defending the right to express even disagreeable opinions. Leftists, however, are portrayed as leading efforts to suppress speech they consider hateful or offensive. For example, the cancel-culture phenomena.

6. **Western Civilization:** According to Prager, liberals have a deep appreciation for Western civilization and its contributions. Leftists, however, are often critical of Western civilization, sometimes viewing it as synonymous with white supremacy.

7. **Religion:** Prager states that liberals respect the Judeo-Christian roots of American civilization, even if they are not personally religious. In contrast, he argues that leftists have contempt for traditional religions, particularly Christianity and Judaism, while sometimes showing tolerance toward Islam. (This certainly argues well to explain CUPE point of view and their alignment with the Palestinian cause.)

Prager's arguments aim to clarify that the values and principles of leftism differ significantly from those of liberalism, and he calls for liberals to recognize these distinctions and ally with conservatives against leftist ideologies.

The domino mask was a masquerading accessory by Venetian party goers in the 16 and 17th centuries. While it did not hide the person, it hid the upper face where only the eyes could be seen. This mask gave partygoers a sense of anonymity so they could be someone who in regular social circles they could not be. I call these leftist imposters posing as modern liberals the "Domino Cover Up" hiding the true nature of their radicalized, power-drunk ideology.

The poisonous rhetoric and aggression toward Israel and Jewish people is typical of what leftists have come to represent. They have shown their double standard when it comes to Jews. Just look at the campuses, the biased media reports, some of the fringe political voices, unions, and entertainers. The more left, the more you will see hatred of Jews and Israel.

It is the conservative-centric movements today that are now countering the rise of scary leftist-Nazism, which is sponsoring and inflaming dangerous rhetoric reminiscent of 1933 Germany. While I very much dislike comparing any event or person to the Holocaust or Nazi Germany (there is no equal to this brutal period for the Jewish people and shameful part of human history) there are no better words I can think of to aptly describe what is going wrong with the corrupted liberal ideology duped by the left in the wake of Ten-Seven.

THE LIBERAL LICENSE TO JIHAD

The "liberal" woke has adopted the belief that agents of Jihad, such as Hamas, are the underdog against the seemingly all-powerful Israel. It's no longer good versus evil; rather, it's oppressed versus oppressor (or their twisted perception of such). Similarly, unions and social movements have adopted rhetoric under the liberal banner that supports the "liberation of Palestine." This is code for "eliminate Israel." They are either willfully blind or morally bankrupt to not know this is the same aim as Jihadists.

What is not discussed is that Palestinian society is completely at odds with the fundamentals of liberalism. This is as much covering the rights of women, the LBGQT+ community, religious freedoms, freedom of speech, and the rights of minorities. In the Jihad world, rape is an accepted tool of the revolution. Conscription of child soldiers as young as 10-years old in Yemen is an accepted tool of the revolution. The kidnapping by Hamas on October 7 of innocents—children as young as 10 months old and of seniors in their late 80s—is an accepted tool of the revolution. The indiscriminate murder of people in their homes in brutal and sadistic ways, including beheading and dismemberment, is an accepted tool of the revolution. Using human shields and conducting military operations under the cover of schools, hospitals, mosques, international facilities, and housing, is an accepted tool of the revolution.

In what truly liberal world are all these things okay? Apparently, when it is happening to the Jews, liberal sensitivities do not apply. It is time for the liberals of today to acknowledge what they have become. A discriminatory, hate-mongering, antisemitic, anti-Christian, anti-humanist movement, hiding behind its own disillusioned dissonance. To the misguided and unintended liberals who have been duped by the left, you have become something you never intended to be. The movement you are part of is a trainwreck. I would jump now before you no longer recognize who you have become.

YES MINISTER! THOSE DAMN CANADIANS

The social (d)evolution of leftist fanaticism is running rampant. Canadian politics has traditionally consisted of slighter variations between the left and right policies. Today, however, the divide seems more extreme than a centrist balancing act. The Liberal Party of Canada, when helmed by Justin Trudeau, hurled itself ever further toward the radical left. The New Democrats made good bedfellows in their coalition. There remains some distinction with the Green Party of Canada, with their consistent and dominant focus on environmental and sustainability issues, which would be tolerable if it did not seek to excoriate and protest Israel at every opportunity. Perennial Green Party leader, Elizabeth May, said in a speech that she "takes marching orders from the Palestinians." Neither her, nor her party, could even bring themselves to condemn the Houthis after causing environmental disasters in the Red Sea. On February 18, 2024 the Houthi launched an anti-ship ballistic guided missile, compliments of Iran, which sank the British-owned cargo ship Rubymar. The ship was carrying over 41,000 tonnes of ammonium nitrate fertilizer, which spilled into the water, threatening to cause the worst ecological disaster in the Red Sea's maritime history, affecting marine ecosystems and impacting food chains and coastal communities.

The chaotic events occurring across Canada appear to support leftist narratives, which are propagated through liberal channels. These narratives include calls for the dismantling of Israel, and by extension promote animosity toward Jews worldwide, potentially triggering a widespread ripple effect of hatred.Canada lost its way so acutely that Hamas felt empowered to release a video on December 12, 2023 thanking Canada for their support in calling for an immediate ceasefire.[1]

Canada took things a step further with its post-Ten-Seven arms embargo against Israel, though I doubt the House of Commons stopped to consider how ridiculous the entire motion was. In December 2023, Israel exported $42 million of military goods from Canada, compared with the $118 million Canada purchased from Israel. The previous year, Israel purchased $506 million Canadian military products, compared to the $1.33 billion worth that Canada purchased from Israel[2]. Canada needs Israel far more than Israel needs Canada, yet the Canadian government happily jumped on the runaway train of anti-Israel sentiment.

---

1   "Hamas Thanks Canada for backing ceasefire in Gaza". *The Deep Dive.* December 21, 2023. https://thedeepdive.ca/hamas-thanks-canada-for-backing-ceasefire-in-gaza/

2   The Observatory of Economic Complexity

JEWISH CLAIM TO THE LAND

THE INDIGENOUS PEOPLE OF ISRAEL

DOCUMENTATION AND ARCHEOLOGY

The entire Jewish claim to the land of Israel is verified in two different ways: documentation and archeology. The Merneptah Stele, also known as the Israel Stele, is one of the most significant ancient steles that mention the tribes of Israel or ancient Hebrews. Discovered in 1896 by Flinders Petrie in Thebes, Egypt, this stele dates back to approximately 1208 BCE and commemorates the military victories of the Egyptian Pharaoh Merneptah. It contains the earliest known extra biblical reference to Israel, marking it as a notable piece of evidence for the presence of a people group identified as Israel in the ancient Near East. The Hebrew Bible is the oldest document that verifies the Jewish presence in the land of Israel, dating back 5,000 years, starting with Abraham. Post exodus from Egypt, the Jewish kingdom was established. While documentation can be argued, archaeological evidence is a science that unearths a story, which supports and complements the documentation. Countless historical sites have been unearthed that establish the presence of the Jewish people over thousands of years within Israel.

At the time of Sarah's death, Abraham insisted on paying Ephron the Hittite[1] for the burial plot, though the latter was more than willing to offer it to Abraham and his family for free. Abraham wanted to make sure there would never be a dispute about this land deeded to him and his ancestors. And at the time of his death, there was, as he had hoped, no dispute over land ownership or inheritance.

The Bible does not state any disagreement when the two sons, Isaac and Ishmael, one the father of the Jews and the other the father of the Arabs, unite to honor the death of their father and bury him in the cave of Hebron. There is no rivalry, and no dispute of Isaac's status as Abraham's rightful heir.

According to the Quran, after the mourning period, Ishmael goes to Mecca, where he lives out his days and where he and his mother are eventually buried. The Bible documents that Isaac is buried alongside his mother and father in Hebron. These are very significant events taking place that must be considered when examining present day claims to Israel. People of ancient times made contracts just like today, but they also relied heavily on symbolism and established presence. There is evidence of several generations of Hebrews buried in the Cave of the Patriarchs at Machpelah, to the east of Mamre, which is today's Hebron, in the modern State of Israel. Burial places and property rights are intertwined, and this

---

[1] Ephron the Hittite, in the Bible, sold the Cave of Machpelah and the surrounding field to Abraham as a burial site for Sarah. This transaction, detailed in Genesis 23, marked Abraham's first land ownership in Canaan, which became the family burial site.

place validates ownership of land. The affidavit of the Hebrew Bible is one of the oldest accounts of humanity, with records going back several thousands of years, which also falls within modern law's interpretation of possession.

THE PROMISED LAND

The redemption of the Israelites from slavery in Egypt (circa 1,300 BCE) saw the formal establishment of a nation and the subsequent conquering of the lands west of the Jordan River to become the homeland of the Jews. This is well documented in every religious text and is widely accepted by the archaeological community.

Having arrived at the staging ground for the battle to come, the Israelites gathered at the plains of Moab, east of the Jordan River, (present-day Jordan), and awaited the sounds of the shofar to enter into the promised land.

Joshua, the successor of Moses, conquered Canaan, on what is now Israel. The Jewish nation quickly divided the land into provinces by tribe, initially establishing the valley of Shiloh as the temporary religious center until Jerusalem became the more permanent center of life. By the 13th century BCE Israel had been thoroughly established by the Jewish people.

THE CITY OF DAVID

The first and second holy Temples of the Hebrews are located in Jerusalem, which further solidifies Jewish claim on the land, going back three millennia.

In 1003 BCE, Jerusalem was built up by King David, who made the city his capital. For 400 years this city, where the first Jewish Temple was built and housed the holy of holies, was the center of the world. There is no dispute as to its rightful heritage as the capital of the Jewish people. Amongst its other names it is known as the City of David and the City of Gold. The Babylonians destroyed the first temple and conquered Jerusalem in 586 BCE, and the Jews were exiled to Babylon for 70 years, until the Persian king Cyrus the Great conquered Babylon in 539 BCE and allowed the Jews to return. The Jews rebuilt the temple and lived in the land with Jerusalem as its capital for the next 550 years. This period is known as the Second Temple period.

The Romans conquered Jerusalem in 70 CE and destroyed the second Temple in the first of the Jewish-Roman wars. Christianity became the official religion of the Roman Empire, and Jerusalem became a major Christian center. The Dome of the Rock was built in 691 CE, and the Al-Aqsa Mosque around the year 700 CE, constructed on the Temple Mount during the early Islamic period. It was then that the city's Muslim significance was established. Islam dominated the region for the next 400 years, until in 1099 CE the Crusaders showed up, marking the beginning of the Crusader Kingdom of Jerusalem. This Christian kingdom lasted until 1187, when the Muslim leader Saladin recaptured the city. So began a period with several different armies or dynasties colonizing the land. The Christians were continually obsessed with retaking Jerusalem and did so for short periods at different times. It was not until 1517 that the Ottomans offered some relative stability to the region; they remained the overseers of Jerusalem, and the region, until 1917. After World War I, the Ottoman Empire, on the losing side of the war, surrendered their territory to the Allied world powers, who had been given rights to set new boundaries for new nation-states.

The 1920 San Remo Conference endorsed the Balfour Declaration (1917), supporting the establishment of a Jewish national home in Palestine under British mandate, thus providing legal and international legitimacy. The conference's resolutions incorporated into the League of Nations further strengthened Jewish claims to Israel by recognizing their right to establish a national home while ensuring protection of civil and religious rights for all inhabitants.

Many countries in recent years have extended a sensitivity, fairness, and accountability to the claims and admission of land grab from the Aboriginal people. Australia, the United States, and Canada are examples of this. Righting the wrongs of the past, to recognize the First Nations peoples claim to land from which it is indigenous. Special status and exemptions are provided to anyone of Aboriginal heritage. In a stark but not unexpected contradiction, this same concern is not extended to the Jewish people, who today are considered by some to be occupiers of a land that was always rightfully theirs. The land was a heritage and inheritance legally taken back in 1948. The Jews did not conquer Israel; it has always been the land of the Jewish people.

INDEPENDENCE

Israel claimed its independence on May 14, 1948. Within days, the surrounding Arab countries pounced on Israel in what is known by Israel as the War of Independence, and named by the Palestinian Arabs as *Al-Nakba* "The Catastrophe." This label creates the victim status of the Palestinians and serves to distort the history of events that took place.

The first war launched against the young country was the beginning of a trend that has continued throughout the last 75 years of Israel's history and will no doubt continue until true peace in the region is achieved. All wars involving Israel have been the result of targeted aggression, forcing the nation to defend itself. Hence the name of the Israeli military, the Israel *Defense* Forces. This is an important point to acknowledge. Israel is a defender of its land and the Jewish people. Israel has never warred for the purpose of conquering.

The Six Day War was a swift pre-emptive strike by Israel due to the relentless bombardment against Israel by Egypt, Syria, and Jordan. The closing of the Straits of Tiran was a critical event leading up to the 1967 conflict between Israel and its Arab neighbors. The Straits of Tiran are a narrow sea passage between the Sinai Peninsula and the Arabian Peninsula, connecting the Gulf of Aqaba to the Red Sea. This waterway was vital for Israel, as 90% of its oil imports passed through these straits to reach the port of Eilat. On May 22, 1967 Egyptian President Gamal Abdel Nasser closed the Straits of Tiran to Israeli shipping. This action was seen as a blockade and considered by Israel (and the UN) to be an act of war. It was seen as a direct challenge to Israel's sovereignty and right to free navigation. Nasser's decision came amid rising tensions in the region and followed several other provocative moves:

1. Egypt had demanded the withdrawal of UN peacekeeping forces from the Sinai Peninsula.

2. Egypt had mobilized its army and redeployed troops to the Sinai.

3. A mutual defense pact was signed between Egypt and Jordan on May 30.

Israel won that defensive war, along with various parcels of land seen as critical defensive buffers for the security of Israel that had been used by her enemies to launch attacks, kill civilians, and undermine the sovereignty of the Jewish state. Those lands won were the Golan Heights (from Syria), Gaza and Sinai (from Egypt), and what is today known as Judea and Samaria (The West Bank) and East Jerusalem (that had been illegally held by Jordan for nearly twenty years).

The Golan Heights, which Israel annexed in 1981, was land that Israel was constantly defending itself against—a strategic high point used by the Syrians to launch attacks on Israel. Israel returned Sinai territory as part of the Camp David Accords peace deal with Egypt in 1978.

NO NAME TO CLAIM

Ancient Philistines (no relation to Palestinians) hailed from the Greek islands, and occupied what is today Gaza. (Incidentally, the

Hebrew word for Philistine is "plishtim," meaning invaders.) This tribe was completely destroyed around 600 BCE by King Nebuchadnezer II of the neo-Babylonian empire. Around 70 CE, after the fall of Judea at the hands of Roman emperors Vespasian and Titus, the Romans changed the administrative name of the land from Judea to Palestine. It was to add insult to injury to name the land after the Jews' enemy, the Philistines. The Quran never once in all its text refers to Palestine by name. In the early twentieth century, the British Mandate for Palestine was simply a territorial name. 'Palestine' is a word that has no historical connection to any culture or people.

To all those rallying to establish a Palestinian state, there is no legal, historical, cultural, or religious significance between the people who lived in Israel prior to 1948 and what is referred to as Palestine today. As we have explored in detail, the term *Palestinian people* is a placeholder that was used to refer to a refugee situation that began in 1948.

Up until the 1960s and until the creation of the Palestine Liberation Organization (PLO) there was no nationalist Palestinian movement to speak of.

THE WAY OF THE LAND

THE STRUGGLE

Israel is the add-on name given to Jacob as he struggles through the night with an angel, who then, upon their defeat, bestows Jacob the name "Israel" (translation: *they* who struggle with God). This is where the reference to the Jewish people as *Sons of Israel* comes from.

The struggle of Israel is very much alive in the Jewish state's deliberation between the secular and its traditional culture, battling with the more ancient religious observance that finds its way into modern living.

Named Israel, I have some understanding of this struggle. I have lived the meaning of my name and have struggled with God (who hasn't?), but I have come to understand that this is not necessarily a bad thing. In fact, the "struggle" is actually a beautiful gift that makes for an authentic life of growth. We are all born to struggle. When Jacob struggled with the angel, he did so for the future of what was to come. He struggled in the name of God, to better serve his creation with purpose, intention, and empathy for all humanity. This is ingrained in the DNA of the Jewish people.

The State of Israel is the only democratic country in the region of the Middle East that can be considered by western standards as advanced, pluralistic, and liberally progressive. The right end of the political spectrum is mainly associated with the smaller minority parties, who are typically representative of the significant religious population. The far left, also small minority parties, has a more secular focus and dislikes anything religious. I found it frustrating to be personally caught up in this polarity and spectrum of confusion every time I would visit Israel. I was either way too religious for my secular family, who would mockingly call me *the Rabbi*, or considered an outsider by my religiously observant family, who would carefully query me on any foods we would bring or outright shelter their children from the risk of my outside influence.

While Israel is not theocratic, the country is highly influenced by religion. Trains do not run on the Sabbath. Jewish lineage, the question of "who is a Jew?," determines one's right to marry in Israel and the status of one's children, monopolized by the national Rabbinical authority; whereas the "right of return" is a more secular interpretation of who is entitled to automatically become a citizen of Israel. Kosher certification is another example of the confusing landscape and influence of religion by the various Rabbinical authorities. However, at the same time, Israel is openly accepting and tolerant of alternative family structures and is the only country in the Middle East where LGBTQ+ people are socially accepted and supported. I am particularly baffled when I see activism from abroad vilifying Israel and joining the Palestinian cause. How tolerant will a Muslim

Caliphate be of the LGBTQ+ community? Homosexuality is illegal in Islamic countries, often punishable by death. Is this what the *Queers for Palestine* are looking forward to?

THE WAY OF THE LAND

There is a detailed account of the Jewish deliverance to their homeland throughout the Hebrew Bible. Promises are made to the forefathers[1], and then again to Moses[2], recounting the blessing of the land if the path of good is followed or the curses that will come should the people lose their way.[3] There is a cornerstone of Jewish life called *Derech Eretz,* which translates to the "Way of the Land." This idea is foundational to the Jewish people and the State of Israel.

The Way of the Land describes how people are treated by one another, and how Jewish people exist within the world. It governs moral conduct, honesty, and accountability in how life is lived and how people interact with each other. The Hebrew words *Gemilut Chasadim,* when translated, means acts or deeds of loving kindness, encapsulating the essence of performing selfless acts of kindness and compassion, which are highly valued in Jewish tradition and thought.

The Way of the Land also refers to the 613 commandments of

---

1   **Genesis 12:1-3:** God promises Abraham that he will make him a great nation, bless him, and make his name great.

    Genesis 15:18-21: God makes a covenant with Abraham, promising his descendants the land from the river of Egypt to the Euphrates.

    Genesis 17:1-8: The covenant of circumcision, where God promises to give Abraham's descendants the land of Canaan.

    Genesis 26:3-5: God reaffirms the promise made to Abraham to Isaac, ensuring his descendants will inherit the land.

    Genesis 28:13-15: God reiterates the promise to Jacob in a dream, promising him and his descendants the land on which he is lying.

2   **Exodus 3:16-17:** God tells Moses that He will bring the Israelites out of Egypt to a land flowing with milk and honey, as promised to their forefathers.

3   **Leviticus 26 and Deuteronomy 28:** These chapters detail the blessings and curses associated with obedience and disobedience to God's commandments.

the ancient Bible's instruction on observances. "Live your life in The Way of the Land, and you will be blessed" is the idea. This is not just a spiritual idea. The Way of the Land is incorporated into the educational system of the Jews, and is fundamental to the syllabus of the Jewish curriculum. In Israel, with the Way of the Land as a guide, we are raising generations of people who are taught to respect and love others and themselves. Even the most secular person will practice various observances that remind them of their Jewish roots and responsibility under The Way of the Land. I am always warmed by the attention of strangers to someone who might have taken a misstep on the street. You will rarely see a person turning a blind eye in Israel. Equally as beautiful is how this sense of responsibility for each other extends beyond Israel's borders. It is called *Tikkun Olam,* which translates to "repairing the world." Israel can be counted on to save lives in any major natural disaster.

Following the 2010 devastating Haiti earthquake, Israel was the first to respond, sending a large delegation of rescue and medical personnel. The Israeli team was noted for its rapid response and the high level of medical care it provided. After a powerful earthquake struck Nepal on April 25, 2015 Israel sent more than 250 people to assist in the aftermath. The Israeli team established a comprehensive field hospital, providing services such as surgery, intensive care, and maternity care, significantly aiding the local medical response capacity. Following the devastating earthquakes that struck Turkey and Syria in early February 2023, Israel quickly offered assistance to both countries. To Turkey, Israel sent a search-and-rescue team of 150 engineers, medical personnel, and other aid workers. Israel also sent humanitarian aid to Syria, a country which is a self-proclaimed sworn enemy of Israel. These instances exemplify Israel's readiness to provide humanitarian aid and disaster relief across the globe, regardless of its political or diplomatic relationships with the countries involved. This is the Way of the Land.

THE PRIDE TO SERVE

The IDF remains a significant agent in building Jewish unity across cultural and racial barriers, and is a focal point of pride and duty for many Israelis. Mandatory conscription does not mean one is less proud or determined to serve, and many soldiers, my son Eitan included, join voluntarily. When Eitan announced he was leaving Canada to join the IDF, I was not entirely on board, and our many arguments over his decision often resulted in shouting matches. Eventually, he confessed to me that he could not be the Jewish person I raised him to be if he did not sign up. He saw the IDF as his personal obligation. The essence of his soul and purpose was aligned with the security of Israel. Being born outside of Israel did not reduce the deeply-ingrained sense of responsibility he felt to his people. When he told me this, I knew I had lost the argument. I recognized Eitan was evolving to become everything we raised him to be. My next words were "How can I help?" Eitan has given me a gift that would change my life. He has inspired me to renew my own commitment to Israel and the Jewish people. This book exists because of his decision to invest in our people, our family and in our land. He has earned not only my highest respect, but that of a nation and of world Jewry. We experienced great pride sitting under the hot July sun as he was called forth and awarded the *Chayal Mitztayen*, the soldier of excellence. He would receive this accommodation a second time during a far more private ceremony after October 7.

"A world built on lies cannot stand. The pursuit of truth must be at the heart of our efforts to create a just and decent society."

RABBI JONATHAN SACKS (1948-2020),
THE FORMER CHIEF RABBI OF THE UNITED KINGDOM
AND A PROMINENT PHILOSOPHER AND THEOLOGIAN

DEBUNKING THE LIES

FROM THE FIRE OF TODAY'S ANTISEMITISM, the words *occupier* and *colonizer* have risen to the top of the rhetoric pyramid. These words are being completely misused, both by people who should know better and others that have no clue what they are talking about. These words have been spread amongst campuses across North America and used in misleading propaganda regarding the Israel-Palestinian conflict. The term "occupier" and "colonizer" have specific historical, legal, and political connotations, yet are being thrown around as careless untruths with the intent of demonizing Israel and galvanizing the moral footing of the Hamas attacks.

These terms have been embraced, sponsored and promoted as go-to slurs by leftists infiltrating liberalism ideology.

Canadian Union of Public Employees' (CUPE) handbook describes Israel as a colonizer and accuses Israel of genocide. Both claims are the subject of a human rights claim against the union, filed by 80 Jewish members alleging discrimination and anti-semitism, including recent messages seen as cheering for the deadly Hamas attacks on Israel.[1]

"OCCUPATION" AND THE GREEN LINE

In international law, particularly under the Fourth Geneva Convention (1949), an "occupier" refers to a state that exercises control over a territory that is not under its sovereign jurisdiction following an armed conflict. The Convention is often thrown around by those who are ignorant, as if Israel was guilty of violating an international treaty in Judea and Samaria (West Bank.) For example, Article 49 outlines how it is prohibited to transfer a civilian population into the territory conquered. But Israelis move there voluntarily. Furthermore, various accords, including Oslo, maintain that the area's future status will be determined by bi-lateral negotiations. And most importantly, even though Jordan held the area illegally, and Israel won it in a defensive war, Jordan relinquished any claims in its peace treaty with Israel in 1994. In the best of terms, it might be considered "disputed territory", owing to the fact that no other state had legitimate sovereignty previously.

The area within the Green Line is the demarcation lines set out in the 1949 Armistice Agreements between Israel and its neighbors (Egypt, Jordan, Lebanon, and Syria) after the 1948 Arab-Israeli War. Judea and Samaria (The West Bank), after the Oslo Accords,

---

1   Humphries, Adrian. "Jewish union members file claim against CUPE alleging discrimination and antisemitism". *National Post*. November 6, 2023. https://nationalpost.com/news/canada/cupe-jewish-members-antisemitism

became a semi-autonomous area under Palestinian rule. Within it, significant cities have been established by both Arabs and Jews. Due to the infiltration of suicide terrorists into Israel and the targeting of vehicles on highways bordering these areas, Israel built a security fence roughly along the Green Line,[2] which has greatly reduced the number of terror incidents.

I believe that some explanation is necessary to understand that Israel's situation in the territories known as the West Bank is a pragmatic reality, not one of military rule. This is an important point to make because when claims of "occupation" of these areas are made against Israel, they are unfounded in the definitive sense of what occupation entails.

Unlike Gaza, which is a defined single area, the Judea and Samaria areas are not consistently connected, but wind through Israel, bordering and sometimes cutting into the Green Line. The West Bank has come under intense global debate, and is certainly a complicated matter. The Arab population of these areas have not been granted Israeli citizenship, and Israel has not announced any plans to change this. The annexation of these lands would be problematic, with its more than 2 million Palestinians threatening a demographic shift that could weaken Israel's Jewish majority. Conversely, Jews can, and do, build and live in authorized settlements within the areas of the West Bank. This is often seen as a strategy to bring more Jews into these disputed areas to strengthen the Jewish presence, making the possibility of a two-state solution even more complex. Some of these settlements have become significant cities. The "settlers", as they are known (sometimes pejoratively), see living there as a responsibility to Jewish presence, although economic reasons can also play a role, as these homes come relatively cheap in a country known for its out-of-control housing prices. Many of

---

2   The Israeli West Bank border consists of fences, walls, and ditches, varying in height and structure, with some sections reaching up to 26 feet high.

these settlements have become built-up suburbs of major city centers.

The town of Tekoa is 15 minutes drive from Jerusalem; 10 minutes of that drive is spent on a newly-paved highway within the "occupied" areas, surrounded by Arab cities that connect the area of the Gush to Jerusalem. Tekoa was established over 30 years ago and is home to nearly 5,000 residents that live in beautifully built single detached homes typical of any suburban dream neighborhood with parks and community centers. There is a heterogeneous mix of people living here, mainly modern orthodox Jews and young families who have relocated here for its proximity to Jerusalem and its affordability. What may have started out as a settlement community has become a thriving dynamic city town with industry and community, surrounded by incredible views of the area's rolling hills and the backdrop of King Herod's ancient castle.

Israel supplies most of the water, power, and other resources to these areas. Non-Israeli residents of the West Bank are also able to work in Israel. The security risks, and the history of terrorist attacks coming from these towns, make this a highly complex and combustive situation. Israel must provide borders and security for the safety and protection of its own citizens. While these areas are governed internally by the Palestinian Authority (PA), it is plainly obvious with every terror attack that the PA is not capable of, or not interested in, providing the necessary security on its own.

The lack of centralized Palestinian control, not to mention their non-recognition of Israel and the commitment to push all Jews into the sea, further compounds the security situation. There is also a perpetuation of terror as the PA continues to endorse a pay-to-slay policy. Terrorists' families receive special ongoing compensation after a terror attack against Israelis. Israel has instructed that this policy cannot continue. Counter measures on the Israeli side include the policy that the homes of terrorists be demolished, as well as lawfare, that is suing those responsible for abetting the attack. As long as there is radicalization and terrorists using these territories to launch attacks against Israel, and the PA continues to reward these activities, Israel has no choice but to maintain a strict security barrier.

In summary, these are 7 points that highlight the impossible situation that Israel is forced to deal with:

1. Israel disengaged from Gaza Strip in 2005. Hamas was elected and had the opportunity to build a viable independent nation state. We all know what choice they made.

2. There is a reality of security issues, born out of the lack of willingness to accept Israel's rightful existence. This forces Israel into a policing effort to protect its citizens.

3. The territories are a mishmash of zig-zag borders that connect and disconnect. There is no continuous border between these villages and towns that would create one land in Judea and Samaria.

4. The continued establishment of Jewish settlements (in particularly contentious areas) will continue to frustrate any effort toward the previous point.

5. Israel must provide the life line of resources to these territories, which have no ability to sustain themselves.

6. These territories are governed by Fatah, which is essentially a dictatorship. There are no elections that comply with democratic objectives.

7. As long as there is radicalization, and terrorists using these territories to launch attacks against Israel and the PA continues to reward these activities, Israel has no choice but to maintain strict security barriers.

Beyond the complex and evolving landscape of Judea and Samaria, Arabs who live in Israel enjoy the same rights and benefits of their fellow citizens, such as the right to vote and state protection. They are issued Israeli passports and are completely free to travel within and outside of Israel. This is hardly the nature of an occupier, and a complete contrast to the implication of the derogatory rhetoric used to attack Israel's legitimacy. The Washington Institute reported that according to its polls the majority of Israeli-Arabs feel a sense of belonging and are proud to be Israeli citizens. Additionally, many Arab-Israelis prefer living in Israel over a potential Palestinian state. In a 2023 poll, 82% of respondents expressed a preference for living under Israeli rule rather than Palestinian authority. This preference is often attributed to practical reasons such as better job opportunities, higher income, and access to a more reliable social safety net, including healthcare and pensions.

Contrary to the Arabs who were permitted to remain in Israel after 1948, Jews were expelled from Iraq, Syria, Egypt, and other Arab lands in response to the establishment of the State of Israel. These countries penalized their Jewish citizens, forcing their migration with only what they could carry. People whose families had lived there for generations and even millennia, owned land, businesses, and homes, were evicted by force. Those who did not leave were massacred, the survivors detained. Yet none of this comes up for discussion by the world bodies, or is recognized by the people accusing Israel of the alleged dispossession and displacement of the Palestinian people in 1948. Perhaps those protesting in the streets of Toronto or London or New York, screaming 'occupier!' and 'colonizer!' should look at the Arab world, where occupation and colonization is a widespread rule rather than an exception.

COLONIZER

The word *colonizer* refers to a state or its citizens that take control of land and people, often in distant lands, and establish a colony.

This usually involves the subjugation and economic exploitation of the native population, and is historically associated with European expansion from the 16th to the 20th centuries. Britain and France, for example, are famous colonizers. Israel is not. To make this claim is to completely misunderstand the term, its context, and its meaning.

The modern state of Israel has existed for 75 years, and, as I have pointed out in every legal respect, Jews have established title to the land in several recorded events. There is no centralized government or state in another part of the world pulling the strings. Calling Israel a colonizer is simply bizarre rhetoric, false, and part of the lying propaganda used by people bent on discrediting and finding any way to turn the narrative against Israel. The claim that Israel is a colonizer is completely incorrect:

1. Jews have maintained a continuous presence in the land for 3,000 years, with a deep historical and religious connection that predates the advent of modern colonial movements. This connection is documented in religious texts, historical records, and archaeological evidence. Thus, the Jewish return to Zion is viewed not as colonization but as the return of a people to their ancestral homeland.

2. Legal Immigration and Land Purchase: Much of the early Jewish immigration to what was the Ottoman Empire, and later British Mandate Palestine, was legal, facilitated by the purchase of land from local and absentee landlords. These transactions are cited as legal and legitimate, differentiating Jewish settlement from colonial expropriation of land without compensation or legal basis.

3. International Legal Sanction: The establishment of a Jewish homeland in Palestine was supported by international law and agreements, as stated earlier.

4. Jews, being indigenous to the land of Israel, have exercised their right to self-determination not as a foreign imposition, but as the realization of the rights of an indigenous people to self-governance in their ancestral land.

5. Unlike classical colonial powers, which sought to exploit colonies for the benefit of their homelands, Israel is a national home for the Jewish people established in response to centuries of persecution and displacement. The mission for the modern state of Israel is to establish sovereignty for the Jewish people in their own country.

6. Classical colonialism involves the expansion of power from a mother country to overseas territories (colonies). Israel does not fit this model because it was not founded as an extension of a foreign power, but rather emerged from the aspirations of the Jewish people for national revival in their historic land.

Critics who point to the displacement of Palestinian Arabs, the characterization of the occupation of Palestinian territories, should read the several widely available books on the history of the Arab-Israeli conflict and history of Israel.[3]

I never cease to be amazed by the people who rally for a cause and yet have no idea what the hell it is that they are rallying for. I have a message for them. Ignorance is not bliss. In this case, it is actually complacency and complicity. For those shouting for the destruction of the Jews, or supporting the very syllabus that promotes terror and hate, they are indeed guilty of feeding the virus of extremism. They have become an evil useful idiot for Global Jihad.

---

3 Recommended reading: *My Promised Land* by Arie Shavit. *Israel* by Noa Tishbi. *Six Days of War* by Michael Oren. *Beirut to Jerusalem* by Thomas Friedman.

GENOCIDE & BABY KILLERS

The definition of genocide was originally termed in 1944 by Raphael Lemkin (1900-1959) a Polish-Jewish lawyer. Born in Belarus, educated in Lviv, he practiced in Warsaw, and after a stint in Sweden eventually settled in the United States as a professor of law at Duke University, North Carolina. He was deeply affected by the atrocities committed against the Jews in the Holocaust, which he understood as the cleansing of people defined by culture and ethnicity by other people, usually via mass murder. Combining the Greek word "genos" (race or family) with the Latin suffix "cide" (killing) he coined this term, and dedicated his career and life to establish an internationally recognized and supported violation of human rights. His efforts culminated in the adoption of the United Nations Convention on the Prevention and Punishment of the Crime of Genocide in 1948.

Genocide is defined as the deliberate and systematic destruction, in whole or in part, of an ethnic, racial, religious, or national group. There were five criteria established to form the claim of genocidal activity. These are:

1. The arbitrary and random act of killing a targeted group.

2. Causing serious bodily or mental harm to members of a specific group.

3. Deliberately inflicting on a group of people conditions calculated to bring about the physical destruction in whole or in part of its culture and life.

4. Imposing measures intended to prevent births.

5. Forcibly transferring children of the group to another group.

Some clear examples of genocide in recent history would include:

Armenian Genocide (1915-1923): The Ottoman Empire systematically exterminated 1.5 million Armenians through mass killings, forced marches, and starvation.

Holocaust (1941-1945): Nazi Germany, led by Adolf Hitler, orchestrated the genocide of 6 million Jews, along with millions of others, including Romani people, disabled individuals, homosexuals and political dissidents.

Rwandan Genocide (1994): In just 100 days, an estimated 800,000 Tutsis and moderate Hutus were killed by extremist Hutu forces in Rwanda.

Bosnian Genocide (1992-1995): During the Bosnian War, Bosnian Serb forces targeted Bosniak (Bosnian Muslim) civilians, resulting in the deaths of approximately 100,000 people, including the Srebrenica massacre.

More recently, but not yet proven in the international court, Russia has been accused of forcibly transporting Ukrainian children from occupied territories in Ukraine to Russia.

When Israel is accused of genocide, it is a blatant lie. Propagating this non-truth at protests, in the media, or by non-governmental organizations is an incitement of antisemitism, and willfully ignorant of the real situation on the ground.

Furthermore, there is no legitimate documentation of genocidal crimes by Israel, and there is no verdict accusing Israel of genocide by any court. The accusations against Israel are simply born out of the bias and corrupted discriminatory presumption of guilt.

There are 8 clear reasons that debunk the baseless claims of genocide against the Palestinian people by the State of Israel. These are evidence-based facts that are in complete contradiction with any possible criteria for genocide as described in the 5 points above.

1. **Lack of Intent:** There is no clear evidence of an intent by Israel to destroy, in whole or in part, an ethnic, racial, religious, or national group, which is a necessary definition of genocide.

2. **Self-Defense:** Israel is managing its internal security threats like any other sovereign country under attack. IDF actions are in response to armed attacks by Hamas.

3. **Targeting Combatants:** In every military operation, Israel's IDF targets combatants and military infrastructure, not civilians, although civilian casualties do happen. Israel takes extensive measures to minimize civilian casualties, such as warnings before attacks. If not for Hamas's strategy to embed itself within civilian populated areas and infrastructure, much collateral damage could be avoided.

4. **Humanitarian Efforts:** It is well documented that Israel provides humanitarian aid and medical assistance to Palestinians. There are hundreds of trucks making their way into Gaza along an Israeli created and protected humanitarian corridor everyday, carrying aid and relief.

5. **Legal and Democratic Processes:** Israel is a democratic state with legal and judicial systems that investigate and prosecute violations of the law, including military conduct. Every incident involving casualties is thoroughly investigated by a special independent arm. I have discussed the MAG Corps earlier on, an independent body within the IDF responsible for investigating allegations of misconduct, including inci-

dents of civilian casualties. It operates independently from the chain of command to ensure impartiality.

6. **Population Growth:** The Palestinian population has grown ninefold in nearly sixty years—that's a very poor genocide. In fact, the Palestinian territories have higher birth rates compared to Israel. For example, the total fertility rate in the Palestinian territories is around 3-4, while in Israel, it is approximately 3.

7. **International Scrutiny:** Israel operates under intense international scrutiny and numerous investigations by international bodies, which would almost certainly have identified conclusive evidence of genocide if it were occurring.

8. **Peace Efforts:** Israel has engaged in various peace efforts and negotiations with Palestinian representatives, indicating a willingness to coexist rather than an intent to destroy.

The accusation of genocide against Israel is untenable, baseless, and easily refutable. Whereas, there is no subtlety in the messaging of the Jihad, whose genocide message is clearly at the top of their agenda when it comes to Jews.

"Hey, are you happy being a baby killer?" "You fucking baby killers." "You are a baby killer." These are the crazed shouts delivered by masked keffiyeh protestors. I cannot believe the scene in our neighborhood as a Caucasian young woman in sunglasses, wrapped in a keffiyeh and wearing a face mask in an attempt to hide her identity accosts my dumbfounded neighbor on our street. "Baby killer" she yells at her.

The term "baby killers" has become yet another meaningless slogan of the protesters attempting to smear Israel and the Jews. Any parent would find the idea of the killing of children abhorrent under any circumstance. Except for a certain part of the world. In a disturbing twist, some Palestinian mothers whose children have died in conflict react in an unexpected way. Rather than mourning, they distribute sweets and celebrate their children's deaths, hailing them as "shahids" or martyrs. These mothers proudly proclaim that their children's lives were sacrificed in the name of jihad.

As for this "genocide," the fatalities numbers offered by the Gaza Ministry of Health, run by Hamas, does not distinguish between combatants and civilians. In May, 2024 The UN's Office for the Coordination of Humanitarian Affairs (OCHA), as reported by BBC News made tweaks to the numbers that suggested inaccuracies in these numbers. The Washington Institute of Near East Policy, in March, 2024, published a study called "Gaza Fatality Data Has Become Completely Unreliable," showing that, for example, the reported numbers are far too steady and even to have taken place in a war zone.

As pointed out, the IDF attacks military targets and terrorists, however, because Hamas insists on embedding itself amongst the civilian population—in schools, hospitals, community centers and residential neighborhoods—there are unintended civilian casualties, all of which are investigated independently. Israel is quickly accused and criticized of situations involving civilian casualties that are often the result of Hamas missiles falling short of targets inside of Gaza's populated areas. The on-the-ground reality of these situations is often vastly different to what is initially reported in the media. It is these media-distributed 'facts' that are seized by the public and gullible politicians, who wrongly accuse Israel of unacceptable atrocities.

There are going to be challenges in urban warfare, and especially where militant groups' use of civilian infrastructure for military purposes lead to civilian casualties and conflicting narratives about responsibility. The IDF uses pamphlet drops, messages on Telegram, signage, and other means to provide information and instruct citizens of restricted areas and humanitarian corridors. These measures are used to protect non-combatants.

In May 2024, an explosion at the Al-Shati Refugee Camp, which killed several members of a Palestinian family, was immediately blamed on an Israeli airstrike. The IDF later provided evidence that the explosion was caused by a misfired rocket launched by Palestinian militants. In the same month, Israel was accused of causing the deaths of numerous civilians in Al-Wahda Street. Further investigations revealed that while Israeli airstrikes were conducted in the area targeting Hamas tunnels, the extensive civilian casualties were partly due to secondary explosions from Hamas' military infrastructure located in civilian areas.

Several incidents have occurred during the present conflict with Hamas where Israel has been blamed without any formal investigations. The Oct. 17, 2023 explosion at the Al-Ahli Arab Hospital, where civilian casualties were first reported in the hundreds, was blamed on an Israeli airstrike. Only after the media frenzy accusing Israel of this attack was evidence made clear, including intercepted communications, that indicated the explosion was caused by a misfired rocket launched by the Palestinian Islamic Jihad. The rocket landed in the nearby parking lot, not the hospital itself, as initially reported, and about 50 people were killed, not the 500 reported by Hamas.

In the last days of October, 2023, Israel was once again charged with targeting a densely-populated area in the Jabalia refugee camp, leading to significant civilian casualties. The IDF clarified that the airstrike targeted senior Hamas commanders who were operating within the camp, and subsequent evidence suggested that secondary explosions from Hamas' munitions stored in the area contributed to the high number of casualties.

Even once the facts are known and the information is released to establish the true story of each incident, the press is mute, and the politicians have moved on. All this information just feeds the Jew-hating narrative, and no one seems to acknowledge the connection between the continued false narratives and the increased hate-mongering.

The obvious bias is difficult to ignore in the face of mounting evidence and the bizarre narration of events taking place. On June 8, 2024 in a daring operation reminiscent of the Raid on Entebbe, Israel successfully rescued four hostages abducted from Israel on October 7. Three were held in the residential home of Abdallah Aljamal, a former Al Jazeera journalist, who along with his physician father, Dr. Ahmed Aljamal, detained and kept Israelis Almog Meir Jan, Andrey Kozlov and Shlomi Ziv captive. In the rescue of these men, along with Noa Argamani, the IDF special forces fought their way out of central Gaza's Nuseirat area to waiting helicopters. It was initially reported that 94 people, mainly terrorists, were killed in the gun fight, which also claimed the life of Arnon Zmora, the leading commander of the rescue effort, now known as operation Arnon. Despite the facts broadcasted, the Canadian Broadcasting Corporation, repeatedly reported that there were "dozens" of innocent Palestinians killed during the raid. At first not even mentioning the rescue of the four hostages, they instead focused on painting the IDF as murdering without cause. They were fighting hundreds of heavily armed "civilians" firing automatic machine guns, RPG rockets, and launching grenades—none "innocent."

WAR IS HELL

There are no winners in war. There are going to be civilian casualties. The loss of innocent life is a tragedy, and it is especially disheartening for the death of any child. Israel faces a challenging situation: balancing the security of its citizens with the safety of civilians who are used by terrorists as human shields. The solution does not lie in blanket condemnation of Israel, or exploiting the tragedies involving children to intensify Palestinian protests. Until there is world wide recognition of the truth, and cessation of support for Hamas, innocent people will pay the price with their lives. The people who continue to support the lies of Hamas are the enablers of the terrorists who are the real killers of babies.

UNDER THE IRON DOME

IN MAY 2023 I was enjoying lunch at a beach restaurant in Tel Aviv with my wife and son when I heard sirens going off. I casually looked up and saw a missile being shot out of the sky by a counter-defensive rocket. As a few customers moved toward the public shelter, a waiter holding a portable payment machine intercepted them almost as fast as the Iron Dome intercepted the missile. Okay, there are missiles flying overhead, but man, you gotta pay your tab. The British couple sitting next to us asked me if they had to leave.

"What are the chances this is going to happen again before you finish your lunch?" I casually replied.

Looking up from your cup of coffee or through your office window and seeing rockets flying overhead, then explode as they are destroyed by the Iron Dome, is an almost daily occurrence for the Israelis. There used to be a time when this was purely a North or South problem, but today's incoming projectiles can reach deep into the country. There is no longer anywhere in Israel that is safe from attack. The air defense system has now become a crucial and normalized way of life.

High-pitch sirens go off whenever the Dome predicts an increased risk of a strike, urging people into bomb shelters. Israelis typically have 15-30 seconds to find refuge in one of these shelters. In some parts of the country, even less time.

Israel's building code requires all homes, offices, and public buildings to have access to a bomb shelter. Most buildings have a *Miklat, a* bomb shelter for public use, or a *Mamad,* a safe room, built into each residential unit. The room can double as a functional room, and is often a bedroom or den. This is a specially constructed line in the building that will remain standing independently of the entire structure. These rooms have thicker walls, steel doors with special seals and locking mechanisms, and air systems that filter out smoke and other gasses. There is a special unit in the IDF that must approve the plans for shelters of any new construction.

These rocket attacks create a constant fight-or-flight stress response that Israelis must endure. Acute stress response involves the release of stress hormones like adrenaline and cortisol, which prepare the body to either fight or flee from perceived danger. The human body is not designed to stay in a constant state of stress, and a prolonged stress activation can lead to many health issues, such as cardiovascular disease, immune, digestive, and sleep issues, as well as contributing to a host of other ailments. Needless to say, there are high levels of these stress-related illnesses amongst the Israeli population. The reality of daily life in Israel is creating entire generations of people with some form of PTSD. Such is the reality of living under constant siege.

No other sovereign entity in the world would tolerate, or be expected to tolerate, an indiscriminate bombardment of rockets into its territories. Yet Israel must build infrastructure around these constant attacks, while any move to defend itself is immediately placed under a microscope to determine if its actions are disproportionate and deserving of a reprimand from the UN or its Western allies. If the United States was under attack, even one strike would be enough to warrant the harshest possible blow; there would be no debates over America's right to protect itself.

The danger of air-strikes has, as of the summer of 2024, forced over 200,000 Israelis from their homes. There are 25 communities in the south within four kilometers of Gaza and 28 communities in the north within two kilometers of Lebanon that have been entirely evacuated. This is unprecedented in Israel's history, and opens up major concerns over the safety of the general population. These are not sparsely-populated fringe communities. Entire cities have been emptied overnight. Incredibly, and another anomaly that sets Israel apart from any other nation state, every evacuated person has a roof over their head. Many of the evacuees are being hosted in hotels across the country. There is nothing excluded. Five star accommodations with full board are being paid for, compliments of the Israeli government. Though the novelty of a hotel stay for a family runs its course; being forced from one's home can be very traumatic. Many families have been put up by other families in their home without any compensation. Not only are these people being housed, but they are being fed as well. Makeshift schools have opened for kids, and communities have added several new public places for the displaced. You have to come to Israel to experience the village that takes care of its own.

Ilan operates a fruit and vegetable store in Tel Aviv, just up the street from our apartment, opened hastily after the October 7 attack. On that day in Sderot, a city of 30,000 people, it took the

Gazans less than 15 minutes to get from the border to the gates of this peaceful community. During the attack, terrorists entered Ilan's home. As he and his terrified wife, sons and daughter held the door of their *Miklat* firmly closed, they could hear the horrific screams of their neighbors. After some time had passed and things had gone quiet, Ilan left the shelter, figuring the worst was over. As he crossed the travertine speckled floor to the kitchen, he heard the distinct dialect of Gazan Arabic slang spoken by voices coming from outside his garden door. The terrorist's plan was to smoke out his family. Without thinking, he grabbed a large kitchen knife, still in the sink after last night's meal, a family moment that seemed now in another world. He seized the first terrorist as the man came in through the door. With incredible strength, he blocked the door with his leg, pushed the invader against the wall and repeatedly stabbed him. He then let the door fly open, wrapping his large hands around the second terrorist's neck, while smashing the third one with his body. In moments, all three terrorists were dead. Later, Ilan would go outside and find his neighbors brutally murdered. He showed me pictures of them on his phone, pictures I would rather have never seen but now cannot erase from my mind. He pointed to a picture of the Torah cover he placed over the body of a child, his voice raised into an angry shout.

"Where is it okay to dig the grave and bury an eight year old boy?"

I told him I have a son in Israel, in the IDF, and he grabbed my arm. "We are all going to die. Take your son home, now."

Then he paused, and with a straight face said in Hebrew, "But for now, buy some produce, it's the best."

Jacob, Ilan's 20-year old son, helps him with the store. I observed him for a moment; the large pupils of his deep black eyes staring into the distance of his own mind. I made a shuffling sound to let him know I was there. He was at first startled out of some memory, then suddenly he revealed this wonderful smile, and his eyes danced with the acknowledgement of my presence in his store.

"*Ma Koreh, Yaakov?*" (What's doing, Yakov?) I spoke in Hebrew, and he came to me for a warm embrace. I hugged these two men daily. What else could I do for them but embrace, listen, and buy some produce? But even these small acts, for now, may be enough. I have come to realize that the people of Israel need to be heard, to feel they have not been forgotten. I saw people from the community filling into this small store, sitting and drinking coffee, giving Ilan the space to tell his stories over and over again. I am touched by the affection and emotion of the village here in Tel Aviv by the sea. I felt like this is the reason I was here.

It remains unclear when Ilan, like most of Israel's displaced, will be able to return with his family to their home. While some of those from the south are beginning to return, others are entirely traumatized and refuse to go back home. Many homes have been completely destroyed. Some of those that remain standing, like in the village of Be'eri, will need to be cleansed of blood and repaired from fire damage and bullet holes before they can be reinhabited. And while this physical damage can be patched, filled, cleaned, painted over, there is a deeper damage that cannot. Many Israeli citizens may never feel safe again after the horror of Ten-Seven. For those in the south whose homes and villages were invaded, how can they ever return home without suffering every day as the blood of their neighbors and families, though scrubbed from the walkways, continues to bleed in their souls? How do you convince these first hand witnesses and victims this will never happen again? The people of the South and North will always feel like sitting ducks, with the foreboding sense of an attack that could happen at any time. They will never sleep safely in their beds, always waiting for *them* to come blazing through the door. What will it take for the people of these communities to feel safe once again?

For the residents of the north, the situation is no less volatile, and it is unlikely that any Northerners now displaced will return home soon. Border skirmishes in the north are serious concerns to

Israel's security. Israel will need to offer more than just verbal assurances to its people that they can safely return. And yet a war with Hezbollah will be a full-scale military operation that will widen the conflict regionally and further the dependency between Israel and the United States and Hezbollah to Iran.

On Aug. 25, 2024 Israel took significant actions and conducted pre-emptive strikes on Hezbollah to avert a pending large-scale strike against Israel. The US has moved a number of warships, including two aircraft carriers, into the Gulf of Oman and the Eastern Mediterranean. They are sending a very strong message to Iran to think twice about expanding the conflict further after the assassination, in Tehran, of Hamas's leader Ismael Haniyeh. Though nothing has been publicly stated by Israel, the message is clear: there is no safe place for murderers to hide.

Lebanon is not the Gaza Strip, and Hezbollah is not Hamas. Lebanon is 29 times the size of Gaza. And Lebanon's population is three times larger than Gaza's. The larger the population and size, the messier a military campaign. It will not be a short conflict and will come at a great cost to both sides.

Eventually, countries will have to declare sides, especially Turkey, whose leader Erdogan has made no secret of his dislike for the "terror state" of Israel. Turkey is a member of NATO, and regardless of its rhetoric, any siding against Israel militarily would be against the United States and a direct violation to the pact. It is ultimately unknown what this country, caught between the progress of Europe and the digress of the Middle East, will decide if push comes to shove, but a side will have to be declared.

The truth is that none of these conflicts should come as a surprise to anyone who has been watching the south and north provocations. Neither Hezbollah's leader Nasrallah nor Hamas's former leader Haniyeh have been secretive about their intentions when it comes to their designs on Israel.

"I am not angry with Hamas," Rubin, who I met at the Tel

Hashomer hospital in Tel Aviv, told me. "They were always clear about their intent to kill me. I am angry with the government, who is well aware of this threat and did not do enough to protect me."

Rubin's hospital roommate, Gal, a jovial, intelligent 22-year old built like a brick house, chimed in. "They (the leadership) made a critical error. On the next day (after October 7) they should have carpet-bombed Gaza and taken out 200,000 of them. We showed total weakness in our initial response, and this will cost us dearly now with Hezbollah in the North. We lost the momentum from the start of this, it was our only opportunity to send a very clear warning and make Nasrallah shit his pants. But once again, our leadership is scared of what others will think and are too scared to do what needs to be done."

I am taken aback by his candor and articulation. What he said may have been uncomfortable to hear, but no less true. Gal has had more than five months in recovery to consider his words after losing half his leg to shrapnel. One look at the deep creviced scars on his back tell his story.

During another one of our visits to Tel Hashomer hospital, I also met Boris, who I saw coming toward me with ease on his crutches. His left leg was amputated after an RPG strike during a surprise Hamas attack a few days into the war. He is a young man with a wonderful sense of positivity. Striking looks, tall and strong—I felt safe and comforted in his presence, even though I was there to offer him my empathy. Boris is from Ukraine and is an *Oleh* (a Jew recently immigrated to Israel).

"War seems to follow me," he laughed. With a wisdom that transcends his 27 years, he continued, "Wars always come to an end, and heroes are forgotten. What I am really concerned for is the 19-and 20-year old kids here who have not even gotten their lives started." He gestured around the long-term care center, at the patients, and at those who were volunteering. "They will need people here for them once all of this is gone."

Today, I continue to keep in touch with Boris, who proudly shows me his new prosthetic leg over video. He is excited to soon move into a new apartment in Tel Aviv and get back to living his life. Not once has he played the victim in any of this, even though he has every right to, and nowhere has he shown a trace of anger or regret. He loves his country, he loves his life, and he is determined to continue to protect and care for others. He is an Israeli hero.

"Never since the Holocaust have the Jewish people been under attack as they are today," said Alick, as we sat together at one of Tel Aviv's laid back beach cafes. I met Alick at a yoga studio in Neve Tzedek, a recalibrated, gentrified area of Tel Aviv. "I simply cannot understand why there are those who truly feel the message of inclusion does not apply to us Jews. When it comes to the liberal humanitarians, they will protest against every violation by anyone for any cause or people, except when it comes to the Jews."

What he says is true. We cannot help but to be unified as a people who are pursued. We have no time to establish the differences between us, even if we wish for it; even in the most divisive times we are brought together by others who want to destroy us.

"The offenses to the body, the rape and the mutilation," Alick motioned with his hands, encircling his crotch, upsetting our *Cafe Hafuch* (cappuccino), which spilled over on the worn wood. He has been deeply moved by the last few months, the stress worn into his young face. "I have lost six friends. I have been to many funerals and shivas. But I am glad they were not taken captive. That, I do not think I could stand to agonize over."

Alick is not the only one who feels this way. Knowing the barbarity of Hamas, it does not leave much to the imagination of what these hostages could be subject to. Thomas Hand, the father of 9-year old Emily, claimed to be relieved when he was told of her suspected death. Thomas was overwhelmed, as seen around the world, as his daughter appeared, essentially from the dead, in the first batch of released hostages. I recall his interview months later, the subtlety of his Irish accent still apparent within the mix of Hebrew and English, explaining his love for the land that gave him his daughter but took his wife.

Alick, a 3rd generation Israeli, is a person seemingly formed by his grandparents' Holocaust survival.

"You cannot escape what happened to our families back then. I cannot believe that this is happening again. 75 years later, and they are still looking to mutilate us. Put that in your book!" He stammered, then fell silent, rolling another cigarette and staring out to sea.

"I will," I promised. And here it is.

AN OPPORTUNITY FOR CHANGE

POLITICAL AND JUDICIAL CORRECTION IN ISRAEL

THE PROBLEM WITH FUNDAMENTALISM is that there is only one way. The problem with radicalization is that it cannot be reasoned with. The problem with people is that we are all subject to human nature; alone among Earth's creatures possessing the ability to make conscious choices against the laws of our nature. Such is the dilemma of leaders who give into the power of their power. Such is the consequence of a public that falls to apathy of their present situation. Such is the importance of agency on an individual level and as a collective where an event has the power to unify us in a way that we thought was forever lost.

The disunity within Israel prior to the 7th of October 2023 was both caused and created by dysfunction. There was a distinct and destructive erosion of faith in government, in purpose, and in each other. I question the philosophical idea that everything is *meant to be*, however I am a believer in events that, when looking back, seem to contrive with fate to determine a path of destiny. There is no one who will convince me that the Holocaust needed to happen for Israel to become; however, the Holocaust did happen, and in their survival, those left came together in Israel to achieve a dream that would protect us from ever again being hunted down and persecuted. October 7 was a terrible tragedy, but it happened, and we are now in the aftermath, at the crossroads, and on the cusp of a wake up call. Once again, Jewish survival depends on adaptation, evolution, and growth. Israel must fix itself from within so that the future of generations to come can be secured. To do so, we must believe in the impossible, and we must act.

There are a number of fundamental social and political challenges facing Israel. Ten-Seven is a symptom of Israel failing in its social contract. Pointing this out is perhaps the easiest step on the path to change, but it is a no less critical step. I believe there are 7 key challenges to Israeli society today:

1. Israel does not have a constitution. The good news here is that there is a plain canvas that can be drawn upon. The bad news is that because there is no constitution, the only way to get there is via complete majority government.

2. The Israeli political electoral system is flawed. There is too much power given to minority interests. The result: a forced collusion to form a coalition government. The popular vote is often ignored in favor of varying smaller minority interests.

3. The judicial system is not functioning as it should and needs reform. (This is a heated topic that I will explain further in this chapter.)

4. Like everywhere else in the free world these days, Israel has created a vacuum for good leadership. No one in their right mind wants this job.

5. Voter apathy. There is disenchantment around the power of the individual voter. Israel needs to get people back to the polls.

6. The demographics of Israel are risking the balance of power and the balance of moderation and reason. With religious birth rates overwhelming secular families there must be a constitution to protect what will become the minority.

7. Israel's reliance on the United States often leads to deal-making by inexperienced, misguided, or politically-motivated leaders, routinely forcing Israel to act against its own best interest.

Israel's democracy is at risk because of its own misshapen structures, diverse interests, codependency, corruption, and lack of leadership. To fix Israel, the country will need a majority government who can usher in the changes required, and to get there, it first needs a leader who can build unity and trust. This is the only way that the country can make the necessary changes to its electoral system and justice system and, while we are at it, write a constitution that will provide a political solution to a highly diverse society and ensure that the government truly reflects the interests of the people. Perhaps this is wishful thinking for the utopian nation state, but unlike other countries, the Jewish State is a village that raises its children. The people of Israel are a people of love, the people of a book. Whether or not you follow that book, it is ingrained in the DNA of every Jew, and in times of challenge the goodness of that book always comes out in the souls of the people. Israel is a small enough country that six degrees of separation is not an anomaly, it is the social reality. Talk to any Jewish stranger and you will find a connection within the first three minutes of conversation. If there is anywhere that such acute change can happen, it is in Israel, in the land of miracles. If not for ourselves then for our children and future generations we must do this. The people of Israel must come together, come forward, and accomplish the impossible. Israel has survived 75 years of war. Its people are the children of Israel (Jacob), and overcoming the impossible is built into our character.

Presently, there is an all-time loss of confidence in the current Israeli government. Despite this, it is not surprising that Netanyahu continues to survive his leadership. Most will grudgingly admit that as a war-time leader he is doing a good job and holding firm to his military goals. Even as the narrative quickly shifts in the West, and world leaders one by one turn against Israel, Bibi soldiers on.

Immediately following the events of October 7, Netanyahu made two significant political maneuvers. One, he brought Israel's competing political parties together in a national unity government that formed a special wartime cabinet, during which an emergency government was sworn in. This froze any discussion of an election and suspended all court decisions, essentially shutting down the Knesset, while the war in Gaza continues. Netanyahu buys time to show what he can accomplish, and has the opportunity to shift public opinion on his leadership. His political prowess secures his power and place in history. By delegating a shared leadership during this full-scale war, he has secured his position with more strength and power than his previous governments. No wartime PM has survived a failure in military security. Golda Meir's government quickly crumbled following the Yom Kippur war in 1973, as did Menachem

Begin during the Lebanon war of 1982. In both instances the Prime Ministers resigned voluntarily, providing the country a time to heal and form new leadership. The story of Netanyahu is yet to be written. He is a populist leader who seems to break the barriers, which may have as much to do with a lack of desirable alternatives as it does with an underestimation of his hold on power.

Netanyahu is nothing if not a controversial Israeli leader; he seems to closely parallel the Trump phenomena, though he is nowhere as crass, negligent, or off-the-handle. Trump's presidency was the work of pure populism, whereas Netanyahu is undoubtedly a mastermind at his craft. Both leaders, however, have a rising stack of judicial issues that could eventually see them slapped with criminal convictions. Both leaders are also the result of political systems that failed to attract viable leadership to the table, and neither properly represents the interest of the majority of voters. Though to the credit of the United States, there are some checks and balances there that do not exist in Israel.

Netanyahu is one of Israel's great leaders, and that is beyond his own ego and the corruption that comes naturally to leaders who hold on to power for too long. He has represented Israel perhaps better than any other leader on the world stage. But, alas, it is time for him to go. All great leaders struggle with this. His final act of service would be a graceful exit into the sunset to prompt and provide the succession for this country's next great leader.

The wartime Knesset plenum is perhaps the most unified government Israel has seen in the 2020s. Following October 7, the Knesset plenum used its powers to pass a number of bills successfully and without opposition, to fund the economy, amass the largest active army in its history, continue the unprecedented Gaza campaign, secure Israel's borders, and take care of its people. The public has been warned that Israel faces a long-term military offensive and that its impending actions against Hezbollah, the Houthis, and Iran will go on for months, if not years.

Israel needs strong, fresh, determined leadership to unify the country. If there were such a person, and this person finds this calling and puts themselves forward to endure the public scrutiny and exposure for the good of the land and its populations, they would still need to form a government by majority vote. This would require voter involvement to increase beyond the apathy that is taking hold today. In 2018 the voter turnout was 56%. In 2022, even less at 49.5%, an indication of voter exhaustion, apathy, or not caring about the outcome. These levels are much lower than the US (66%) or Canada (62%). Every vote does count. To make changes, Israelis must all feel the importance of being a part of the democratic process. It is time now for Israel to unify, to step up and make the impossible happen. The people of the book must believe that there is a path forward.

As I mentioned earlier Israel does not have a formal constitution, rather a set of basic laws that serve a similar function and can be seen as a gradual compilation of legislation through the Knesset that covers various aspects of government and civil liberties.

In a democracy, a separation of powers provides for no single person to dictate the rule of law, though many see the influence, corruption, and persistent reign of Netanyahu to be approaching dictatorial territory. Israel, like other healthy democracies, has branches of power that create checks and balances for government. There is an executive branch of the government made up of the Prime Minister and their cabinet. The executive will form a government through deal-making that goes on behind the scenes with the several other parties who make up the coalition. This practice is the most significant crisis of democracy within Israel, because the government's prime purpose is survival. In such a coalition the government can easily become a slave to the minority interests of fringe parties who make up a tiny fraction of the popular vote but receive a disproportionate say in government. At any time, the government can be brought down by an aggrieved partner, which adds to the instability.

THE DISPROPORTIONATE PROPORTIONAL PROBLEM

The system that Israel has known for 75 years is problematic. The balance of power generally shifted between two main parties, Labor and Likud. During the current Gaza war, the governing party, Likud, had 32 seats in the Knesset out of 120 parliamentary delegates. It is clear that no single party holds a majority, reflecting the fragmented nature of Israel's proportional representation system.

Member's of the Knesset (MK's) are not elected directly by the people, but rather indirectly. Candidates run on a *slate* of delegates. This means that the higher up a candidate is on the list of delegates the greater the chance of holding a seat in the legislature. Delegates become MK's proportionate to the share of vote of their party. For example, if a party receives 20% of the national vote, then 20% of its slate from the top down become legislators. By comparison, in constituency democracy, the members of parliament are elected by the constituents representing various registered parties within the riding. The result is that the people choose their representative, and the parliamentarian's first responsibility is (ideally) to their constituents, not the party. This can make a significant difference in outcome to representation. In Israel, the system of proportionality is flawed in that it represents the interests of the party first and there is no direct representation at the federal level of specific localities. Though a small country geographically, Israel is heterogeneous, with a highly diversified spectrum of religious, economic, and security concerns depending on where people reside; the people of Tel Aviv are going to have different needs for representation than those in Jerusalem or the Golan. Zooming in closer, for example, the residents of the German colony neighborhood in the greater Jerusalem area are going to be vastly different economically and culturally than those of the religious neighborhood of Mea She'arim. Then there is the Old City, which is one of the most diverse communities in the world, catering not only to the spectrum of holy city residents but also to several major religions. Like everything else in Israel, population diversity is a complex matter.

There are 30 different parties vying for power in the current Israeli political landscape. That is quite a dilution of vote, and most of these parties would not qualify to register in Canada, which is at most five parties, of which one is exclusive to the province of Quebec. In the United States, the choice comes down to just two main rivals. The more parties, the less likely that the popular vote will result in the government and policies of the people's choice. In the 2022 election, Netanyahu's Likud party garnered only 23.53% of the vote. The ultra orthodox party, UTJ, enjoyed a seat at the table despite representing less than 7% of the popular vote. Contrast that to the 13% of votes earned by Yair Lapid's Yesh Atid, a centrist-secular party, which even though it received more votes than UTJ, has a lesser say in policy due to not being included in the ruling government. In the flurry of deal-making that occurs in the days following an election, the party with the most votes will generally have first opportunity to present their preferred coalition deal to the President of Israel, which will mainly draw from other parties on or near the spectrum of the leading party's policies. However, in 2021, Naftali Bennett, historically a right-wing ally and protege of Netanyahu, alienated his key support base by a joint Prime Ministership dealmaking move with Yair Lapid. It was a desperate measure to unseat Netanyahu and create a stable coalition, a political risk, yet one which I believe finally provided greater representation and fairness to the voters. While this arrangement did not serve Bennett well, (Netanyahu returned to power two years later) the Bennett-Lapid deal is an example of how creative the back room can get when it comes to power-brokering leadership in the Holy Land. Many other democracies use proportionate representation, including Germany, Italy, Netherlands, Belgium, India, Norway, Finland, Denmark, and Sweden; and even constituency representation can result in minority governments, such as the Liberal-NDP coalition in Canada. However, this does not mean that Israel is in good company and cannot do better for itself. The sheer volume of parties is what contributes to its complex political relationships, which often lead to dysfunction.

THE ISRAEL JUDICIARY: MUCH TO DO ABOUT SOMETHING.
The judiciary reforms is a significant subject, and requires some background to understand the deeply divisive and polarizing effect this has amongst the people of Israel. In fact, I believe, and so do many others, that this division was so severe that it has compromised Israel's security. Scores of military personnel have spoken out against the government, something unheard of. You think Hamas was not listening? Israel's enemies were very tuned in to its disunity.

The Israeli Judiciary has been the subject of much controversy. The issue of judiciary reform has brought Israel as close to civil disunity as it has ever been in its 75 years. The massive protests in response to the proposed reforms are of significant concern to Jews around the world, who otherwise thought the Jewish State to be well above this type of public infighting. Israel is the head of the global Jewish family, and the protests are seen as an embarrassing situation akin to washing the dirty laundry in public. That being said, protesting, when done in a constructive and respectful way, is an example of democracy and free speech at work. Israel's citizenry are not a silent people, and they feel compromised by the failing of its electoral system to elect a government of the people. It is a frustration widely felt, and there is little patience for what is seen as political corruption that above all puts the security of the people at risk.

The complexity and severity of the divide over the issue of the judiciary is another symptom of the need for electoral and political reform in Israel. We are at this juncture in Israel's history because its government structure may be too simple for the work it must do. Currently it lacks the confidence of controls needed when it comes to making changes in the basic laws of the land with a normal coalition majority of 61 votes in the Knesset (51% of the vote). Compare this to the United States, where a constitutional amendment requires a two-thirds majority vote in both the House of Representatives and the Senate. Again, this can be a significant risk to democracy, and is especially concerning with a populist right wing agenda whereby, because of the representation, or rather *misrepresentation,* of its people, there can be a significant trampling on civil rights and freedoms. This is why when in 1995 the Supreme Court of Israel reformed the judiciary power it ruled that the court has the power to strike down Knesset legislation that is not compatible with two of the country's Basic Laws, later expanded to include all Basic Laws. This ability has been used by the court to protect human rights in Israel and the territories it controls. It has also frustrated the right wing in Israel, which claims that the court is perpetuating a left wing agenda, frustrating legislation by the right wing majority coalition. This, contends the Netanyahu government, is stalling progress and the will of the people.

JUDICIARY BACKGROUND

The Israel Supreme court is made up of 15 judges, who are appointed through the JSC (Judicial Selection Committee), which is made up of nine members: two government ministers, two members of the Knesset (one each from the coalition and the opposition), three Supreme Court judges, and two lawyers from the Israel Bar Association, a set up designed to guarantee that neither the government nor the opposition has an automatic majority. The Basic Laws of Israel, yet another complexity, form a de facto constitution, but is not in actuality a proper constitution. These are 14 laws that have been added one after the other over the years (all other laws are considered "ordinary" laws.) One would think that the basic law is superior to the ordinary law, however this remains under debate as there is no basic law indicating so, leaving the order of priority ambiguous. The basic laws deal with foundational issues of the country, the very first being the law of the Knesset's 120 members.

Other basic laws deal with Israel lands, the Office of the President, the formation of government, the State Economy, the state comptroller or ombudsman of the country, the individual's freedom of occupation, the law of referendum, and more. The last addition to the list of basic laws was in 2018 declaring Israel as the *Nation State of the Jews.* It is easy to see how the courts, who are not elected by the people and are meant in Israel to be the protectors of civil liberty, can frustrate a government that operates on the opposite end of the court's sensibilities. In response, the Netanyahu government recently legislated the highly controversial "unreasonableness law" to offset the power of the current judiciary. What this means is that the sitting government can deem that the court's ruling, meant to protect the basic laws of the people in a government that has real checks and balances, as unreasonable and thereby voided by the ruling coalition majority of the Knesset, undermining the entire purpose of the court's independence and threatening to make them redundant. With our dysfunctional Knesset, we continue to spiral down the rabbit hole, applying bandage after bandage to an arterial wound and hoping the bleeding will simply stop on its own. When it doesn't, the government shrugs and applies yet another bandaid.

Israel's electoral system is a house of cards, and the wind is getting stronger. The simple 61 vote majority rule does provide for a quick escalation and passing into law of legislation, but also means that each majority coalition in cahoots on extreme ends of the spectrum can repeal important groundbreaking work from previous governments and use its own unreasonable power to further its own agenda and alienate minority interests on the other side. Democracy is not designed for the majority rule, but to ensure the protection and rights of the minority. When this functions effectively, the true essence of a democracy is at work. Israel has one house of representatives. One house that, if the stars align, can do some real damage without checks. This is why the 1995 provision of the Supreme court was necessary, to thwart unfair self-serving government interests and conflicts in power. But the potential to handicap an ineffective system of government is in itself just another bandaid. True reform is required to heal the wound. Such are the perils of a concentration and centralization of power.

On the other side of the coin is decentralization. Decentralization of power is achieved by operating multiple independent branches of the government. In the United States the upper chamber (the Senate) is independently elected by the people, as is the lower house of representatives (Congress). The Executive branch, the President and their appointed cabinet, operates outside of the houses. The United States has a legal constitution that cannot be simply modified by a majority vote by one house, as is the case with Israel. In Canada, the upper house is not elected, rather appointments are made by the sitting government when vacancies become available. It is the Senate's duty to veto or provide approval of legislation of the lower house. In both the US and Canada, Supreme Court judges are appointed by the leaders of the day, but not before undergoing an exhaustive screening process. Given the sitting government's influence, you can assume that the judges, who will likely outlive the government, are the choice of the people of the day. This is why most Presidents of the United States take these appointments very seriously. Donald Trump, who stacked the court in his favor during his tenure, saw dividends on the other side of 2020. This does not insinuate that judges are partial to any one person, and the judges who sit on the US Supreme Court today may not approve of or care about Trump one way or the other. Yet their values, interpretations of law, and ideals, can help preserve the legacy of the outgoing President's party beyond their government. In the exceptional and unprecedented situation of Trump today, it is as if he foresaw the challenges to his next leadership run. The moral framework of the Supreme Court of Justice weighs in his favor and entitles him to another run at the White House, a clear annuity to Trump for having stacked the courts. Frankly, I do not know if any court would have upheld the reason for disqualification of a President based on an obscure Civil War-era law, but appointing some of the judges on the panel certainly has not hurt him. Regardless of these questionable elements of the system, it is these independent branches of government that exist to provide the essential checks and balances needed to protect democracies that Israel lacks. Israel has one house, and there is nothing independent about its branches. The Israel Supreme Court acts as the only check to a government that threatens *true* democracy. The judiciary of Israel was never meant to become a political check to the system, but rather a lawful body to decide and set precedent for the legal issues of the country.

HIPSTER OR HASID?

One of the most divisive demographic differences within Israeli society is the exemption of the mandatory army conscription of the religious *Haredi* community. Conscription is one of Israel's most significant basic laws, requiring each able-bodied person from the age of 18 to serve in the army. For the far right religious community, this requirement was historically waived. Yet the army is actually a healthy melting pot of Israeli society that provides the opportunity for people from all spectrums of society to learn to live and work together. There is the humble servitude of the higher purpose to defend the land and thereby the Jewish people. Some of the strongest relationships a *Chayal* (soldier) will form is with those they have served with. There are many in the right wing religious community who do not believe that the secular State of Israel represents the Holy Israel referred to in the Bible and therefore do not accept its authority. However, they will certainly accept its welfare. What is at odds here is that if there wasn't an army protecting them, there would not be the religious institutions that have flourished over the past 75 years. In the time of the reclamation of the Second Temple, the most famous armies were the Macabee defenders, who were the most religious and strongest adherents to Jewish practice and culture.

There are, indeed, many religious soldiers in the IDF. In fact, the most fierce of them are from the *Yishuvim* (settlements) or territories. Many Israelis, both secular and religious, feel that the waiver of conscription for the far right is abused, and that this waiver should not exist. At the very minimum, the alternative to perform *Sherut Leumi* (community service) should be mandatory. "Why should my children be put in harm's way to protect those who do not support or contribute to the security of the state?" is a common and reasonable sentiment of any soldier's parent, including myself, who must endure half-sleeps and the constant anxiety of knowing that at any moment there could be a phone call or knock at the door that can change my life in an instant.

On June 25, 2024 the Supreme Court of Israel made the historical move announcing that all ultra-orthodox males of the age of 18 must be included in the law of conscription. This comes on the tail of a protracted war with Hamas and the need to replenish the army. It will be interesting to see if this law is countered with the unreasonableness law of Netanyahu's government or if it proceeds as intended.

PROTECTION OF RIGHTS AND LIBERTIES

One only needs to visit the land and experience its vastly diverse ideals to appreciate that Israel is a veritable island of freedom in the Middle East. Freedom of speech, freedom of the press, access to information, right to privacy, freedom of assembly, and freedom of religion, are not God-given rights to be taken for granted. In a democracy, these are the fundamentally *protected* rights of a society that is accountable to its members and whose members are accountable collectively to the greater good of the social contract they enjoy. Israel is the only democracy in the Middle East. It is the only country in the region that protects the rights and liberties of its citizens and those in disputed areas. It is not a pleasant neighborhood they are part of. To be gay in Gaza, or in other Middle-Eastern countries, is akin to a death sentence. Syria's Assad has killed thousands of Syrians with chemical agents. Turkey harbors terrorists, and President Erdogan takes every opportunity to call on the destruction of Israel, even though the two nations are significant trading and tourist partners. It would take another book to list the well-documented human-rights violations and the countless illegal detentions and murders of Iranian citizens by the Iranian government, the largest supporter of international terrorism. There is not one country in the region that will not stop at nothing to maintain its power base, whose leaders do not seem to enjoy lifetime rule.

Israel, on the other hand, protects and nurtures the rights and liberties of its citizens. You can be who you are, voice your opinions, and believe me when I say this, Israelis are not shy about stating what they think. There are several religions that are respected and whose right to practice is the very fabric of the land. From the Bahai in Haifa, with its beautiful treasured temple, to the Bedouins, who are deeply integrated into the deserts of the Negev. Muslims are free to pray at their 400 mosques; all sects of Islam are granted the same opportunities of expression. Muslims, outside of the ruling sect, or those who are not adherents, do much better in Israel than the Islamic countries they hail from. In Israel, gay Muslims may walk hand in hand with their partners. Women do not have to cover their hair and face, no one is watching the citizenry and enforcing Sharia law. Israeli Arabs, of all genders, have the same opportunities as Israeli Jews to attend universities. Muslims are not required to serve in the Israeli army, however, some Israeli Arabs choose to, and like their fellow soldiers loyally and bravely defend their country. The Druze are a special sect of Muslims that are very strong and loyal supporters of Israel. Up until recently the Druzim have had their own IDF units. They are known for their bravery. The Druze Arabs are trusted Israelis and a fabric of Israel society.

Walk through the Old City of Jerusalem and you can find yourself walking upon the very stones that Jesus did. As you venture through the narrow streets of the Christian Quarter you will come across various denominations, including the Eastern Orthodox, Roman Catholic, Armenian Apostolic, Coptic, and Maronite Churches, among others. Protestant communities such as Anglicans, Lutherans, and Evangelicals are also present. All of these people, and the many that come from afar to visit, are respected and given free reign to contribute to the diversity that makes up the Jewish State of Israel.

Since the last King of Israel and the destruction of the Second Temple, Jews were often restricted from freely practicing Judaism and visiting their holy sites. Upon gaining control over Jerusalem fully in 1967, Israel has put an end to this prejudice. Israel is the only caretaker of Jerusalem that has safeguarded and restored the city's holy sites. Excavations and restorations include all sites of all religions, including the Al-Aqsa Mosque[1]. It is ironic that Israel, being the only country in the world who must defend its right to name its own capital and further defend its right to defend itself, is the only caretaker of Jerusalem that has refurbished it to its glory and has democratized it completely for all peoples of the earth. If it moves you, feel free to come and be close to your interpretation of your God in the holiest land on earth.

THE RIGHT OF RETURN

Anyone who identifies as a Jew, within the definition of who is a Jew[2], is instantly approved for citizenship. This is perhaps one of the most unique basic laws and unlike any immigration practices of other countries; it entitles anyone from anywhere that can prove Jewish heritage the right to citizenry, known as *Aliyah*. The word means

---

[1]   The Al-Aqsa Mosque, built in 705 CE by the Umayyad Caliph Al-Walid I, is located in Jerusalem's Old City. It is one of Islam's holiest sites and part of the Al-Haram Al-Sharif complex, also known as the Temple Mount.

[2]   Under Israel's Law of Return, a Jew is anyone with a Jewish mother or who converted to Judaism and isn't another religion's member. The law also includes their children, grandchildren, and spouses.

to go up, transcend, and rise. We use this word when someone is called to the Torah, beginning at 13 years of age, and to describe someone's bodily passing and ascension of the soul to the heavens. A person who has immigrated to Israel is referred to as an *Oleh Chadash*, which translates to "a new immigrant." This status comes with many benefits to entice the people to utilize the right of return. The question of who is a Jew is the subject of some controversy, and is the beginning of the debate regarding the floor and ceiling when it comes to separation of religion from state. According to tradition, Jewish lineage is matrilineal; however, to take advantage of the Right of Return for Israeli citizenship the requirements are more secular. But those having a Jewish father or grandfather, who converts to Judaism by either Orthodox, Conservative, or Reform movements, are considered Jewish insofar as the Right of Return. However, to marry within Israel, one needs to prove lineage exclusively according to Orthodox interpretation. This aligns with the idea that Jews are a people, who belong to our own religion called Judaism.

DIVERSITY, GOVERNANCE, AND POLITICS

Having spent enough time amongst Israelis, I am happily mistaken for a native, at least until I shamelessly speak in error-riddled Hebrew. I notice with pride the beautiful spectrum of people bustling through one of the most dynamic, active, and exciting places in the world, the interaction of so many different people without concern for their difference. There is a common Moses moment, the tags worn around people's necks declaring support for the hostages: *Let our people go!* I feel this universal unity amongst the people, an inclusion without judgment of a family concerned with staying together and learning to live with differences. I happened to be in Tel Aviv on the day of municipal elections, and throughout the city I saw many voting stations, as well as manned tables on the sidewalks and streets, calmly and peacefully supporting the slate of candidates in the lead-up to the vote. This is a social system of involvement and participation in political life without fear, another tenet of a democracy at work.

Just as I am proud of my spiritual homeland, I also feel a huge sense of privilege for having grown up in a free and democratic country. Government accountability and free speech are the rights of every citizen under the social contract. There is much debate on limits to expression and where the line is crossed. We can plainly see this in the growth of anti-Israel protests and encampments. Or what former Israeli government spokesman Eylon Levy calls the *tentifada*.

UNWELCOME IN MY OWN HOME

These protests have clearly crossed the line from an exercise in free speech to a call for violence. There is a difference between peaceful dialogue to bring attention to a matter of concern by a social strata, and the blatant threats used by pro-Hamas protesters. These protests are normalizing violence against Jews. It is only a matter of time before that violence becomes real. I believe that the situation has come to the crescendo of the obscene.

Prejudice and discrimination of Jews were the "welcome mat" to those that fled Eastern Europe for a new life in the early twentieth century. Many young men struggled with getting jobs and entering into universities with these strange *Yiddishe* names. It was 100 years ago, and the established citizens of America were not quite ready for this influx of Jews. That necessitated the effort to assimilate with name changes and the easing of observant adherence. Many felt that this is the New World, and we have to become more like *them*. My grandfather came over with the name Elishevitz and woke up to children with the name of Ellis. My friend's grandfather turned Goldberg into Gordon, and was then able to get a job. The stories are many, and they are all about the direct response to prejudice, not a threat to personal injury or one's life. This has now become about a fear of violent reprisal against the Jew. It is antisemitism in its most nefarious form.

Jews everywhere are feeling at risk. It has come to a place where I must now consider my safety before telling someone my name. This is the difference between then and now. It is abhorrent that anyone should feel unsafe and intimidated because of their heritage. I am a 3rd generation Canadian; for me to have to concern myself with the consequence of my name or a display of Jewish pride, to the point that I must fear for my well-being, is a sad place that we have come to. I remain very proud to see the level of restraint and calmness that continues in the Jewish collective voice. We need to believe that reason will prevail, that truth will be known, and that our governments, neighbors, and friends will come to understand that what is afoot here is a coordinated effort of the Jihad at work.

These encampments and protests by Kaffiyeh-masked participants raising signs of hateful slogans like "Globalize the Intifada" will ultimately encourage violence and promote the genocide of Jews. Nonetheless, these are the challenges of democratic free societies; sometimes even shutting them down and making arrests potentially conflicts with the right to demonstrate. The useful idiots of Hamas mock the moral compass of the social contract to taunt the police, government, and society.

An additional layer of provocation is that these protests are not always happening organically, but rather financed by bad actors who aim to destabilize and disrupt. The money trail has been much reported on, with trainloads of funds coming from terror-sponsoring nations and hard-left charitable organizations.

The organization "Plenty Collective" in Victoria, B.C., a recipient of public government grants, has been distributing significant amounts of money to individuals and groups participating in anti-Israel rallies. These funds reportedly go toward providing professional signage, banners, and logistical support, creating the appearance of more widespread grassroots support than might actually exist. The collective is said to disperse up to $20,000 a month to support these activities.[3]

In the United States, millionaire tech mogul Neville Roy Singham and his wife Jodie Evans are implicated in funding pro-Palestinian protests through organizations like the "People's Forum." These groups have been linked to organizing anti-Israel protests and spreading related propaganda.[4] These antisemitic marxist millionaires are using the money they have earned from the American dream to test the limits of free speech as they indirectly promote hate and genocide against the Jewish people.

A lawsuit filed in Virginia by victims of the October 7 attack alleges that organizations such as American Muslims for Palestine (AMP) and National Students for Justice in Palestine (NSJP) are not merely advocacy groups, but act as propaganda arms for Hamas. This suit claims that these groups provide material support to Hamas and coordinate protests and other activities on college campuses across the US[5]

One of the most controversial figures in the funding of Pro-Palestinian protests through organizations like Students for Justice in Palestine (SJP) is the billionaire George Soros. Through his Open Society Foundations he has reportedly funneled millions of dollars to groups following the events of October 7, 2023. Soros, born György Schwartz on August 12, 1930, grew up in Hungary, hiding his Jewish roots to escape persecution. He moved to England in 1947, where he studied at the London School of Economics under philosopher Karl Popper, whose ideas on open societies influenced Soros deeply. He went on to become one of the most influential and successful hedge

---

3   cija.ca/victoria_queer_activist_group_paying_pro_palestinian_protesters_loses_grant_true_north

4   heritage.org/global-politics/report/how-the-revolutionary-ecosystem-sustains-pro-palestinian-protesters-and-the

5   washingtonexaminer.com/news/justice/2989266/hamas-victims-sue-pro-palestinian-organizations/

fund managers in the United States, earning him the moniker "The Man Who Broke the Bank of England." Soros's philanthropic path is rooted in causes of social justice, likely influenced by his experience as a young Jew on the run from the repressive and violent regime of his native Hungary. He has been a controversial figure, especially as he has departed from his Jewish loyalties. He is accused of turning his back on his people; his support of anti-Israel sentiment has him labeled as a self-hating Jew. I know nothing more of the man than what I can research. It is about unaffiliated, uninformed, and apologetic Jews who get swept up in the liberal wokeness of the day and lose sight of both the impossible situation the Jewish State finds itself in and her right to defend and survive.

Just as there are people who will hate, there are also people who can freely choose to stand up and support Israel. On June 9, 2024, 50,000 people took part in the Walk with Israel in Toronto, and amongst them were Christians, Iranians, First Nations, and others who plainly see the injustice against Israel and the Jews. A peaceful march, celebrating with love and unity. No one wore masks or held threatening placards.

Democratic free society has the freedom to state the facts, voice opinions and concerns, and publicly investigate everything from misuses of funds to who is sleeping with whom. Try voicing concerns in Putin's Russia, Khomeni's Iran, Kim's North Korea, or XI's China. The list goes on: Saudi Arabia, Qatar, Bahrain, UAE, etc. In these countries, pushing for accountability can get you killed. Any dissent in the Palestinian controlled areas including Gaza are often met with the same result. In recent years, there have been a multitude of "accidental" deaths of business people and opposition leaders in Russia. Apparently, many people are affected with extreme vertigo, causing them to fall out of high-rise windows. The silencing of the lambs is a trait of closed societies. You would be challenged to find even one example of this in Israel. The demonstrations are loud, and for good reason. Israelis are not a quiet bunch. People have the freedom to camp outside of the Prime Minister's residence, unabated by his security team. The educational syllabus teaches governance and systems to growing generations of future citizens so that they will know their rights and feel empowered to exercise them.

ELECTED TO SERVE–WHAT A NOVEL CONCEPT

Just as other nation states have evolved, Israel needs to evolve, in this case to protect its future self from its current self. The voice of the general majority needs to be heard through its elected government. The United States has gone through several constitutional changes since 1791, generally in response to events that challenged its very existence, such as the Civil War and Reconstruction Amendments (1865-1870). Many other countries have made changes to their constitutions based on changing realities. For example, Finland and Sweden, traditionally neutral, have now pursued NATO in light of Russia's invasion of Ukraine. Since World War II and the cessation of colonial rule across the globe, many of the independent states that have emerged in the last 100 years have written constitutions. Israel is not the same society it was in 1948. The population is far more diverse and complex, and these demographics challenge democracy. Significant change is needed to safeguard Israel's future generations and the future generations of all Jews.

I firmly believe that October 7 was a result of the disunity of Israel (something which I will talk more about in the following chapter). It is of my opinion and likely shared by many others that this period of disunity eroded the morale of the people, and the army, and led to many of the security concerns that I posit will most certainly come out in the aftermath of a public commission of how Israel's borders were breached and over 1,200 Israelis were murdered. This disunity of Israel, I propose, is the direct result of a very much flawed electoral system, which I have now referred to a number of times.

As a political scientist and someone who has participated as a working member in Canada's electoral reform in the 1990 Lortie commission under the Mulroney government, and as a person who has watched closely the degradation and failures of where Israel's system elects its government and how that government governs, I submit that the transformation of Israel starts with the formalization of its basic laws into a constitution, and the electoral reform from a proportional to a constituency system.

A constitution by nature is more permanent, and does not waiver in the wind of political change. Having secured the rules of play, it will curtail the potential for increased disunity, which will result in ensuring that the national security of Israel will be prioritized. It will thus ensure the army's efforts are focused on security and defense, not a reflection of political motivations.

The current system of proportional representation supports extreme minority interest of the country over the popular sentiments of the electorate. This leads to political deal-making, whereby unqualified people may end up in highly sensitive areas of the country's security apparatus. Doing away with the current electoral system in favor of first-past-the-post in a parliamentary democracy will ensure elected representatives will represent the people. The priority of a politician should always be to serve their country first, their constituents second, the government third, and lastly their party.

Such changes will allow Israel the antidote to a host of other challenges the Jewish State faces. For example, to impose term limits on the PM, or allow changes to the judiciary.

Power is a drug, against which no man can avoid addiction. History has proven this.

The people need more say in who judges the nation, and with the change in political systems they will be able to do so unabated by the influence of the few.

INTO THE FUTURE

My son Eitan sometimes complains to me how bizarrely inefficient it is to do personal banking in Israel, deal with government licensing, or manage social insurance programs for health and welfare. He grins and says, "Aba, you would blow a gasket if you moved here and had to deal with all this stuff." This chapter has focused on the elements of Israeli government and society that highlight its democratic and socially inclusive values and structures, many of which could do with an overhaul; but outdated government structures and tedious banking processes do not make for a bad or undemocratic nation state.

Despite all the challenges the Jewish State faces internally, these frictions are because Israel is a democracy. Can this democracy work better? There is no question it can. The perfect storm has happened, which has exposed many gaps and weaknesses that Israel is now becoming painfully aware of. And the biggest chink in this armor, more a missing component than a weakness, is political leadership, which has failed to prevent and protect Israelis.

Politically, the single most fundamental challenge is the electoral system. It is a dated institution that no longer serves its masters. In 1948, Israel was a homogeneous society. There were small gaps between the left and the right in the political system. I do not think the many diverse interests and needs of today's ideological spectrum, with large polarizing gaps to contend with, were envisioned 75 years ago. The path for change in Israel becomes a complex and sensitive matter. There are simply too many special interests, and the spectrum between the haves and have nots, secular and religious, attitudes of passivity and those of action and demographics, continues full of the rich and colorful diversity of what it means to be an Israeli today; all of these are differences that have the potential to be divisive.

THERE ARE 3 THINGS THAT MUST BE CONSIDERED FOR THE FUTURE OF ISRAEL:

1. Israel's security and social services are the highest priorities in its hierarchy of needs. It is therefore critical that the military and the social policies of this country are given the best available tools to be successful in their missions.

2. Israel's Defense Forces need to be inclusive of all citizens. This means that all citizens, including the highly religious sects, must undergo conscription for military or social services. It is no longer sustainable for these populations to be given a pass. If a person benefits by the social contract of welfare and security, they must do their part. Another key area for military evolution is how women are treated and respected within the IDF. One of the main failings of October 7 was direct reports from a womens' intelligence battalion being ignored due to gender bias.

3. A strong democracy cares for its most vulnerable and provides the maximum opportunity for its citizens to flourish, to have families, and to grow old with dignity. The Ministry of Welfare and Social services is critical for Israel's internal survival, and must address its value in a realistic and equitable manner for all. The military and social services are linked, and will be strengthened when the Jewish state has a government of the people, elected by the people.

Ultimately, Israel must return to its roots, achieve unity, and come together once again with a common vision for social collaboration and the respect that binds us and protects the *Derech Eretz,* the Way of the Land.

JEWISH DISUNITY

WHEN THE ISRAELITES WERE PREPARING to finally enter the land of their forefathers and claim their divine inheritance, Moses stood before his people. As one of his last acts before his death and succession by Joshua, he reminded the children of Israel that they were once slaves in Egypt, and, as they gathered on the precipice of nationhood, they would no longer be strangers in their own land. That they would prosper in peace, and that their people had the knowledge and power to become great unto themselves and amongst the other nations of the world. For this future to be realized, there was just one condition: so long as the People of the Book followed the basic laws of the *Way of the Land* they would receive divine protection. The way of the land depended on one seemingly simple foundational element, to "love your fellow as you would love yourself." Respect, consideration, and empathy were the cornerstones to a healthy, thriving community. And along with this guidance came a stark warning: disobeying this one grounding principle of the Jewish nation would bring a litany of curses upon the people. In the Hebrew Bible[1] curses include illness, defeat by enemies, foreign interference, drought, crop failures, mental suffering, and physical afflictions. Within this guiding testament can be found one of the oldest adages of a recipe for defeat: *be divided and you will be conquered*.

This biblical prediction seems to have held true in several instances of early Jewish history when the chosen fell from their perch. In 930 BCE, following the death of King Solomon, ancient Israel split into the northern kingdom of Israel and the southern kingdom of Judah. This division weakened their collective military and political strength, making them more vulnerable to external threats. The northern kingdom was eventually conquered by the Assyrians in 722 BCE, and the southern kingdom by the Babylonians in 586 BCE. After a successful revolt, the Maccabean uprising against the Seleucid Empire in the 2nd century BCE, internal divisions emerged from both political infighting and differing religious views, leading to weakening leadership and vulnerability, culminating in a 63 BCE conquest by the Romans. The Bar Kokhba[2] uprising against the Roman Empire (132-136 AD) resulted for a brief time in an independent state of Israel. The period is known as the last major nationhood period of ancient history, but internal

---

1   Leviticus 26 and Deuteronomy 28

2   Simon Bar Kokhba led the Jewish revolt against Roman rule from 132 to 136 AD, known as the Bar Kokhba Revolt. He emerged as a messianic figure, heralded as the "son of a star," and briefly established an independent Jewish state where he enacted religious and national governance.

divisions over leadership and strategy, as well as harsh Roman responses, led once again to failure. The aftermath was an 1,800-year dispersion and diaspora of world Jewry that lasted until the creation of the modern state of Israel in 1948.

The establishment of modern Israel came on the tail of one of the most horrific and devastating periods of Jewish history. Thirty-six percent of world Jewry—6 million souls—were murdered by the Nazis and their collaborators. 1500 years of rich Jewish culture was almost wiped from Europe.

When Israel became a recognized nation state in 1948 it was led for the next nearly 50 years by Holocaust survivors; people who understood firsthand the terrible price of the rise of antisemitism. Yitzhak Rabin and Menachem Begin, both former Prime Ministers of Israel[3], who as young men were orphaned by the Holocaust in Europe, found themselves washed up on the shores of Palestine. They fought the Nazis and then fought the British.[4] They understood that as long as there was a Jewish State there would never again be the wholesale murder of Jews. At the time, Jews everywhere became unified by the common cause of their survival, the blessings and curses of their people fresh in their minds.

When post-Holocaust survivors took the helm, such as Prime Ministers Ehud Barak, Benjamin Netanyahu, and Ariel Sharon, these were men experienced on the battlefield of Israel's major wars. They understood the neighborhood they lived in and the reality of the enemy knocking at the door. However, even survivors of the worst Jewish tragedy since the 15th century and battle hardened soldiers can slip over time from being realists to idealists, with a dream that everyone can become a partner in peaceful coexistence.

---

3   Yitzhak Rabin served as Prime Minister from 1974-1977 and 1992-1995. Menachem Begin served from 1977-1983.

4   Yitzhak Rabin and Menachem Begin fought against British rule in Palestine leading up to the 1948 declaration of independence and establishment of the State of Israel. Rabin was a member of the Haganah, and Begin led the Irgun. Their efforts were part of the Jewish insurgency to end British control and establish Israel as an independent state.

I suppose when you see enough death in war, you want to believe there can be a different reality. And while I would like to join the ranks of thinking this way, the reality is that as long as the lovers of death are determined to murder innocent Jewish souls, it remains an *us* or *them* equation. "Better their mothers cry at their son's grave than our mothers cry at ours," the simplified moniker of being a soldier in the IDF. The People of the Book, made in the image of God, struggle with such pragmatic realism. The duty of defense is not an easy route for the Jew, who is naturally a lover of life, and the taking of a life, for any reason, even in the defense of your own, is a deep tarnishment of the soul that for many becomes too much to bear. This is, I believe, the ultimate root of the disunity. Beyond religious observance, there are many who value life to the extent that they cannot live with the cost of defending themselves. It is this very foundation of humanism that the Jihad manipulates so well.

The modern Jewish State of Israel stems from a political movement called Zionism, coined in 1890 by Nathan Birnbaum, an Austrian-Jewish nationalist and journalist. Birnbaum used the term to describe the nationalist movement aiming to establish a Jewish homeland in Palestine. It comes from the word *Zion,* which is a biblical term for Jerusalem and, by extension, the land of Israel. Theodor Herzl (1860-1904), an Austro-Hungarian journalist and playwright, was deeply influenced by the Dreyfus Affair, which he covered as a young journalist. The Dreyfus affair was a political scandal in France in the 1890s involving the framing and wrongful conviction of Jewish officer Alfred Dreyfus because he was a Jew.[5]

---

5   Alfred Dreyfus was exonerated after a lengthy legal battle. Following his wrongful conviction for treason in 1894 and imprisonment on Devil's Island, new evidence emerged in 1896 indicating that Major Ferdinand Walsin Esterhazy was the actual culprit. This led to a second court-martial in 1899, which again found Dreyfus guilty despite the evidence in his favor. However, intense public outcry and advocacy by prominent figures, including writer Émile Zola, who penned the famous "J'Accuse...!" letter, kept the case in the public eye. In 1899, Dreyfus was pardoned by President Émile Loubet and released from prison, but it was not until 1906 that a civilian court fully exonerated him. The French Supreme Court annulled his previous convictions, and Dreyfus was reinstated into the army with the rank of major. This exoneration was a significant moment in French history, highlighting issues of antisemitism and injustice within the military and judicial systems.

The event highlighted antisemitism, prompting him to advocate for a Jewish homeland. Herzl became the prominent leader of the Zionist national movement following the publication of his 1896 manifesto *Der Judenstaat* (The Jewish State), in which he argued that the solution to the "Jewish Question" was the establishment of a Jewish State. This work laid the philosophical foundations for Zionism, advocating for Jewish migration to Palestine and the establishment of a national homeland as a response to global antisemitism and as a place for Jewish cultural rebirth. Herzl was instrumental in organizing the First Zionist Congress in Basel, Switzerland, in 1897, which established the World Zionist Organization and declared its aim of establishing a home for the Jewish people in Palestine secured by public law. Herzl was elected as the first president of the Zionist Organization, a position he held until his death in 1904.

The early days of independence marked some key divisive issues within Israel that set the stage for tensions between religious and secular ideology—the social division between the Ashkenazi and Sephardi Jews, and right/left ideological polarities, especially when it came to politics and the peace process.

There were differing organized approaches to the realization of the Zionist dream. These were coordinated and divided into three main approaches: Practical, Labor, and Revisionist Zionism. Practical Zionism focused on infrastructure building over political lobbying and creating a viable Jewish society on the ground. Labor Zionism, headed by such prolific figures as David Ben-Gurion (1886-1973), Israel's first Prime Minister, and Berl Katznelson (1887-1944), a thought-leader of his time, focused on the socialist principles of equality and workers' rights, and was instrumental in building the economic and social structures that would support a future state, including the Histadrut (General Federation of Labor). Revisionist Zionism was founded by Ze'ev Jabotinsky (1880-1940), advocating for a more militant approach to establishing the Jewish state. Jabotinsky believed in the use of force, if necessary, to secure

Jewish rights and territory. This approach led to the formation of Jewish defense organizations like the Irgun, which were more radical and military-oriented than the mainstream Haganah, which later evolved into the Israel Defense Forces.

The Haganah (meaning "defense" in Hebrew) was the main Jewish paramilitary organization and was closely aligned with the mainstream Zionist leadership and Labor Zionism. In contrast, groups like the Irgun and Lehi (Stern Gang) broke away from the Haganah due to ideological differences, advocating for more aggressive tactics against both British authorities and Arab populations.[6] Haganah, Irgun, and Lehi differed in tactics and ideology. Haganah favored defense and cooperation with the British. Irgun, more militant, opposed British rule directly. Lehi, the most extreme, targeted British and Arab forces alike. Their divisions reflected varying approaches to achieving Jewish independence. These divisions reflected broader ideological disputes within Zionism about the best path to Jewish statehood, ranging from purely diplomatic efforts to grassroots settlement, and from defensive military strategies to offensive military tactics. The differing strategies often led to internal conflicts, but also provided a diverse set of approaches that ultimately contributed to the establishment and defense of the State of Israel. When Israel was established, so was a unified defense force known as the Israel Defense Forces (IDF). The word *Defense* is not some accident of branding. It is intentional: the blending of ideologies from these three early military factions, that while Jews will never again be led to their deaths like sheep, they will also respect the humanity from which they are born.[7]

---

6   The Haganah was established in 1920, the Irgun in 1931, and the Lehi in 1940. All three were Jewish paramilitary groups fighting the British and Arab factions in British Mandate Palestine, now the Jewish State of Israel. They were integrated into the Israel Defense Forces (IDF) in 1948, shortly after Israel's declaration of independence.

7   It's important to note the main descriptor word "Defense". Israel has always been a force of defense for the protection of the Jewish people. Never has the IDF been used as an aggressor force to acquire or expand its lands other than for defensive reasons.

SECULAR VS RELIGIOUS

The early Jewish refugees, many of whom grew up in the Eastern European *Shtetl*,[8] came from religious families. For some, the bond with God had been broken in the loss and tragedy of the Holocaust. Others doubled down on religious observance lest they abandon themselves to a non-observant life, which was seen as the ultimate victory for the Nazis. Freedom from the village by the way of a secular life became a Jewish ideological movement that clashed with Jewish religious observance. In the country's early days, the focus was agrarian and military; farming was a kickstarter to the economy, and survival on the battlefield was key to survival of the country. The pressing need to house, feed, and heal a population overtook peoples' ideological and cultural differences for a time. As the country matured and developed, however, the division between secular Jews and the ultra-Orthodox Haredi community deepened. Issues such as military draft exemptions for Haredi students, public transportation on the Sabbath, and the role of religious law in civil matters are still material points of contention. Today, there remains very little middle ground in Israel when it comes to religion. As a modern traditional Jew, I am viewed as very religious by the secular, and not religious enough by the fervently observant.

ASHKENAZIC AND SEPHARDI JEWS

The expulsion of Jews from the Pan-Arab world almost immediately following the newly established state of Israel created a significant welfare problem for the young country. Within a very short period of time, Israel was put into a predicament to house, clothe, and feed the 1 million people who arrived after 1948 until well into the 1980s. The more established Ashkenazic Jews saw the arriving Sephardic Jews with differing customs, prayers, and mode of dress. They

---

8   A shtetl was a small town in Eastern Europe with a dense Jewish population, central to Jewish life until World War II. Characterized by close-knit communities, they revolved around synagogues, local markets, and Yiddish culture. The Holocaust largely eradicated these towns, symbolizing a lost era of Jewish history.

were described as Arab Jews. This discrimination was embarrassingly ingrained into the social fabric of Israeli society and still exists in many ways today. The Eastern European Jews saw themselves as more educated and civilized in this new secular world, and the Sephardic Jews were often looked down upon. Much to the credit of the IDF conscription, as I have mentioned earlier on, the forced arrangement of Ashkenazic and Sephardic Jews to work together for their survival and form a brotherhood beyond their origins is the melting pot that has eventually blended the socialization between these two groups. However the struggle between them has left deep scarring in Jewish unity.

In the 1980s, following the exodus of Jews from Ethiopia in Operation Solomon, discrimination once again flourished between the newly-arrived black Jews and their hosts. Again, it has taken a couple of generations for cultural assimilation to take effect, though cultural and racial division almost certainly remains to some extent.

SHAKE UP AND WAKE UP IN THE IDF

While Israel has mandatory conscription, for most, it serves as a point of pride and passage. The army has a very disciplined structure, and there is no place for politics within its ranks. "If anyone expresses an interest in political ambitions, they are not serving under me," stated an IDF general, my close friend. Dissent in the IDF is almost unheard of; any of its leadership will disagree with the attempt to leverage military assets to protest the government. However, during the height of the judiciary reform protests, it was unfortunate to see a moment of dissent among military ranks. Reservists in the air force and military signed letters refusing to serve under the current government. The IAF chief, Major General Tomer Bar, acknowledged the significant damage these statements caused to the force's cohesion and readiness.[9] These public com-

---

9   Fabian, Emanuel. "Gallant decries 'dangerous' refusal threats by reservists: 'a reward for our enemy.'" *Times of Israel.* July 11, 2023. https://www.timesofisrael.com/liveblog_entry/gallant-decries-dangerous-threats-by-reservists-not-to-show-up-a-reward-for-our-enemy/

ments are a departure from the unwritten rules of the IDF. As I have mentioned earlier, there are those who have gone so far as to blame the timing of Ten-Seven on the disunity in Israel during the judicial reform crisis. One of those is Middle East scholar Mordechai Kedar. He explained his theory in a National Post article of July 3, 2024:

"But Hamas smelled weakness and a fissure in Israeli society when 200 Israeli F-15 pilots were boycotting training to protest judicial reforms in March 2023. The in-fighting and mass demonstrations 'destroyed the image of Israel as a powerful country' to its neighbors. 'It inflated the Jihad glands in the bodies of our neighbors. They went out in the streets to celebrate. "No fighters, no pilots!" It encouraged them to start the war,' Kedar said."

In the aftermath of Ten-Seven there will likely be a significant IDF shake up, resulting in the departure of the entire top slate of military leadership. And so there should be, as there are no second chances when it comes to Israel's security. I expect and hope to see a much-hardened military command akin to the days when Holocaust survivors filled these positions, fresh from the reality of the murder of 6 million Jews and equipped with the resolve necessary to effectively protect the Jewish State. Israel now needs the unquestioning dedication and follow-through of a military that honors the roots of its inception, without exception, without distraction, and without influence from an external world that does not care for Israel's best interests and in many cases actively opposes them.

HUMBLE AS YOU ARE, I THANK YOU!

My son Eitan will most certainly criticize me for writing his praises. He will say to me, "Aba, this is not the way we operate. We do not need your praise. What I do is part of a collective obligation. It is a duty, and it is the *Way of the Land.*" And yet, to be honest, I cannot help my overflowing emotions to thank the people of the

IDF for their courage and heroism. Thank you to all of my heroes. It is because of their sacrifices that I as a Jewish person can live anywhere with my head held high and have the agency to call out antisemitism without fear.

THAT WHICH BINDS US–MIGHTY AND GREAT PEOPLE

There are common beliefs that bind the Jewish people, beginning with us standing at the foot of Mount Sinai, where the Ten Commandments were delivered. When Jews achieve unity they are worthy of nothing less than the direct proclamation by God that we are "a mighty and great people", together, and not apart.

Jews are a resilient bunch. Stubborn, but charitable. Like any family, there will be disagreements. But there will also always be that softer place in our hearts that is written into our DNA. We are lovers of life. We live and build for the next generation. It is time for the Jews and for Israel to remember Jacob's determination. The Jewish struggle is for the love of all humanity. And for the Jews alone, there is one undeniable fact that binds us in the fight for survival; so long as the Jewish state of Israel exists there will never again be a time that we are led like sheep to our deaths. The words *Never Again*[10] depend on the continued existence of Israel. For this reason alone we must act in concert to protect our future. *Achdut,* (our) togetherness will always be our greatest weapon against evil.

THE SCAPEGOAT NARRATIVE

A strong, united stance against threats to Jewish people is our best defense against harmful ideas that could lead to violence.

Starting with the Covid pandemic in 2020 and growing into a roller coaster of economic concern, paired with what I see as the

---

10   The phrase "never again" originated post-World War II, prominently used by Holocaust survivors and Jewish leaders to vow that genocides like the Holocaust would never happen again. It gained prominence through speeches and memorials, particularly after the Holocaust.

collapse of Western governments' meaningful ability to lead, the narrative of scapegoating the Jew is happening. The ideas and claims being made are bizarre, but, like the Elders of Zion authorship, reality is what you make of it, and eventually becomes truth in the minds of people looking for a target to blame. It is easier to dismiss a bunch of extremely disillusioned and angry people passing them off as a fad of sorts. But as they march through the streets of our cities, their faces covered, and the constant messaging which promotes violence to the Jews. We cannot afford to make that mistake of not seeing it for what it truly is. The echoes of a past right out of the Jew-hate playbook.

We must be vigilant to ensure the survival of Israel, because by extension the Jewish State of Israel is the single most defensible barrier to Global Jihad.

THE WAKE UP CALL

I MET WITH MY SHIN BET CONTACT, Jacob, in the stylish Kempinski hotel cafe. Outside, beyond the floor-to-ceiling glass, people walked, ran and cycled along the Tel Aviv Tayelet, the sea shimmering blue behind them. The background was beautiful and joyful, the conversation not so much.

"In every military campaign there is a front line of defense," Jacob said, his words calm, matter-of-fact. "Israel is the front line of defense for the world. If we fall, so does the world."

He allowed me a moment to absorb this, then continued with almost smug certainty. "The world needs not worry about being invaded." A thin smile stretches his stern face. He gently slaps my knee for emphasis. "The invasion has already happened!"

If Israel is the front line of the world, then the front line of the world is under heavy attack, and the enemy grows stronger every day. Israel is surrounded by the Party of Terror from every side: Hamas, Hezbollah, Houthi, and Syria are proxies of Iran, loudly vowing for Israel's destruction. Violent attacks can happen within Israel at any time. The entire country lives under constant fight or flight stress; children are growing up with the trauma of expecting life-changing, destructive events in the flash of a moment. Public confidence in the safety net is at an all time low. There are protests all over America and Europe, thousands of people calling for the destruction of Israel. Encampments on university campuses have become well organized (and funded) campaigns, attracting large crowds calling for the outright purging of Jews. The Jews of the world, justifiably, are increasingly feeling isolated and betrayed. Betrayed by police, politicians, and heads of state—who either turn a blind eye or fail to address the growing calls for violence. The worst of the betrayals comes from Israel's strongest allies, who have only stood with Israel on condition, hold Israel closely under a microscope, jump to conclusions shaped by a biased media, and maintain that this conflict is two sided—giving credence to Hamas. The call for a ceasefire supposes that there is someone legitimate to sit down and talk with. Often, the terms do not deal with the release of all hostages and the demilitarization of Hamas. It is madness to assume a situation where terror is given the opportunity to rearm and survive to kill another day.

There is a looming state of being unsafe, which festers for all Jews, as the message of Jihad is normalized. I worry for my children and for my home. "I will not be caught off guard," I tell myself. "We will pack up and leave… but where shall we go?" I cannot believe I am having these thoughts.

The *National Post* reported that the McGill University encampment offered a 2024 summer camp. This was the headline:

"McGill encampment to host an anti-Israel revolutionary youth summer program. We pledge to educate the youth of Montreal and redefine McGill's 'elite' (institutional) legacy by (transforming) its space into one of revolutionary education."

The social media image for this advert was accompanied by an image of men wearing keffiyehs and clutching machine guns.[1] Though the event never happened, the fact that the very idea was taken seriously by some may have encouraged others to take actions. Perhaps, the Canadian from Alberta who flew into Israel to attack border guards with a kitchen knife was made to believe that his actions were okay and, in some bizarre way, rewarded.

COMPLETE SILENCE FROM OUR POLITICIANS

If these useful idiots and the Jihadists of evil are not stopped now, something terrible will happen. Neither the lone wolf or the organized terror cell will discriminate.

The funding of aid relief into Gaza must be properly audited, with incorruptible safeguards in place to make sure this aid is not intercepted by Hamas or any other radical organization for the use of terror. Hamas has built over 300 miles of tunnels, created manufacturing capabilities for mass destruction, radicalized an entire population, and sullied an entire generation, all under the noses of the United States, Canada, Europe, and Israel, the latter of which may have arguably prostituted themselves through compromises. Qatar and the Pan Arab world have provided an open checkbook to Hamas.

To do this, the Islamic Republic of Iran, the ultimate sponsor of terror, must be neutralized. Indeed, for the safety and peace of the world and for the Iranian people. The door US President Barack Obama purposely and naively opened must finally be closed. Obama's subservient bow was a license to terrorize. To negotiate

---

1   National Post Staff. "Police probing McGill encampment's 'revolutionary youth summer program'". *National Post.* June 15, 2024. https://nationalpost.com/news/anti-israel-summer-program-mcgill-university-encampment

with terror is to legitimize terrorism. We will pay dearly for the consequence of not listening to the messages they are brazenly sending to our streets and neighborhoods around the world. They are raising their middle finger and taunting our love for life, and we are unable to respond because we cannot acknowledge the evil it brings. Must we add more dates of terror to our calendars to remind us of where current events are leading us?

Ignorance is complicity, and is not an acceptable defense when it comes to human lives. Haters have the choice not to hate. There is a choice to include *everyone* in the diversity, equity, and inclusion the left proudly stands by. These treaties must equally apply to the Jewish people, without which the participants of these movements become the worst discriminators and haters. It is particularly unfortunate that the good people of social justice and equality have been duped into believing that to advance their own cause they must scapegoat the Jew.

We must stop the victimization of the Palestinian people and hold their leaders accountable for failing to take the many opportunities offered for true and lasting peace. The only "peace" the PA, Hamas, Hezbollah, Iran, and Syria are willing to negotiate includes the complete destruction of Israel and the annihilation and capitulation of the Jewish people. When Western leaders call for a ceasefire, or smile for the camera alongside known terrorist leaders and middle-eastern dictators, this is what they are legitimizing.

In the face of the non-truths and hateful sentiment sweeping across the Western world, Israel remains the safety net of the world, the front line of defense from Jihad. Israel will always be a safe haven for those who seek the freedom to be Jewish and the freedom for all religions and orientations to be themselves. To ensure its security, Israel must undergo change, return to its roots, come back together as a family, and evolve our leadership to better serve its people and find inclusivity for all. I have the faith that we can get there. This will take a miracle, but Israel is the land of miracles.

HEALING

IN THE FIRST PAGES, I stated that this was the book I would have preferred not to write. The ideas came pouring out of me in answer to the night terrors that would wake me well before the first light. I was cold and drenched in a fearful sweat for the well-being of my son serving in the IDF; for all our sons and daughters of the village. For a nation utterly devastated by what happened on October 7, a day now marked in history forever, and for a world Jewry that is reminded every day since Ten-Seven of the Global Jihad agenda to annihilate the Jewish people. The rise of global antisemitism is happening on a level never before experienced by most people alive today. The betrayal of the world is reminiscent of other dark times in Jewish history.

No person being chased by the beast should be left to fight it off on their own. The Jewish people and any good Christian and Muslim stand united together to call out the terrible deeds of those who propagate senseless hatred, Jewish exclusion, and terrorism.

October 7 should be a traumatic jolt for anyone who is a lover of life. We must stand united and resolved to make the world a safer place for the future generations that will follow. For if the lovers of life cannot heal the hate, we are truly lost at sea.

I met George, a doctor from Germany, at a healing retreat on Koh Phangan, an island in the south of Thailand. During the first of our many conversations, I described some of the ideas that would later become these chapters, and in answer to his piqued interest I went on to explain to him the events that took place in Israel on October 7 and the theater of the world since. We got around to the existential question on what it takes to save our world from itself, and both readily agreed in the simplicity that peace comes from love. And to love is to heal. Our conversation turned to philosophy and the infinity of the cosmos. It's the kind of place that leads you into these thoughts. I brought up the biblical story of Jonah, the unwilling oracle, who warned the people of Nineveh, who repented without question because they came to understand the severity of the warnings and the opportunity to change. I asked George: Where is today's Jonah to tell the haters wrong from right? to warn us of the consequences of hate?

The next morning George sat beside me and told me had he reflected on the prior evening's discourse.

"I agree," he said with slow, carefully chosen words. "*Both sides need to heal.*"

He saw my body tense up at the reference to "sides." The idea of shared moral equivalence between Israel and Hamas is a typical red herring of those that will not fully condemn Hamas and stand for Israel. George gently raised a placating hand and asked me for patience. "Can you for a moment accept that there is a part of Hamas within you?" I caught my breath.

We sat in silence while I pondered this and took effort to examine George through a different lens. He has no connection to Israel; he is not affected by what happened on October 7 except that he is a lover of life and a healer and he is saddened that this event has happened in a world he deems has turned itself upside down. He lives his life in a bubble, not intentionally, but rather because he was born into it; a privileged Western bubble with all the trappings, including the luxury to question his existence and the next steps in his life. He is a good person. He is not committed to any specific ideology, except for his life and those of his patients. He is not a liberal nor does he consider himself a conservative. He will not take up a placard and join a protest. He believes that all people should live together in peace. He stays out of business that is not his to judge, because he knows his opinion will have no effect on the outcome. It occurred to me that his apathy is part of the challenge the world faces; he places his complete trust in his government to manage the situation. He corrected me when I suggested this, and instead claimed it is humanity itself that he trusts. "Humanity will *eventually* find their way, they always do," he said. But I disagreed. "This is not a stream of water trickling through the path of least resistance," I said. "To avoid long and painful consequences, we sometimes must act to protect humanity from and for itself."

The impossibility of the situation Israel finds itself in is a predicament for the free world. To counter the epidemic of Global Jihad will require some sacrifice of liberty, and this can be a slippery slope. And yet, it has already begun. The UK has the most extensive and sophisticated closed-circuit video monitoring system of its kind in the world, complete with facial recognition and AI capabilities. There are few places left in London where you can escape someone watching you. This invasion of privacy is the compromise for security. But this does nothing to weed out the problem of radicalization by its roots. These bandaid solutions will only drive the Jihad further underground into the metaphorical and literal tunnels. The only long-term solution depends on overhauling how the next generation comes to see their world. Confronting the hold that the radicals have institutionalized over young people, dismantling the arenas for hate, and policing the spread of lies and calls to Jihad, is of the most critical importance. Like the cameras in London, it is not pretty to impose law and confront hate.

I returned to the present with the clang of a spoon against my metal cup. George waited for my answer. Can I accept that there is something of Hamas in all of us? It is a difficult question, because on the face of it it seems a bizarre and hurtful theory by someone who knows little about the situation on the ground. But I have come to respect George, and I knew he was not playing with me. What he asked me is if we are all capable of playing the part of Hamas if we were wearing the shoe on the other foot.

I looked across at George and asked him thoughtfully if he has siblings. "Yes," he answered, not really sure of where I was going with this. "I have a sister, she is eight years younger than myself." I asked him if he ever felt jealousy toward her. He assures me that he did. When she first arrived home, the focus of his entire world shifted to her. "Did you ever have evil and violent thoughts about how to deal with that? Did you plan to kill her?" I asked, to his wide-eyed look. Of course, this is extreme, but relevant. "I love my sister to this day," he stammers. "I would never harm her." He takes a slow breath in and admits "regardless of how much she may have infuriated me as a young boy."

In the story of Cain and Abel. Cain, the older brother, is jealous at the acceptance of Abel's' sacrifice to God, and in response he kills him. Cain is new to all these powerful emotions, being only the third person to ever live, he has no context for *dealing* and how to manage these feelings. Leading up to the act, he could not have understood the consequences of his actions, yet as his brother lay unmoving beneath him, he realizes immediately by some intuitive force that he has committed a grave transgression. "Am I my brother's keeper?" he responds to God, when questioned of Abel's whereabouts, a clear defensive diversion away from the moral consequence of what he has done. There are direct lessons that can be interpreted from this story; the moral wrongness of murder, the accountability, the shame and regret, and the divine justice that follows.

In my own paraphrasing of Genesis 4:11-12, I quote; "Cain, the earth received your brother's blood from your hand, thereby the ground will give you nothing in return, and you are banished and will walk the earth without home." This is a very clear and powerful statement that is made, one that neither Jews, Christians, or Muslims will disagree with. A person who commits murder will become a wanderer, a refugee wherever they go. They are Cain, who was deserving of justice, even though no lawbook had ever told him murder was wrong.

What happened on October 7 was a collective sociopathic act that crossed a line from which there can be no return, not just for the Hamas terrorists that came armed with guns and bombs, but for the people of Gaza who supported the invasion and followed in its wake, rampaging through residential areas, pillaging, burning, and committing barbaric acts of rape and live dismemberment. The people of Gaza, everyday citizens, came to set fire to buildings with people still inside. If you poll Gazans today, the majority will support Hamas and celebrate the events of October 7. If you survey the Palestinian people in the lands controlled by the PA, chances are there will be a strong empathy for the Gazans whose immorality brought them to their own destruction. If you poll the Pan Arab world, you will likely find an alarming number of people in support of Hamas. The October 7 attacks ignited global outrage, revealing deep-seated hatred and a disturbing lack of empathy. Those who march in support of Israel's destruction or celebrate Hamas's violence are morally complicit in these heinous acts. Like Cain, who committed the first murder despite having no explicit prohibition, these supporters cannot claim ignorance as a defense for their actions. And this is the difference between a terrorist, a terrorist sympathizer, and a fundamentally good person. The masked people holding placards celebrating Hamas and chanting for the genocide of Jews, participating in protests and encampents, these are not just the useful idiots of Hamas, these are useful evildoers *for* Hamas.

"So no, George," I say with finality in my voice. "Thankfully, there is not one particle of Hamas that can be found within me." I continued, "For two sides of healing to exist, there must first exist two aggrieved parties that play by rational and reasonable rules. As soon as one party crosses the line into terrorism, they forfeit the privilege of being a *side*."

A man murders his ex-wife. He is unrepentant, and yells at the court as he is hauled away, "I would do it again!" Has he not forfeited his side at the negotiating table? Does he have any opportunity to come back to a side that can heal?

The only way that there can be "another" side is where there is responsibility and accountability. This is the only way that *they* can be included in a process of healing. Once terror is denounced and terror groups like Hamas and Hezbollah are disbanded, demilitarized, and shunned; once there is a declaration of a willingness for coexistence; once Israel's right to exist and defend itself as a sovereign nation is recognized, only then can there be two sides.

What better place to write about healing than in a place of healing? The knowingness of what I must say comes through my writing. I am overcome with a depth of sadness I have not known before. There is a tear in my heart and my throat closes with fear, different from any other loss or anxiety I have ever experienced. I am a ship adrift on the reality of what is, my brain desperately trying to navigate the sorrow my soul endures for the senseless loss of life in Israel that took place on October 7. The aftermath of the truth is the realization that we are a world bleeding without a mechanism to clot. This is Ten-Seven.

How do the people of Israel heal? How do they defend their lives whilst staying true to the moral compass that values life and protects freedom? I know the answer will be found, and am even more confident of the truth, as I am surrounded by the observation of young Israelis honed to this place from where I write this closing chapter. I see the love and affection, I see healing in motion, bright minds peeking through eyes that remain vibrant even though they have eulogized family and friends. They have come here to return the apple to the tree, to give back the knowledge they do not want to know, the scenes they wished never to see, to come back to the authenticity of their innocence.

The Jewish nation will eventually heal. The children of Israel, who struggled with the angel in the dark of the night and was bestowed the blessing of God. But what is our price for survival? To tarnish our souls for what must be done in self defense? For what is the price we must pay if we are an island in our healing and the world does not listen? The world must listen to what is already known, but refuses to acknowledge the truth. The whole of Israel's hearts and all decent people of the world are torn by the cries of those remaining hostages, whose parents, grandparents, cousins, and friends cannot bear each day.

I met Nerene, a 33-year old mother of three boys under the age of five. Her husband was born in Kibbutz Magen, a small community less than 2 kilometers from Gaza. Magen is where they have lived, this was their home, where they were raising their children. On October 7 she was enjoying an early morning coffee in solitude when the sirens started blaring. Several members of her community were murdered. Terrorists tried to break into her safe room, where she sheltered with her children, thinking at any moment they would die. The residents have all been displaced since that day. Some were moved to hotels, others went to relatives. Nerene eventually *escaped*

Israel with her husband and children to this faraway Thai island. She began to cry as she looked down at her middle son, asleep on her lap, playing nervously with his golden curls. She cannot go back. She cannot imagine living anywhere else than in her Kibbutz in Israel, but now her home is gone.

"I do not trust them (the government). I do not believe anything they will tell me. I know it will happen again. How can I return, when any moment it can happen? I am alone here, with no help. I feel forgotten." My heart is wrenched by her words and despair.

I asked her, if she could make demands so she could feel safe to return, what would they be?

"Our military was supposed to be the strongest. They have become weak and overconfident. How could they let this happen?" She was visibly struggling with our conversation, her suffering is so painful to observe, I feel guilty for forcing myself into this intimate space.

"You have to look after yourself," I said to her. "Nerene, you must ask and find the help you need, that is most important. Ask for help."

She smiled thinly through her tears and told me she will think about her list of demands for her safe return. She never thought of this, and it made her feel more in control of the situation, if only just a little.

Leor and I met at a co-working space on the island. Unlike Nerene, she is fortunate that she works remotely and can afford to travel. Not so for many other displaced Israelis, families who must cram themselves into a government-issue hotel room.

"I am from Kiryat Shmona," Leor smiled. "I'm a Northern girl."

Leor was evacuated from her home on October 7. She loves her home, yet cannot return with missiles flying overhead every day and no time to reach a shelter. She appreciates that she can enjoy this beautiful paradise, but she misses her family and her way of life. Leor considers herself part of a generation of Israeli peace activism. I asked her, as I asked Nerene, what needs to happen for her safe return.

"I want to understand them (the Palestinians). I am against war, but the reality is I am now running, and I cannot return home to be blown up at any time." She looked down, almost embarrassed by what came next. "We must remove the threat by any means. This is the saddest thing I can say."

Ilan, my grocer back in Tel Aviv, has salt and pepper hair, sandpapery skin, and enormous, powerful hands that, when they envelop mine, they radiate with warmth. But when he talks about October 7 and where his life is today, it is in a distant, almost dissociative manner, as if telling me about things that happened to someone else. Ilan held his safe door closed for eight hours. He killed three terrorists with his own hands. He buried 53 people. He is about my age, perhaps younger, yet you would think him much older. I am worried for him and his family. He has not yet started to feel. Perhaps he knows better than to open that door. I hope that soon he will find the courage to accept what is, what has happened, and begin, slowly, to heal. I hope our brief talks and hugs at his fruits and vegetable store have helped him.

For an Israeli, allowing oneself to feel vulnerable is a luxury in short supply. Israel lives surrounded by enemies actively working on their destruction. Life goes on, vibrancy reappears, buildings are rebuilt, but the terrible stress of this reality will remain, just as the memory, trauma and loss of Ten-Seven will remain. I see it in the eyes of so many people I have talked to, and my heart aches not knowing if I can bring comfort to them.

While in Israel, listening and learning, I fought against the guilt of disturbing the deeply private places of people I spoke to. I forced myself to ask the hard questions and to listen to the answers, because I know this vulnerability is a step on the road to healing. Healing must come to the people whose family and friends did not come home on October 7; to the Israeli soldiers who are haunted by the feeling of not doing enough, even though they are all heroes and have done more than asked of them; and to those that feel unsafe, isolated and abandoned. All of these people need the help and support of the village so they can find a way to live on and heal in the aftermath of this destruction.

The story of the aftermath of Ten-Seven will continue for years to come. It is difficult to write an ending to something that is evolving, and for many there will never be a period that can be placed at the end of this sentence.

I have struggled deeply with a sense of imposterism throughout the journey of writing this book. I do not live in Israel and deal with the everyday fight or flight stress. I am, afterall, a tourist, an observer, and I cannot help but question my authority to fill these pages. However, like many Jews around the world, I felt a strong need to do *something*. Writing this book answered that calling with the intention of bringing understanding to those unaffiliated with the impossible situation Israel faces, and to provide solace and comfort for those who feel isolated and betrayed by a world gone crazy.

MY PRAYER

To the soldiers and command of the IDF: be strong and faithful. Carry out your duty with responsibility and moral guidance. To the people of Israel: I pray you unite peacefully to demand change in a system that will work for the future. To the political powers and leaders of the free world: I pray that you pursue truth, support Israel's right to defend itself, and do what needs to be done to permanently disband terror from the reach of our borders. Finally, to the citizens of this world: if you love life, then please educate yourselves. Denying Israel's right to self-defense is not a reasonable path. Do not preach an agenda that applies only to some while preaching hatred to others. If you are truly tolerant, then be tolerant of all who are good, kind, and humane, including Jews. Live the life you love, but do not sacrifice it in conflict with your humanity.

THE BEGINNING AND NOT THE END

I am almost embarrassed to say that the denials and the betrayals by my neighbors, my government, my country, and the media have caught me off guard. I feel angered by being unwelcome in my own home. When it comes to the Jews, all reason, fairness, objectivity, and the pursuit of truth and justice seems to be compromised with the increasing normalization of hateful anti-Jewish and anti-Israel rhetoric.

The worst of it all, post-Ten-Seven, is fighting the instinct to go into hiding. As that chant to Jihad becomes louder, my discomfort becomes stronger. As a Jew I am feeling increasingly unsafe. When my youngest son hung an Israeli flag in his window at his university residence, I was concerned by him bringing unneeded attention his way. "Lay low," I found myself saying. He put the Israeli flag up anyway, and I'm proud of him for being proud of who he is. His small act of defiance to the haters, strengthened my resolve not to hide. I will not hide my necklace displaying the Star of David, I will not remove the Kippa from my head, and I will not be embarrassed to say my name.

Looking back in my rear-view mirror, I now understand what being persecuted means. The echo of the words of the last people of a generation of modern persecution leave us with witness to what could be and must never happen again.

I need not apologize for my birth, my land, my history, and the truth. My name is Israel—do you have a problem with that?

עַם יִשְׂרָאֵל חַי

THE NATION OF ISRAEL LIVES!

www.ingramcontent.com/pod-product-compliance
Ingram Content Group UK Ltd.
Pitfield, Milton Keynes, MK11 3LW, UK
UKHW021705190726
13853UKWH00001B/428